THE EUROPEAN UNION SERIES

General Editors: Neill Nugent, William E. Paterson

The European Union series provides an authoritative library on the European Union, ranging from general introductory texts to definitive assessments of key institutions and actors, issues, policies and policy processes, and the role of member states.

Books in the series are written by leading scholars in their fields and reflect the most up-to-date research and debate. Particular attention is paid to accessibility and clear presentation for a wide audience of students, practitioners and interested general readers.

The series editors are Neill Nugent, Professor of Politics and Jean Monnet Professor of European Integration, Manchester Metropolitan University, and William E. Paterson, Honourary Professor in German and European Studies, University of Aston. Their co-editor until his death in July 1999, Vincent Wright, was a Fellow of Nuffield College, Oxford University.

Feedback on the series and book proposals are always welcome and should be sent to Steven Kennedy, Palgrave Macmillan, Houndmills, Basingstoke, Hampshire RG21 6XS, UK, or by e-mail to s.kennedy@palgrave.com

---

General textbooks

Published

Desmond Dinan **Encyclopedia of the European Union**
[Rights: Europe only]

Desmond Dinan **Europe Recast: A History of European Union**
[Rights: Europe only]

Desmond Dinan **Ever Closer Union: An Introduction to European Integration** (4th edn)
[Rights: Europe only]

Mette Eilstrup Sangiovanni (ed.) **Debates on European Integration: A Reader**

Simon Hix **The Political System of the European Union** (2nd edn)

Paul Magnette **What is the European Union? Nature and Prospects**

John McCormick **Understanding the European Union: A Concise Introduction** (4th edn)

Brent F. Nelsen and Alexander Stubb **The European Union: Readings on the Theory and Practice of European Integration** (3rd edn)
[Rights: Europe only]

Neill Nugent (ed.) **European Union Enlargement**

Neill Nugent **The Government and Politics of the European Union** (7th edn)

John Peterson and Elizabeth Bomberg **Decision-Making in the European Union**

Ben Rosamond **Theories of European Integration**

Forthcoming

Laurie Buonanno and Neill Nugent **Policies and Policy Processes of the European Union**

Dirk Leuffen, Berthold Rittberger and Frank Schimmelfennig **Differentiated Integration**

Sabine Saurugger **Theoretical Approaches to European Integration**

Esther Versluis, Mendeltje van Keulen and Paul Stephenson **Analyzing the European Union Policy Process**

Also Planned

The Political Economy of European Integration

Series Standing Order (outside North America only)
ISBN 0–333–71695–7 hardback
ISBN 0–333–69352–3 paperback
Full details fr---

Visit Palgrave Macmillan's
EU Resource area at
www.palgrave.com/politics/eu/

The major institutions and actors

Published

Renaud Dehousse **The European Court of Justice**
Justin Greenwood **Interest Representation in the European Union** (2nd edn)
Fiona Hayes-Renshaw and Helen Wallace **The Council of Ministers** (2nd edn)
Simon Hix and Christopher Lord **Political Parties in the European Union**
David Judge and David Earnshaw **The European Parliament** (2nd edn)
Neill Nugent **The European Commission**
Anne Stevens with Handley Stevens **Brussels Bureaucrats? The Administration of the European Union**

Forthcoming

Wolfgang Wessels **The European Council**

The main areas of policy

Published

Michelle Chang **Monetary Integration in the European Union**
Michelle Cini and Lee McGowan **Competition Policy in the European Union** (2nd edn)
Wyn Grant **The Common Agricultural Policy**
Sieglinde Gstöhl and Dirk de Bièvre **The Trade Policy of the European Union**
Martin Holland **The European Union and the Third World**
Jolyon Howorth **Security and Defence Policy in the European Union**
Johanna Kantola **Gender and the European Union**
Stephan Keukeleire and Jennifer MacNaughtan **The Foreign Policy of the European Union**
Brigid Laffan **The Finances of the European Union**
Malcolm Levitt and Christopher Lord **The Political Economy of Monetary Union**
Janne Haaland Matláry **Energy Policy in the European Union**
John McCormick **Environmental Policy in the European Union**
John Peterson and Margaret Sharp **Technology Policy in the European Union**
Handley Stevens **Transport Policy in the European Union**

Forthcoming

Karen Anderson **Social Policy in the European Union**

Hans Bruyninckx and Tom Delreux **Environmental Policy and Politics in the European Union**
Jörg Monar **Justice and Home Affairs in the European Union**

Also planned

Political Union
The External Policies of the European Union
The External Economic Relations of the European Union

The member states and the Union

Published

Carlos Closa and Paul Heywood **Spain and the European Union**
Alain Guyomarch, Howard Machin and Ella Ritchie **France in the European Union**
Brigid Laffan and Jane O'Mahoney **Ireland and the European Union**

Forthcoming

Simon Bulmer and William E. Paterson **Germany and the European Union**
Brigid Laffan **The European Union and its Member States**
Baldur Thórhallsson **Small States in the European Union**

Also planned

Britain and the European Union

Issues

Published

Derek Beach **The Dynamics of European Integration: Why and When EU Institutions Matter**
Thomas Christiansen and Christine Reh **Constitutionalizing the European Union**
Robert Ladrech **Europeanization and National Politics**
Cécile Leconte **Understanding Euroscepticism**
Steven McGuire and Michael Smith **The European Union and the United States**

Forthcoming

Christina Boswell and Andrew Geddes **Migration and Mobility in the European Union**
Wyn Rees **EU/US Security Relations**

Gender and the European Union

Johanna Kantola

First published 2010 by
PALGRAVE MACMILLAN

Palgrave Macmillan in the UK is an imprint of Macmillan Publishers Limited, registered in England, company number 785998, of Houndmills, Basingstoke, Hampshire RG21 6XS.

Palgrave Macmillan in the US is a division of St Martin's Press LLC, 175 Fifth Avenue, New York, NY 10010.

Palgrave Macmillan is the global academic imprint of the above companies and has companies and representatives throughout the world.

Palgrave® and Macmillan® are registered trademarks in the United States, the United Kingdom, Europe and other countries

ISBN 978–0–230–54232–7 hardback
ISBN 978–0–230–54233–4 paperback

This book is printed on paper suitable for recycling and made from fully managed and sustained forest sources. Logging, pulping and manufacturing processes are expected to conform to the environmental regulations of the country of origin.

A catalogue record for this book is available from the British Library.

A catalog record for this book is available from the Library of Congress.

Contents

List of Tables and Boxes

Tables

Boxes

List of Abbreviations

ALDE	Alliance of Liberals and Democrats for Europe
CATW	Coalition Against Trafficking in Women
CEDAW	Convention on the Elimination of Discrimination Against Women
CEEC	Central and Eastern European Countries
CFSP	Common Foreign and Security Policy
COPA	Committee of Agricultural Organizations
DG	Directorate-General
DG V	Directorate-General on Employment, Social Affairs and Equal Opportunities
ECHR	European Court of Human Rights
ECJ	European Court of Justice
ED	European Democrats
EDF	European Disability Forum
EEA	European Economic Area
EES	European Employment Strategy
EHRC	Equality and Human Rights Commission
ENAR	European Network Against Racism
EIGE	European Institute for Gender Equality
ENOW	European Network of Women
EOC	Equal Opportunities Commission
EOU	Equal Opportunities Unit
EP	European Parliament
EPACVAW	European Policy Action Centre on Violence Against Women
EPP	European People's Party
EPWS	European Platform of Women Scientists
ERRC	European Roma Rights Center
ESF	European Social Fund
ETUC	European Trade Union Confederation
EU	European Union
EWLA	European Women Lawyers Association
FEMM	Committee on Women's Rights and Gender Equality
FRA	Fundamental Rights Agency

GUE/NGL	European United Left/ Nordic Green Left
G/FRA	Greens and the European Free Alliance
ILGA	International Lesbian and Gay Association
ILO	International Labour Organization
IND/DEM	Independence and Democracy
JHA	Justice and Home Affairs
MEP	Member of European Parliament
NAP	National Action Plan
NGO	Non-governmental organization
NOW	New Opportunities for Women
NPM	New Public Management
IOM	International Organization for Migration
IPS	Public Service International
OECD	Organisation for Economic Cooperation and Development
OMC	Open Method of Co-ordination
OSCE	Organization for Security and Co-operation in Europe
PES	Socialist Party Group
PPE	European People's Party
TAN	Transnational Advocacy Network
UEN	Union for a Europe Nations
UK	United Kingdom
UN	United Nations
US	United States
WAVE	Women Against Violence Europe
WHO	World Health Organization
WID	Women in Development
WIDE	Women in Development Europe
WOE	Women's Organization for Equality

Acknowledgements

For the past three years when colleagues have asked me: "What are you working on?" I have replied "A book on gender and the EU." Several times this reply has made mainstream political scientists laugh: "What does gender have to do with the EU?" On one hand, the book is written for those who are unaware of the complex ways in which gendered power structures underpin EU institutions and discourses and inform and construct policies and actors in the EU and member states. It aims to be an accessible text on the key issues that a gender perspective raises in relation to the EU. On the other hand, the vastness of research in this field comes as no surprise to feminist scholars. Here the problem is rather the scattered nature of this research, its spread into various journals, journal special issues, and chapters in edited volumes. For those aware of this diversity and perhaps daunted by it, the aim of this book is to pull the literature together, present the diversity of perspectives and consider issues that often remain separate in conjunction with one another, and thereby shed some analytical light on the big picture of "gender and the EU".

This book would not have been written without the support and encouragement of several people.

I would like to thank my colleagues Kevät Nousiainen, Anne Maria Holli, Milja Saari, Outi Anttila, Linda Hart, Anu Pylkkänen, and Eeva Raevaara in our Academy of Finland funded research project GENIE – The Paradoxes of the Finnish Gender Power Order: Law, Politics and Multi-level Governance. We have successfully combined not just the interdisciplinary study of politics and law but also friendship and work, serious theoretical and methodological discussions with good food, wine and the exchange of recipes.

The Gender and Politics Reading Group in the Department of Political Science, University of Helsinki has kept me up to date with most recent research in the field and provided me with an opportunity to exchange views and ideas directly relevant to this book. In addition to the colleagues mentioned above, I would like to thank Kristina Brunila, Jemima Repo and Maria Svanström for their insights on this book.

Judith Squires gave me some invaluable practical suggestions on how to handle such a big topic when I was just about to start. Steven Kennedy at Palgrave Macmillan encouraged me to carry the suggestions through. Anne Stevens read the final manuscript carefully and gave me detailed suggestions that greatly improved the text. I am indebted to all three.

Karen Celis, my co-convenor of the European Consortium for Political Research (ECPR) Standing Group on Gender and Politics, never tired of asking me how the book was coming along. Our projects, including the First European Conference on Politics and Gender held at Queen's University Belfast in January 2009, and the friendship that followed coincided with the writing of the book. I would also like to thank Karen (again), Sarah Childs and Mona Lena Krook for our work together on substantive representation of women; for bearing with me when I have been too preoccupied with this book to deliver on our other projects; and for our friendship.

The themes of the book cut across so many issues that I owe intellectual debt to a great number of scholars. Of these, I would like to thank Emanuela Lombardo in particular. She has generously shared with me her research and insights and I hope that my debt to her shows in the book. I would like to thank a number of others too for sharing their work with me, for inviting me to conferences and panels, for giving me encouragement, for being enthusiastic about the project and for giving me comments on papers: Gabriele Abels, Claire Annesley, Fiona Beveridge, Maria Bustelo, Rachel Cichowski, Sara Clavero, Yvonne Galligan, Roberta Guerrina, Ulrike Liebert, Petra Meier, Joyce Outshoorn, Elisabeth Prügl, Lise Rolandsen Agustín, Silke Roth, Mieke Verloo, Anna van der Vleuten, Laurel Weldon, Stephanie Woehl and Alison Woodward.

I have had two research assistants, one official and one unofficial, Joe van Troost and Jussi Kantola, and I would like to thank both for their invaluable help at the beginning and at the end of the process.

Most of all I would like to thank my partner Anders Vacklin, who has been enthusiastic about the book although finding out little about it as I have refused to discuss it after work, for always having been keen for me to spend time writing it, for practical help in finding data, and for writer's insights about the beginning, the structure, and the argumentation of the book.

An earlier version of Chapter 3 appeared as 'Women's Political Representation in the European Union' in *Journal of Legislative Studies* 15 (4). I thank the publishers for the permission to use the material they published.

JOHANNA KANTOLA

Chapter 1

Introducing Gender and the European Union

The family portraits of the leaders of the European Union (EU) are familiar to us all. Dating back to the signing of the Treaty of Rome in 1957, they show rows of white men in black suits. By 2007, when the EU celebrated its fiftieth anniversary, little had changed from a gender perspective. Whilst the number of leaders had increased exponentially, only one woman, the German Chancellor Angela Merkel, appeared in the front row among the EU leaders.

Over the decades, the Union itself has evolved considerably and its tasks and competencies have expanded. The EU now is a multi-level polity where 27 member states and the supranational EU level interact in complex ways. The EU has been called a 'success story of economic integration' (Börzel 2005: 219). It has come to hold exclusive competencies in market-making policies (including external trade) to ensure the free movement of goods, services, people and capital. It shares with the member states responsibilities for market-correcting policies that involve the harmonization of national standards on environment, consumer protection, industrial health and security, agriculture and labour markets (Börzel 2005: 219). The member states collectively co-ordinate at the EU level their competencies in macroeconomic policies, justice and home affairs, and foreign and security policy. The EU has less or no competence in redistributive policy, including taxation and expenditure, social welfare, culture and education policy (Börzel 2005: 219–24, Hix 2005, Hooghe and Marks 2001.)

The EU's political integration is often seen as less of a success story. For example, there is no European political party system and no Europeanized media reflecting the strong internal diversity of the EU countries and regions (Swenden 2004: 385). Despite these limitations, the EU has considerable impact on the member states beyond its formal competencies. Even though the EU's redistributive capacity is small, it transfers significant resources through its budget. Its market policies constrain the capacity of the member states for redistribution and, as a result, have an indirect impact on their social policy (Scharpf 1999). Competition rules, the convergence criteria and the Growth and Stability Pact put further constraints on the expenditure policies of the member states (Börzel 2005: 219–24). Finally, new policy-making processes in the form of soft law have increased member state co-operation in the fields of social policy, culture, vocational training and education, where EU competencies are otherwise limited (Swenden 2004: 384).

It is not uncommon to hear politics scholars and students ask: 'What does gender have to do with the EU?' Does the EU matter to gender and, *vice versa*, gender to the EU? The EU's capacity to shape gender relations in its member states has been there from its very beginning. The Treaty of Rome was negotiated and signed by men but it contained a clause on equal pay between women and men. Since then the EU has emerged as a key actor in shaping gender relations in Europe even if this is not evident from its fiftieth anniversary family portrait. In a multi-level governance framework, ideas, norms and policies travel and are transferred from the international and EU levels to national, regional and local levels and back again (Rai and Waylen 2008, Waylen 2008). In this process, the EU sets trends and carries particular normative notions of gender equality as well as promoting certain solutions to perceived gender equality problems. Their impact often reaches beyond the 27 member states of the Union. Actors too, including those studied in feminist research such as women's movements and policy agencies, need to direct their political claims and demands for change to the EU. These processes change the gender relations and regimes as well as the notions of gender equality in member states and in the EU.

There are three interesting and interlocking aspects about the role of the EU in shaping gender relations in Europe. First, the EU has its own *gender policy* as evidenced by its equal opportunities directives, gender policies such as those on family and violence, and general policies such as trade and agriculture (Elman 1996, Haas 2003, Hantrais 2000, Hoskyns 2008, Meehan 1993, Prügl 2008, van der Vleuten 2007).

To characterize the evolution of the gender policy field, Theresa Rees famously distinguished a move from equal opportunities to positive action and gender mainstreaming in the EU (Rees 1998 and 2005). Alternatively, Mark Bell sees equality policy as having evolved from anti-discrimination policy to working towards substantive equality and to managing diversity (Bell 2000 and 2002). Both frameworks show that EU gender policy has expanded in important ways. On one hand, whilst equal opportunities and anti-discrimination policy focused mainly on women's rights in the field of employment, the principle of gender mainstreaming requires that gender inequalities are tackled across *all* policy areas. On the other hand, gender is no longer dealt with in isolation from other bases of inequality such as race and ethnicity, disability and sexuality. Rather an 'integrated equalities' agenda requires consideration of many types of equalities and discrimination and of how together, they can result in 'multiple discrimination'. Both models capture the expansion of the notion of gender equality on which EU policy has been based from a more formal notion of equal opportunities before the law to more substantive and possibly even structural notions. These different stages of the EU gender policy have, notably, not replaced one another but continue to co-exist.

Second, the interaction between *institutions, processes, actors* and *discourses* in the EU and its member states is gendered and gendering. When an institution is gendered, it is underpinned by norms about femininity and masculinity, and hierarchical relationships between them, where what is considered 'masculine' is often prioritized over 'feminine'. Gendering, in turn, refers to processes of feminization and masculinization whereby social and political institutions constantly reproduce subjects that fit these norms. The focus on the EU decision-making institutions and policy-making processes reflects a shift whereby the origin of gender policies has to some extent moved from the member states to the supranational EU level (von Wahl 2008: 23). This means understanding the European Council, the European Commission, the European Parliament and the social partners, as institutional constraints from a gender perspective (Clavero and Galligan 2009). Important policy-making processes with gendered impact include the principle of subsidiarity, co-decision-making, hard law and soft law, and the Open Method of Co-ordination (OMC) discussed below (Beveridge and Velluti 2008). Civil society actors also shape and are shaped in new ways by the opportunity structures provided by the supranational actor. Voice and access, as well as political representation in the EU context, are important questions from a gender perspective. Ideas, discourses and norms about gender are now defined at EU level with very real effects on women and men across Europe (Mazur 2009: 28, Verloo 2007, Lombardo, Meier and Verloo 2009).

Third, the fact that the EU is a multi-level polity signifies that subnational, national and supranational institutions, actors and discourses interact in complex ways to enact gender legislation and policy. The processes of *Europeanization* raise questions about the member states shifting towards common EU standards and about the amount of diversity that should be preserved between different countries in relation to gender. The 2004 and 2007 enlargements with the accession of Central and Eastern European Countries (CEEC) pushed the debate on gender and Europeanization beyond the interaction of the EU gender regime with those of the old member states. It has also raised questions about the depth of EU gender policy, its position and weight, and the EU commitment to the value of gender equality in general. A focus on Europeanization may also shift the focus from policy formulation and outputs in the EU to actual policy implementation, outcomes and impacts in the member states and to the question whether gender relations actually change as a result of transnational gender policies (Mazur and Pollack 2009: 7).

Despite this extensive research on the complex ways in which gender and the EU interact, mainstream literature remains 'virtually untouched' by feminist analysis (Hoskyns 2004: 33). This means that research, textbooks, theories and policy analyses are written largely in isolation from gender analysis, although some collections now include chapters on feminist approaches (see for example, Egan, Nugent and Paterson 2010, Graziano and Vink 2008, Jørgensen, Pollack and Rosamond 2007, Wiener and Dietz 2004 and 2009). However, as gender informs all social relations, the EU cannot be fully understood or explained without a gender analysis (Kronsell 2005: 1036, Locher and Prügl 2009: 182). On a theoretical level, gender analysis helps to explain the role of gendered power structures and hierarchies in EU integration theories and concepts (see Kronsell 2005). In policy analysis, understanding gender shows that policies are often based on a male norm or strong gender stereotypes, whereby, for example, men's employment patterns are 'normal' and women can be seen as mothers and as an atypical workforce. A focus on gender demonstrates that apparently gender-neutral policies have gendered impact. For example, the EU's employment policy may fail to increase employment trends if it does not tackle childcare which is important for women's labour market participation. Sometimes a failure to understand gendered impacts can make laws or policies ineffective.

For instance, ignoring sexual harassment as an important workplace health and safety issue may result in a law that does not address an important problem that many people, especially women, face. Gender mainstreaming has helped to bring this to the attention of policy makers.

The aim of this book is to provide a critical introduction to the issues involved when understanding and explaining the EU from a gender perspective. The book draws upon a field that has expanded tremendously over the past five years and takes stock of and builds upon these findings. Catherine Hoskyns' seminal text of 1996, *Integrating Gender: Women, Law and Politics in the European Union,* has been complemented by a flood of new introductory chapters (Kantola 2010, Locher and Prügl 2009, Prügl 2007), monographs (Askola 2007a, Cichowski 2007, Einhorn 2006, Elman 2007, Guerrina 2005, van der Vleuten 2007, Zippel 2006), edited volumes (Beveridge and Velluti 2008, Liebert 2003, Roth 2008) and numerous articles and chapters on specific aspects of gender and the EU. Elisabeth Prügl (2007) argues that feminist research questions have changed in this process of decades of research on gender and the EU. Whereas feminist research used to inquire 'how and why does the EU adopt and implement gender equality policies?', it now analyzes 'how and why is gender difference constructed and gender inequality reproduced through EU policies?' (Prügl 2007), and, one might add, with what effects on member states' gender regimes.

The goal of this chapter is to provide a background to understanding what we are studying when we study gender and the EU. First, the chapter discusses existing *gender inequalities in Europe and the EU*, reviewing the key issues and challenges to gender equality to which these give rise. Despite similar patterns in the levels and causes of gender inequality in different member states, there is also considerable diversity in member states' gender regimes. This diversity provides the context where the EU policy, institutions, actors and discourses operate and come from. Second, the chapter discusses the *EU gender regime* as evidenced in its binding hard law and non-binding soft law on gender equality. The final section *evaluates* the EU gender regime from a feminist perspective. Whilst pointing to some clear trends, the chapter also highlights the need to be sensitive to the differentiated character of the EU whereby different institutions, actors and policy fields may point to different conclusions about gender and the EU.

Gender inequalities in Europe

'Equality' is a concept debated by theorists, politicians and activists and one that takes on different meanings in different contexts. Politically, there has been a shift from emphasizing 'equality of outcome' to 'equality of opportunities' in policies seeking to address inequalities. Theoretically, debates on equality first moved from theories of distributive justice to theories of recognition as fundamental to equality (Young 1990). Later Nancy Fraser influentially proposed a theoretical framework that addresses both political economy and culture, addressing both redistribution and recognition as equally significant elements of inequality (Fraser 2000), whilst Iris Marion Young has suggested that the two need to be combined with representation (Young 2000). In today's world, a number of scholars and activists share a concern that while political equality is high on the agenda, there is a worrying indifference to economic inequality (Phillips 1999; for a discussion see Kantola and Squires 2010).

Europe has witnessed a number of positive trends with regard to gender equality. Women's labour market participation has increased over the past decade. This has been enabled by changing attitudes, active labour market policies and increases in childcare provision providing more 'equal opportunities' for women. Indeed, Europeans' attitudes to gender equality converge on women's and men's equal right to participate in the labour market, which is the view that gathers the highest level of support in the member states (Gerhards, Kämpfer and Schäfer 2008: 10). In terms of recognition and representation, women today are better represented in political decision-making processes than before (Chapter 3) and their concerns are also kept on the political agenda by an array of women's organizations, movements and policy agencies that have gained access to political decision-making (Chapter 4). This has helped to frame issues such as violence against women as fundamental to gender equality and put them on the European political agenda.

However, a number of serious Europe-wide challenges to gender equality remain. Labour markets in the EU are horizontally and vertically segregated on the basis of gender. This means that there are women's jobs and men's jobs and the latter are better paid than the former. In general, female employment is more concentrated than male employment in the fields of public sector, health care and education (Barth, Røed and Torp 2002: 9). The European gender pay gap has remained at about 15–20 per cent despite 50 years of legislation and policy in the field (Plantenga and Remery 2006: 4–5, Rubery *et al.* 2002), and only a third of all managers across all EU-25 countries were women in 2005 (Eurostat 2006: 4). A third of working women are in part-time jobs, compared to 7 per cent of men, which leaves many women outside social security schemes and makes their pensions smaller. The inequalities in the labour market are partly caused by the unequal distribution of care responsibilities between women and men (Aliaga 2005: 1). This makes the issue of reconciling work and family, maternity, paternity and parental leave policies, and childcare provision central to achieving gender equality (Chapter 5).

The fact that women have lower employment rates than men in EU countries is a key factor contributing to women's greater exposure to poverty and social exclusion. Social welfare systems in many European countries still rely on an implicit policy assumption that women have or should have access to the income of a male 'breadwinner' partner or derive benefits as his dependent spouse (Fagan, Urwin and Melling 2006: 8). It is often black and ethnic minority women who are most at risk of poverty. For example in the UK, only eight per cent of Pakistani and Bangladeshi women have an occupational pension and one per cent a personal pension. Black and ethnic minorities face direct discrimination in European labour markets and institutional racism hinders the careers of many (European Commission 2006: 77).

Gender inequalities remain not just in terms of economic, political and social rights of women but also in terms of civil rights. Feminist scholars have traditionally highlighted the importance to women of bodily integrity, which is defined by such issues as gender violence, reproductive rights, abortion and sexuality. Again, notable levels of domestic violence have persisted in European countries. Women's reproductive rights and the right to abortion remain contested in some member states and criminalized in Ireland, Malta and Poland. Similarly, gender stereotypes in media and advertising as well as in education promoting traditional gender roles are a source of inequalities.

The practices that reproduce these gender inequalities are institutionalized at national, local and international levels in different gender regimes. Elisabeth Prügl defines a gender regime in the following way:

Regimes are institutions, sets of rules that make gendered agencies and structures. As such, regimes are conduits of power: they produce normalized and empowered subjects, but they also routinize power, giving the effects of power permanence and structure. (Prügl 2008: 47)

In Europe, there are local, regional, national, EU and international gender regimes that interact in the multi-level governance framework. At the crudest level, they define who works, who cares, who participates in political decision-making, who has a right to have a family and children (Sainsbury 1999, O'Connor, Orloff and Shaver 1999). Some scholars use more specific terms such as 'an equal employment regime' to describe how states, markets and families interact in relation to gendered work and employment patterns (von Wahl 2008: 21) and others talk about particular care regimes (Lewis 1997).

There is considerable variation in member states' equalities, inequalities and gender regimes. Member states' gender regimes range from the conservative welfare states of continental Europe to the British liberal conservative regime, the southern European 'Mediterranean regime' and the 'Nordic egalitarian model'. These are briefly introduced below to illustrate the different traditions, norms and institutions that continue to shape the European landscape of gender inequality.

The social capitalist, corporatist or conservative welfare states of continental Europe, such as Germany, Belgium, and the Netherlands, appear to be based on a passive or reactive type of welfare policy where the aim is not to change the market logic but merely to temper its outcomes (Esping-Andersen 1990). The fact that social rights are linked to class and status combined with the maintenance of the traditional family results in specific gendered patterns (Bussemaker and van Kersbergen 1999: 17). Social policy and taxation are based on the primacy of the family unit, where the male breadwinner as the head of the family receives benefits. The regime relies on a female caregiver, private care arrangements and a strong division between the public and the private spheres. Wives' rights to benefits may be dependent on husbands' rights, and hence married women lack individual rights to benefits (Sainsbury 2001: 124). The division of labour in the family is reflected in the division of labour in the labour market, where there is the persistence of ideas about men's jobs and women's jobs (Macrae 2006: 526, 540).

Women's employment rates have traditionally been low and women risk poverty at the time of divorce. These issues have been politicized via interaction with the EU equal treatment laws and norms and there is evidence of a slow change towards the EU gender regime discussed below.

Britain is an example of a liberal regime combined with conservative values with a restricted role for the state and heightened emphasis on the individual. This trend was strengthened in the 1980s and 1990s by successive Conservative governments. For gender relations, this means that a number of key issues, such as motherhood and childcare, are considered 'private' and the regime is based on the view that the market should provide what is needed. Social policy in this regime, as in social capitalist regimes, is based on a male-breadwinner and female-caregiver model that promotes 'economic dependence on marriage' (O'Connor, Orloff and Shaver 1999: 7). Women's employment is characterized by high levels of part-time work and long career breaks for mothers of young children. Both Germany and the UK show relatively high poverty rates for single mothers and relatively high gender gaps in poverty (O'Connor, Orloff and Shaver 1999: 20). The New Labour government has changed some of these patterns by providing more support for families since 1997 (Lister 2004). Some commentators suggest that this has signified a move to a 'one-and-a-half-workers model' where women still work part-time and men full-time (Lister *et al.* 2007: 58).

The 'Mediterranean welfare state regime' in southern Europe is based on the central role of the family as an institution which ensures social protection with minimal state intervention. In Italy, this is evidenced by the clear shortage of resources earmarked for family policy as compared with the European average (4 per cent versus 8 per cent) (Guadagnini and Donà 2007: 164). Whilst, for example, Italy had a strong Marxist and socialist culture, the role of the Catholic Church has upheld the centrality of the nuclear family. Women's participation in the labour market is among the lowest in Europe; gender pay gaps and gender segregation in the labour market remain high. Gendered division of labour in the family is strong with women having the responsibility for care work and as a result being penalised for maternity, which leads to the lowest fertility rates in Europe (Guadagnini and Donà 2007: 164–5) .

The 'Nordic egalitarian model' is based on a dual worker/dual carer gender regime that currently places much emphasis on men's caregiving roles. Traditionally, women's labour market participation has been high and it has been actively supported by state social policy, for example in the form of extensive childcare arrangements (Bergqvist *et al.* 1999, Sainsbury 1999). Unlike some of the other gender regimes, the public–private distinction is not as strongly upheld. In terms of welfare state provision, social rights have traditionally been universal rather than means-tested, which has reduced poverty for women as well as men. The process of neoliberalization has also rolled back the welfare state in these countries. Feminist critique has pointed to the remaining problems that include the gender segregated labour market, gender pay gaps, the exclusion of minority women from the official discourse on gender equality and the high levels of violence against women (Lindvert 2002, Kantola 2006). Different studies on the levels of gender equality, however, continue to place the Nordic model at the top. For example, Janneke Plantega *et al.* (2009:30) constructed a 'European Union Gender Equality Index' composed of the dimensions of equal sharing of paid work, money, decision-making power and time. Their findings show that the Nordic countries Denmark, Finland and Sweden come closest to gender equality on the basis of these standards, whereas southern countries such as Greece, Cyprus, Malta, Spain and Italy are still far from achieving gender equality.

The new member states of the central and eastern European countries (CEECs) are usually not included in the traditional welfare state typologies on which the gender regimes characterization here draws. Under the communist gender regime, women of working age had full-time paid employment supported by paid maternity leave, paid leave to care for sick children and heavily subsidised childcare – the key elements of the Nordic model. This changed dramatically in the 1990s with the fall of communism and the processes of neoliberalization combined with new traditionalization evidenced by the prominent role of the Catholic Church in countries such as Poland. Women's unemployment soared and women were made redundant when state-owned companies privatized and restructured (Koldinská 2008a: 120). This exposed the underlying gender hierarchies and inequalities in these societies. Whilst western European countries are moving towards an 'adult worker model', Barbara Einhorn (2006: 101) suggests that the CEECs are on an opposite trajectory from a dual-earner model back to the assumption of a male-breadwinner model. Yet women's full-time employment rates remain higher than in a number of western

European countries (such as Austria, Belgium, UK, Germany and the Netherlands) where women tend to work part-time (Fuszara 2008: 109) and the overall gender pay gap is not as high as in the West (von Wahl 2008: 29), complicating any simplistic portrayals of the situation.

The discussion above is useful in pointing to the sheer diversity in the region. Gender policies are institutionalized in different ways, and the EU norms and legislation face significant challenges, due to these differences, when transposed and implemented at the national level. Furthermore, it becomes evident that the concept of gender equality takes on multiple meanings in different countries (see Verloo 2007). In some countries, gender equality may mean mothers' right to stay at home to care for their children, and elsewhere their right to participate in the labour market. As a concept, then, 'gender equality' is remarkably flexible. It can be filled with different meanings by different actors in a process that has been described as 'fixing' or freezing its meaning, 'stretching' it towards wider meanings, 'reducing' it to particular ones and 'bending' it to fit other goals (Lombardo, Meier and Verloo 2009). Definitions of what constitutes gender equality matter, however, because they have very real effects. In addition to specific political effects, such as too expensive or poor quality childcare or dead-end jobs, they can 'depoliticize or degender' gender equality, neutralizing conflict and masking existing power relations (Lombardo, Meier and Verloo 2009b: 190).

Whilst they are useful in pinning down the differences between countries and traditions in Europe, such broad characterizations may also mask more than they reveal about gendered patterns. First, some countries do not fit the models particularly well. France is a frequently mentioned example where the state plays a central role and the values of universality and equality have long informed public policies. Maternity provision has been good and yet there are persistent gender differences. Countries can change rapidly too. For example, Spain has taken significant steps under the socialist governments since 2004, with a parity government, and new progressive legislation on gender violence, same-sex marriage and gender equality, making Spanish gender policy a frontrunner in comparative terms (Bustelo 2009).

Second, the idea of regional gender regimes masks differences both within regions (for example within CEEC or Nordic countries) and within states. Within states, a focus on different policy fields may generate different results in the extent of gender equality; for example, a focus on violence shows the Nordic countries in a less favourable light (Kantola 2006) although violence is rarely accounted for in comparative models (see, for example, Plantega *et al.* 2009, Ferrari, Occhionero and Nocenzi 2009).

Third, the diversity among women and men and the ways in which gender interacts with class, race, nation and citizenship (O'Connor, Orloff and Shaver 1999), and how states reproduce gender norms through regulation of and through sexuality (Smith 2007) are difficult to grasp with the above models. For example, citizenship rights and responsibilities are not the same for everyone. Belonging and membership can be 'multilayered', which means that they are shaped by belonging to different minorities (Yuval-Davis 1997). The Nordic model has recently been interrogated from the perspective of postcolonial theory. Gender equality is at the core of the discourse on nationhood in these countries and is central to defining who belongs to the nation and who does not. In such a context, gender inequality is easily assigned to other cultures and other racialized bodies (Mulinari *et al.* 2009: 5). A focus on transnational governance patterns may aid such discussions and point to questions about what the gender regimes mean for women from different countries of origin.

The EU gender regime: policies, institutions and actors

It is evident, then, that whilst European countries share some key challenges to gender equality, their gender regimes and definitions of what constitutes gender equality differ considerably. In this context, the EU emerges as a transnational actor promoting particular definitions and solutions to perceived equality policy challenges. In other words, with its expanding competencies, the EU and its institutions – the Parliament, the Commission, the Council, the Court, the social partners – occupy a privileged position in promoting particular policy solutions to gender inequalities and 'fixing the meaning of gender equality' (Lombardo, Meier and Verloo 2009: 13).

The EU gender regime can be discerned by looking at different policies, institutions and norms, and it can be represented by different actors. To provide one way to study the EU gender regime, this chapter briefly maps out EU gender policy and norms in relation to 'hard law' and 'soft law', a distinction followed in a number of chapters of the book that deepen the picture given here. A focus on hard and soft law makes it possible to discern the governance patterns, institutional policy-making mechanisms and their powers and the actors that each privilege. EU hard law consists of primary law, such as treaties, and secondary law, such as directives, as well as the rulings of the European Court of Justice (ECJ) that are binding on member states. Hence they provide definitive ideas about what the EU institutions and member states have been able to agree upon as crucial to gender equality. Soft law, by contrast, is a broader notion and consists of different policy documents, recommendations and declarations that rely on the power of persuasion, the spreading of good practice and softer instruments. Soft law can, nonetheless, be powerful in terms of setting trends, and Fiona Beveridge (2008) cautions against constructing too strong a dichotomy between the two.

Hard law defines the EU competencies for action, the fields where it can enact binding legislation and policy on its member states. In gender policy, Article 141 EC on equal pay (ex Article 119 of the Treaty of Rome) has occupied a prominent place in the primary law and shaped gender legislation. It calls for each member state to 'ensure that the principle of equal pay for male and female workers for equal work or work of equal value is applied'. It gives powers to the Council to 'adopt measures to ensure the application of the principle of equal opportunities and equal treatment of men and women in matters of employment and occupation, including the principle of equal pay for equal work or work of equal value.' Chapters 2 and 5 of this book discuss how the article came about and how important directives, such as the Equal Pay Directive 1975, Equal Treatment Directive 1976 (amended in 2002), the Social Security Directive 1978 and the Recast Directive 2006, were enacted on the basis of this article and implemented in member states. All of these tackle gender inequalities and gender-based discrimination in relation to the labour market. Whilst covering a wide range of issues from equal pay to sexual harassment, the EU gender policy that these directives represent has been criticized for being narrow and restricted to anti-discrimination and employment rights as discussed below.

In this context, the Amsterdam Treaty 1997 represented major developments in EU gender policy. First, Article 141 EC was revised in the Amsterdam Treaty to institutionalize positive action and gender mainstreaming as parts of EU gender policy in addition to anti-discrimination policy in the labour market (Ellina 2003: 52). The EU's gender policy was now officially three-dimensional which removed some of the uncertainties and confusions that had previously surrounded positive action as an acceptable tool in member states' policy-making (Chapter 2). The official adoption of gender mainstreaming, in turn, made a gender perspective and analysis relevant for all EU policy-making processes and policy fields (Chapter 6). Celebrating these developments, some feminist commentators argued that this marked 'the beginning of a new stage' in the development of gender policy in the EU (Shaw 2001: 3) and widened the original commitment of the member states to equal pay for equal work 'to the progressive recognition of equality between women and men as a fundamental principle of democracy' for the whole EU (Hubert 2001: 145).

Second, the Amsterdam Treaty introduced Article 13 EC, which provided a new legal basis for anti-discrimination directives. The article provides new opportunities for attempts to reach beyond some of the confines of the earlier narrow legal basis in gender policy. For example, the 2004 Directive on Goods and Services, enacted on the basis of the article, expanded gender equality legislation in the EU beyond the confines of the labour market and outside the field of employment (Masselot 2007: 153). Its scope includes access to premises that the public are permitted to enter, housing, services of a profession or trade, including banking, insurance, other financial services and transport.

Third, the new article also widened the bases of equality from gender and nationality to race and ethnicity, religion and belief, age, disability and sexual orientation. This has had the effect of pushing for gender inequalities and discrimination to be tackled in conjunction with these other bases of inequality. In this way, the article has been pivotal in developing emerging EU policy on 'multiple discrimination' (Chapter 8). However, Article 13 differs from Article 141 in that the former requires a unanimous vote in the Council whilst when the latter is used, qualified majority voting is applied, enhancing the possibilities for progressive gender directives as discussed below and in Chapters 4 and 5.

In addition to law and policy, the EU gender regime is shaped by the policy-making process by which directives and policies are enacted and the gendered and gendering roles that different institutions play in this process. The process by which the anti-discrimination directives have traditionally been drafted is known as the classic

'Community method' (see Chapter 4). In this process, the role of the European Commission has been strong in the formation and execution of Community legislation, with the European Parliament gaining power and influence. Regulations, directives and decisions reached through this method always have binding force. At the final stage, all legislation is adopted by the Council of Ministers by qualified majority or unanimous vote. During the preparation, formulation and implementation of policies the Commission and Parliament consult private groups and non-governmental organizations (NGOs) for information and expertise on specific issues (Kohler-Koch and Rittberger 2006: 34).

In terms of gender policy, the European Parliament influences its contents by debating Commission proposals, drafting reports and raising questions. One of the 27 committees of the Parliament specializes in gender, the Women's Rights and Gender Equality Committee (FEMM). This Committee organizes the examination of proposals on matters related to women's rights and gender equality and its amendments are then considered in the plenary sessions. The committee appoints a *rapporteur* who follows the legislative proposal throughout the process. On the basis of the work of the *rapporteur* the committee adopts a common position that normally prevails in the plenary sessions. This ensures that agreement is found across political groups (Shackleton 2006: 112–13). In this way, the Parliament pushes for specific formulations in equality legislation, keeps gender equality on the political agenda and raises the profile of such questions as violence against women and trafficking in women. The strengthened role of the Parliament in the co-decision procedure introduced in the Treaty of Maastricht 1992 was welcomed by feminist activists and its restricted powers in the Social Dialogue (see below) lamented (Clavero and Galligan 2009, van der Vleuten 2007).

The European Commission is the manager of EU gender policy and provides political and policy direction in the field. It can use hard law by proposing new legislation and soft law by drafting action programmes or roadmaps. The Commission, for example, issues an annual 'Report on equality between women and men' to the Council and the Parliament, which discusses the state of gender equality in the EU. Its Commissioner on Employment, Social Affairs and Equal Opportunities heads the Directorate-General for Employment, Social Affairs and Equal Opportunities, which has administrative powers in terms of gender policy. It is in charge of ensuring that gender mainstreaming is implemented in all Union policies. The Commission can use the infringement procedure to require recalcitrant governments to transpose equal opportunities directives into national legislation (Chapter 2). Here it has been aided by the European Court of Justice (ECJ), which interprets gender directives. The Court, in turn, expands and gives depth to the equal opportunities directives through case law (Cichowski 2007).

Despite the powers of the Parliament and the Commission, most of the major decisions continue to be taken at European Council level. It provides political guidance across all Union activities, is in charge of the Open Method of Co-ordination (OMC) and amends treaties. The ministers of the member states meet within the Council of the European Union, which passes laws, legislating jointly with the Parliament under co-decision, co-ordinates economic policies of the member states, and constitutes the authority, together with the Parliament, that agrees the Community budget (Hayes-Renshaw 2006, de Schoutheete 2006). The Council meets in nine different configurations depending on the subjects under discussion. There is no configuration for gender, anti-discrimination or equal opportunities. Qualified majority voting introduced in the Treaty of Maastricht 1992 facilitated decision-making but gender equality continues to be hampered by the number of directives that need to be decided with a unanimous vote (Ellina 2003: 54). For example, while legislation adopted under Article 141 can be agreed upon through qualified majority voting and can benefit from the involvement of the European Parliament, legislation adopted under Article 13 requires unanimity among member states in the Council (Caracciolo di Torelia 2005: 340).

The Community method is further shaped by two governance patterns introduced in the Treaty of Maastricht that both point to the tendency to foreground deregulation as opposed to centralized decision-making in the EU. First, the involvement of *social partners* in the legislative process allowed peak organizations representing labour and management at the EU level to prepare draft directives for Council approval (Heide 1999: 385). Chapter 5 discusses the Parental Leave Directive 1996, the Part-time Workers Directive 1997 and the Directive on the Burden of Proof 1997 as examples of equality legislation negotiated by the social partners. Second, the legislative path has been fundamentally shaped by the *subsidiarity* principle, constitutionalized by the Treaty of Maastricht. Subsidiarity requires that, whenever possible, action should be taken at the lowest possible level. In other words, Community action shall be undertaken only if the objective can be 'better achieved' by the Community than by the individual member states. In all other cases, activities should be left within the scope of the nation states (Rossilli 2000: 2).

The enhanced role of the social partners in the legislative process and the principle of subsidiarity are examples of the trend towards deregulation and decentralization in the EU policy-making processes. This governance trend is further strengthened by the various forms of soft law that have gained prominence in the EU over the past decade. The EU gender regime can also be discerned from these soft law policies and processes. Typically soft law is thought to lack the formal characteristics of law, for example by not having binding force or legal sanctions, but can nonetheless have some, often significant, impact on member states (Beveridge 2008: 26). This kind of 'soft law' complementing binding hard law has always been important in gender policy, as evidenced by equal opportunities action programmes and various recommendations (Chapter 2). Soft law has often preceded hard law, as in the case of sexual harassment or trafficking in women, thereby pre-empting a more fundamental change. Gender policy, institutions, actors and discourses are also being shaped by a new soft law tool – the Open Method of Co-ordination (OMC) – which emerged with the European Employment Strategy in the 2000s (Chapters 5 and 6). The OMC is used especially in fields where differences between member states are large and reaching binding EU policy is difficult, such as employment, or where the EU has no competence, such as social policy (Büchs 2007).

The Roadmap for equality between women and men 2006–10 is an example of traditional soft law that lays out the policy priorities of the Commission in relation to gender equality. In contrast to hard law, such policy papers signify flexibility in choosing the policy tools used to achieve the priorities. The six priority areas in the Roadmap included: (i) achieving equal economic independence for women and men; (ii) enhancing reconciliation of work, private and family life; (iii) promoting equal participation of women and men in decision-making; (iv) eradicating gender-based violence and trafficking; (v) eliminating gender stereotypes in society; and (vi) promoting gender equality outside the EU (European Commission 2006). The Roadmap emphasized that EU policy was based on 'the dual approach of gender equality based on gender mainstreaming (the promotion of gender equality in all policy areas and activities) and specific measures' (European Commission 2006: 1). The fields covered were broader than those in the hard law (for example eliminating gender stereotypes in society) and, indeed, soft law has been a way to expand the EU gender regime to cover new areas and issues. Another example is the European Pact for Gender Equality, adopted by the Council in 2006, which represented the Council's political commitment to three fields where it encouraged member states to take action: (i) closing gender gaps and combating gender stereotypes in the labour market; (ii) promoting a better work-life balance; and (iii) reinforcing governance through gender mainstreaming and better monitoring. Reflecting the more conservative nature of the Council in gender policy, these fields are closely linked to equal opportunities in the labour market.

The Open Method of Co-ordination (OMC) that represents a new governance style in the EU defines some economic and social policy goals at EU level, for example in relation to employment or provision of childcare, but decentralizes the reaching of these goals to the member states (Chapters 5 and 6). The goals are not binding and they are formulated as general principles rather than specific policies, which increases the open-endedness of the policy-making process and ensures member state autonomy (Büchs 2007: 19; Pascual 2008: 175). Hence, unlike hard law, the OMC aims to 'achieve a standardization of ideas, visions and political concepts, rather than of institutions and laws' (Pascual 2008: 184). The method enhances the role of the Commission and the Council. Both are subject to less direct scrutiny by the Parliament and the ECJ too has little role to play (Beveridge 2008: 28). National civil society organizations may have difficulty having their voices heard in the process due to its bureaucratic rather than political nature.

The impact of the Lisbon Treaty (discussed in Chapter 10) on this framework remains to be seen. A lot of the feminist debate centres on the position of the Charter of Fundamental Rights of the European Union to which the Lisbon Treaty makes reference. A number of commentators point out that the Treaty of Lisbon would strengthen a human rights approach to gender equality through the inclusion of the reference to the Charter (Beveridge 2008: 14). As a fundamental right, equality is no longer restricted to the internal market, but must be guaranteed in all areas of the Community and within all pillars (Masselot 2007: 155–6). Others remain more sceptical, pointing to potential confusion between the current law and the new treaty as well as the weakening of some provisions, as discussed in Chapter 10 (Koukoulis-Spiliotopoulos 2008: 16, Lombardo 2007, Millns 2007: 231).

Overall, the EU gender regime, as it emerges from hard law and soft law, includes three dimensions: anti-discrimination law, positive action and gender mainstreaming. The EU has traditionally concentrated on advancing gender equality and using these tools in the labour market. However, soft law has expanded this focus to issues such as gender violence and gender stereotypes, and gender mainstreaming has required policy-makers in the EU to understand how gender shapes a wide range of mainstream policy fields, such as trade and development. The expansion of EU gender policy was institutionalized in hard law in the Amsterdam Treaty. The Treaty further expanded the Union's discrimination policy in giving the Community the powers to tackle discrimination on grounds of race and ethnicity, religion, disability, age and sexual orientation in addition to gender (and nationality). This has had consequences for gender policy too, by resulting in a new policy direction that emphasizes understanding multiple discrimination. In the EU gender regime, the shifting powers and roles of the Parliament, Commission and Council in the EU governance shape gender policy.

Feminist evaluations of the EU gender regime

The EU gender regime as represented by its hard and soft law policies on gender, its institutions and policy-making processes, provides both opportunities and challenges for promoting gender equality or progressive gender policy. The first issue to discuss is that this gender regime is based on an anti-discrimination model where the dominance of the Anglo-Dutch tradition on discrimination is evident. On one hand, as discussed above, this has enabled gender discrimination in the labour market and beyond to be outlawed. The anti-discrimination directives drafted on the basis of the model are 'based on individual litigation rights with an emphasis on access to key social goods such as employment' (Bell 2008: 36, Geddes and Guiraudon 2004: 334). Issues such as equal pay are treated in terms of discrimination legislation (in contrast, for example, to the Nordic corporatist model discussed in Chapter 9), and the EU has been a forerunner in defining the notions of direct and indirect discrimination in Europe (Chapter 2). This Anglo-Dutch model has, in turn, been shaped by US legal culture. Its importance can be seen in the EU in, for example, defining sexual harassment as sex discrimination. The transfer of norms is, however, notably not straightforward and here too the EU has added its own definitions by defining sexual harassment in terms of 'violation of dignity' (Zippel 2008: 73).

On the other hand, the dominance of the anti-discrimination agenda has meant that there has been less emphasis on positive measures, such as positive action and gender mainstreaming. These could, however, be in some cases more effective than anti-discrimination in that they do not focus on the discriminated individual but emphasize structural inequalities and place the responsibility to act on society or organizations. For example, intersecting inequalities are being tackled in terms of 'multiple discrimination' rather than more positive action measures in the EU (Chapter 8). Here the EU anti-discrimination policy can, arguably, be extended to fields that could be best tackled through social policy, such as Roma women's poverty, but where the EU competence to act is low (Kantola and Nousiainen 2009). Feminists are also concerned about the emerging hierarchies between inequalities and bases of discrimination (see Chapter 8). For example the fact that protection against gender discrimination in the Goods and Services Directive, discussed above, has a narrower scope than the comparable directive on racial discrimination sends, according to Annick Masselot (2007: 154): 'a message that some forms of sex discrimination and gender inequality are acceptable, while not allowed as far as racial discrimination is concerned' (see also Caracciolo di Torelia 2005: 342).

The second and most persistent feminist critique of the EU gender regime suggests that the Union reduces all questions of inequality and exclusion to problems of employability or the functioning of the economy and the market (Young 2000, Ostner 2000). Here the way in which the EU gender regime prioritizes the labour market and employment issues is highlighted, and, indeed, actions taken on the basis of Article 141 are based on a clear link between the market and economic orientation of the Union (Caracciolo di Torelia 2005: 339). The EU's normative vision on gender and employment is based on an 'adult worker model' where 'all adults – male and female, old and young, abled and less-abled – are required to take formal employment to secure economic independence' (Annesley 2007: 196). Critics argue that as a result of this dominant way of conceptualizing inequality and exclusion, social rights as opposed to economic rights retain a weak position in the EU gender regime.

This holds not only for hard law but for such soft law instruments as the Roadmap for Equality too (Ahrens 2008). The emphasis on the labour market and employment trends arguably constructs gender equality narrowly in that it is based on 'the notion of equality as sameness', where the aim is to provide women with equal opportunities on the basis of the male norm (Macrae 2006: 530–1).

Feminists have long argued that gender equality cannot be narrowed down to gender inequalities in the labour market but that oppression in other spheres – such as family, home, education, media, advertising – supports and constitutes gendered oppression and impacts on women's participation in the labour market (Chapter 2). These evaluations illustrate that feminists struggle with some basic dilemmas in relation to the EU: How compatible are market values, competition, efficiency and productivity with gender equality? Can women's concerns be represented in the EU without them being co-opted to the overall agenda? Is gender equality an issue that necessitates global governance?

In contrast to the identification of these strong models for the EU gender regime, it can be argued that gender equality takes on different meanings in EU policies with diverse gendered effects (Beveridge 2007, Locher and Prügl 2009, Lombardo and Meier 2007, Stratigaki 2004, Verloo 2007). This book provides a number of examples of this trend. Women's participation in the labour market is seen as central to economic growth but also to gender equality (Chapters 5 and 6). Domestic violence is conceptualized within a feminist 'violence against women' frame but tends also to be reduced to a narrow 'public health' issue (Chapter 7). The Commission definition of intersectionality as 'multiple discrimination', in turn, reduces the issue to anti-discrimination policy closing off, for example, class inequalities (Chapter 8).

EU institutions – the Parliament, the Commission and the Council – can be evaluated both in terms of their representativeness and policy outputs from a gender perspective. A focus on women's political representation in these institutions shows that none of them are based on gender-balanced representation (see Chapter 3). Whilst all of them have contributed to the existence and development of EU gender policy, criticisms of them have also been voiced. The role of the Parliament in pushing for more gender equality reforms has long been recognized in feminist research and it is often deemed the most gender-friendly of the EU institutions. The

Commission, by contrast, has been shown to be an initiator of genderfriendly policies but also a bureaucratic actor resistant to gender equality reforms. This has, for example, been evidenced by its failure to implement gender mainstreaming in its own structures (Chapter 6). Similarly, the European Court of Justice (ECJ) has made some controversial rulings, for example by outlawing (automatic) positive action and has, as a result, been seen as an actor harmful to gender equality in the EU. The Council, however, has been deemed the most secretive and difficult site from a gender perspective (Clavero and Galligan 2009). Lack of transparency in its processes has made it difficult to evaluate the negotiations that surround decision-making. However, it is well established that member states' differences and constructions of 'national interests' come into play in the Council negotiations in relation to gender equality, often hampering progressive policy.

The enhanced role of the social partners in the EU legislative process has resulted in further challenges for gender equality directives. Directives enacted after their involvement have not significantly enhanced gender equality provisions in the EU and the member states (see Chapter 5). Similarly, many feminist scholars remain unconvinced about the benefits of the subsidiarity principle for advancing gender equality. They argue that it can lead to non-interference and benefit those actors, such as employers and industries, who prefer 'raising awareness' about gender equality to binding measures (Hoskyns 2000, Nousiainen 2009). For example, in relation to family policy, one can detect a trend of 'double subsidiarity', where, first, the family is traditionally treated as a private sphere where there should be no political interference, and, second, the EU competence to act in the field of social policy and family law is traditionally low and is further reduced by the principle of subsidiarity (Nousiainen 2009). This double subsidiarity means 'double trouble' and increased challenges for any aspirations to strengthen EU policy away from a model of female care givers and towards gender-neutral parenting (Nousiainen 2009).

Whilst EU bodies that use public power may be privileged sites of discourse, which is also why they are studied (Kantola 2006: 44), it is important to note that elites are not the only source of discourses and that citizens and movements exercise discursive power too (Bacchi 2009), as highlighted in the new social movements theory (Tarrow 1998, Della Porta and Diani 2006). Gender equality advocates, women's movements and policy agencies provide counter-discourses and alternative policy solutions at the EU level. Although they can provide important counter-discourses to the official ones, they can also become complicit with the overall policy agenda and priorities. Different chapters in this book study the position of equality advocates in the EU governance framework, and ask what space there is for promoting alternative frames, or whether women's movements have become, for example, technical suppliers of knowledge in the EU polic-making processes.

Soft law and the dominance of the OMC in employment and childcare policy (discussed in Chapters 5 and 6) represent new trends and challenges in the EU gender regime. As a policy-making tool the OMC closely parallels gender mainstreaming in its soft way of functioning and shares some of the implementation challenges that gender mainstreaming has faced (Beveridge 2008: 15, Woehl 2008, Woodward 2005, ch. 6). In addition to democratic and representative issues, gender scholars point to the problems related to the method's 'softness' in that it does not result in any real structural change in gender relations in the member states. Political commitment varies with changes in governments and is also vulnerable to economic recession (Beveridge and Velluti 2008a: 192–3, 198). The open-ended gender equality goals can always be superseded by other more pressing concerns. There are no clear-cut standards, such as the correct implementation of directives, by which to assess member state progress, but rather states can present in their national reports various, often unrelated or old, methods as their ways of working towards gender equality goals (Verloo and van der Vleuten 2009). Overall, the OMC combined with gender mainstreaming has increased the complicity of gender equality with the market-driven notions of what constitutes equality.

Hence, whilst soft law has broadened EU gender policy to tackle issues beyond its direct competency such as gender violence, it has also strengthened the tendency to define gender equality as a way to achieve economic growth, for example via women's participation in the labour market. Soft law has certainly not raised radical new concerns, such as empowerment, eco-feminism or women's rights in relation to childbirth (Hašková 2005: 1092–3), onto the EU political agenda, but rather has strengthened the tendency towards achieving gender equality in terms of quantifiable policy outcomes.

This book

The book covers, first, the question of how gender came onto the EU agenda and how feminists came to study it. Second, it focuses on current gender policies including the institutions and actors relevant in advancing gender equality, and gender mainstreaming (that is, the gender aspects of other policies) and recent moves towards theorizing gender in connection with other bases of equality. Third, it explores how the EU gender model is being exported to old member states (Europeanization) and to the new member states (enlargement). The book maps out where significant progress has been made in relation to gender equality in the EU, and what the remaining problems and blind spots are.

Chapter 2 tackles two questions: how gender came onto the EU agenda and how feminists came to study it. It will thus present the legal developments in the field of gender equality since the Article 119 on equal pay in the Treaty of Rome 1957 and the Equal Treatment Directive 1976. These developments have, for instance, introduced the concepts of direct effect of the EU law, and direct and indirect discrimination.

Chapter 3 focuses on gendered patterns of representation and voice in the EU. It analyzes women's descriptive representation in different EU institutions including the European Parliament, Council of the European Union, the European Commission and the European Court of Justice.

Chapter 4 provides an overview of policy-making processes in the EU and evaluates their strengths and weaknesses from a gender perspective. The chapter tackles basic questions involved in analyzing the formulation of gender policy such as: What opportunities do the EU policy-making processes provide for promoting gender equality? With what political tools is gender equality being advanced and what challenges are there in the process? What role do civil society organizations play in these policy-making processes?

Chapters 5, 6 and 7 move on to discuss three different policy debates from a gender perspective. Chapter 5 discusses the issue of the reconciliation of work and family that constitutes a key EU gender policy debate. The chapter illustrates the interplay between hard law and soft law in formulating policies surrounding the issue and draws attention to the roles of different EU institutions and policy-making processes in these debates. Chapter 6 focuses on ways in which gender has become relevant across all policy-making fields in the EU by discussing gender mainstreaming. The challenges relating to gender mainstreaming are illustrated with a focus on development policy on one hand, and employment policy on the other. Chapter 7 draws attention to a key feminist priority, that of gender violence, which is discussed in terms of EU policies on trafficking in women and domestic violence.

Chapter 8 explores the way in which EU anti-discrimination and equality policy has horizontally expanded to cover other bases of inequality in addition to gender. This, it is argued, has fundamental consequences for gender that now need to be considered in conjunction with other intersecting inequalities. The agenda is new in a number of member states and promoted in them by the EU. Chapter 9 discusses in more detail these processes of Europeanization and the multiple ways in which EU policies interact with old and new member state gender regimes.

Chapter 10 draws conclusions about gender and the European Union and finishes with some reflections on the possible impact of the Lisbon Treaty on the EU gender regime and policy discussed in the book.

Chapter 2

The History of Gender and the European Union

How has gender equality policy developed at the supranational EU level? How did it ever get started in male-dominated decision-making bodies? How did the understandings of the contents of gender equality and the ways of achieving it change? What role did the different EU institutions – the Commission, the Parliament, the Council, the Court – play in this? And did the states implement sex discrimination directives?

This chapter begins to shed light on these questions by exploring the history of gender discrimination legislation and policies in the EU. The inclusion of Article 119 on equal pay in the Treaty of Rome in 1957, discussed in the first part of the chapter, represents a very early beginning of gender policy in the EU. It shows that the issue of gender equality was part of European integration from the beginning although the reasons for its inclusion were economic rather than related to social justice or equality between women and men. This reflects the weak position of social policy vis-à-vis economic priorities in the EU in general. However, the second part of the chapter focuses on the period of intensification that gender policy went through in the 1970s, which illustrates the ways in which gender equality was a field where binding legislation on social policy was often agreed for the first time. In a favourable international and European context, the EU enacted three new equal opportunities directives and created a European women's policy machinery. The 1980s, by contrast, represent incremental, discontinuous and frequently suspended development in the field of gender equality, as illustrated in the third part of the chapter. In the cold climate of neo-liberal market reforms, a number of draft directives were rejected or watered down. Some of them were turned into weaker recommendations or announcements, which, together with the first two action plans on equal opportunities, marked the beginning of the use of 'soft law' in the field of gender equality in the EU. The rocky history of gender is well illustrated in the fourth part of the chapter by the precarious position of positive action in the EU history of gender equality legislation and case law. Indeed, feminist evaluations of EU gender policy remained highly critical for a long time, as discussed in the final part of the chapter.

The beginning: Article 119 on Equal Pay

The Treaty of Rome in 1957 marks the beginning not only of European integration but also of European gender equality policy. The Treaty contained a single article on social policy placing a direct obligation on the member states and even specifying the deadline for its implementation (van der Vleuten 2007: 33). This was the famous article on the principle that women and men should receive equal pay for equal work (Article 119, now Article 141 EC) which stated: 'Each member state shall during the first stage ensure and subsequently maintain the application of the principle that men and women should receive equal pay for equal work'. Pay gaps between the sexes were wide at the time. For example, the Dutch pay gap was around 40 per cent, with many sectors of the economy relying on low-paid female labour. Women's wages were 63 per cent of men's wages in Germany in 1955. One can therefore ask: how was the principle of equal pay incorporated into the Treaty and with what consequences for women and member states?

The drafting of Article 119 has to be understood in the context of two developments. First, the International Labour Organization (ILO) Convention that included a recommendation on equal pay for women and men was an important backdrop to Article 119 (Ellina 2003: 26–7, Hoskyns 1996: 53, van der Vleuten 2007: 35). After the First World War, lobbying by women's organizations ensured that the equal pay claim was on the agenda of the committee that drew up the so-called labour section of the Versailles Peace Treaty. International trade unions supported their claim because they feared that employers would prefer to keep the cheap female workers who had replaced men during the war. In this way, the principle of equal pay for work of equal value was included in the constitution of the ILO in 1919 (van der Vleuten 2007: 35). Second, France had adopted a constitutional principle of equality that was held to require equal pay much earlier than many other countries in Europe. The French legislation alarmed French employers as no similar measures existed in the other member states. This persuaded the

French government to include equal pay in the set of demands on harmonizing social costs in the negotiations of the Treaty of Rome (Hoskyns 1996: 53–5).

The other negotiating partners of the Treaty were not keen to include equal pay between women and men and the treaty debates were characterized by resistance from the Dutch to the idea of equal pay. An equal pay stipulation was in direct conflict with Dutch wages policy. The country alleviated poverty among workers not by providing equal pay for female workers, but by paying all male workers, whether married or not, a 'family wage' (Cichowski 2002: 223). Women in the civil service, including the health service and education, faced dismissal when they married. The German government did not want an extension of the ILO norm either and its representatives resisted all supranational obligations concerning harmonization (van der Vleuten 2007: 38). Eventually, domestic developments made it possible for Germany to agree to French demands on the issue. The Federal Labour Court accepted separate wage categories for physically lighter and heavier work. In practice it meant that women were placed systematically in the lowest paid category. 'Women's work' was redefined as 'lighter work'. Formally women were entitled to the same pay for the same work, but in practice their work was usually defined as 'not the same as men's work' (van der Vleuten 2007: 46–7). The Dutch government could not block the provision without German support, but succeeded at the last minute in unilaterally weakening its obligation to implement it (van der Vleuten 2007: 50). Article 119 was therefore finally included in the Treaty as a result of French demands, domestic changes in Germany and a concession to the Netherlands.

It is clear, however, that the origins of Article 119 were embedded in economic rather than social justice concerns. Countries with equal pay principles were thought to be in an unfair position in market competition when compared to those countries that paid lower wages to women. The interests of women were not raised in the debate (Hoskyns 1996: 57, Pillinger 1992: 80). Article 119 was a piece of legislation by men, drafted in all-male working groups to which women had no access and no channels of influence (van der Vleuten 2007: 50–1). Furthermore, it dealt with equal pay for equal work and not with the broader and more important question of equal pay for work of equal value.

Implementation

It is not surprising, then, that until the late 1960s, not one national government had undertaken domestic policy changes to implement Article 119 (Cichowski 2004: 501). Anna van der Vleuten (2007) has studied the various reasons behind this and suggests that on the positive side, for example, France and Germany believed they had in theory already implemented Article 119. In France, the principle of equal pay was again included in the new constitution of 1959 and it applied to all labour contracts. Germany held that Article 3 of its Constitution already stipulated the equality of men's and women's wages. The Dutch, by contrast, did not show concern about discrimination against women workers but about the economic costs of paying women correctly (van der Vleuten 2007: 52–3).

The Commission and within it DG V, the Directorate-General on Employment, Social Affairs and Equal Opportunities, did take some steps to oversee implementation. Its study of the state of equal pay in the member states confirmed that women's work was systematically undervalued. The problems included job classifications that assigned a lower value to work done primarily by women. Women could also be paid a lower piecework rate because their productivity was thought to be lower than male productivity. Of all the member states, the Netherlands was the most backward. There was no statutory equal pay provision. Collective labour agreements fixed women's wages 25–30 per cent lower than men's wages for the same work (van der Vleuten 2007: 53–4).

The final deadline for implementation of equal pay provisions was 31 December 1964 but the member states violated this. Pressure for implementation increased after 1965 but it was too weak to overcome resistance among employers and governments. The Commission drew up reports, but shied away from taking action against member states. It did not bring a single member state before the Court for fear of losing Council support for its proposals in other domains. Some (male) officials in DG V made efforts to advance the implementation of equal pay, but the Commission was not supportive. The European Parliament supported the criticism of the member states, but lacked any substantial power (van der Vleuten 2007: 67).

Defrenne 1

Defrenne 1 is often regarded as the founding moment in the history of gender and the EU as it rescued Article 119 from oblivion in the late 1960s. The Belgian lawyer Eliane Vogel-Polsky initiated the *Defrenne 1* and *2* legal actions at the end of the 1960s. Defrenne, an air hostess who had worked with the Belgian airline Sabena, was forced to resign when she turned 40 whilst her male colleagues could work until they were 55. This meant a significant loss of earnings and pensions for air hostesses, who in many cases had to search for alternative work. Vogel-Polsky attempted to use the provisions of Article 119 to argue that this constituted wrongful discrimination (Cichowski 2004: 501–2, Hoskyns 1996: 70). The first *Defrenne* case to arrive at the European Court of Justice in 1970 was, however, against the Belgian state for the annulment of the special pension scheme for air crew adopted in 1969 on the grounds that it was contrary to the provisions of Article 119. The new scheme gave 'any member of the air crew except air hostesses' a special deal on pensions amounting to what was virtually full salary on retirement (Hoskyns 1996: 80). The case received surprising amounts of sympathy among the male judges in the European Court of Justice. The matter was completely new to them, but they had some familiarity within their jurisprudence with concepts of freedom, non-discrimination and rights. However, applying these to women in the labour market proved controversial and the court ruled in favour of the Belgian state (Hoskyns 1996: 73).

Despite the negative outcome, the ruling had far-reaching consequences due to two remarks by the Advocate General. First, he believed that pensions which were paid directly by employers were indeed covered by Article 119. The Court agreed that 'social security payments were not entirely separate from the concept of pay'. From this ruling DG V deduced that its mandate concerning the implementation of Article 119 also comprised equality in the area of social security. Second, the Advocate General confirmed the presumption of Vogel-Polsky about direct effect. He reminded the member states that Article 119 imposed an obligation on them that was sufficiently precise to be held directly effective. This would mean that, for example, Dutch women who still had no legal right to equal pay could appeal to the national court and ask for the application of Article 119. However, the Court ruled on this aspect only in *Defrenne 2* (see below) (van der Vleuten 2007: 79). Overall, the case exposed the challenges facing EU legislation on gender equality. It played a role in the intensification of gender policy in the 1970s when three new directives were drafted.

The intensification of gender policy in the 1970s

The process of intensification in the 1970s took place with the enactment of three new directives on Equal Pay 1975, Equal Treatment 1976 and Social Security 1978 and the creation of a women's policy machinery within the EU. Both the European and international contexts were favourable to gender policy at the time. In the EU the favourable developments related partly to the emergence of a European social dimension. When the government leaders met in Paris in October 1972, the German chancellor Willy Brandt and the French President Georges Pompidou each presented a memorandum on the social dimension. Both stressed that a common social policy was essential so that the population could identify with the EU. The Commission was told to present a social action programme before 1 January 1974 (van der Vleuten 2007: 71). The Paris mandate did not mention equal rights policy, but on its own initiative the Commission seized the opportunity to give equal rights a prominent place. In this way the equality of women and men became one of the key objectives of the Social Action Programme (Pillinger 1992: 84, van der Vleuten 2007: 71). The reason for this was perhaps the fact that equal pay and equal treatment in social security, pensions and taxation were costly. Therefore, member states preferred joint action in these fields instead of unilateral national policy. In this way every state would be bound to the same high standard (van der Vleuten 2007: 76).

Equal opportunities policy became an important issue for other reasons too. First, the EU expanded with three new member states: the United Kingdom, Ireland and Denmark. This meant a reshuffle of commissioner duties and the Irishman Patrick Hillery taking over as the Social Affairs Commissioner. He was more ambitious than his predecessor and several conservative top officials in DG V were replaced by officials who wanted to utilize the 'social mandate' of the Commission (van der Vleuten 2007: 72–3). Second, female politicians and bureaucrats and the women's movement were able to exert pressure on the EU in the 1970s (Hoskyns 1996: 78). A transnational equal rights network of national experts and supranational officials developed, bringing in feminist experts who were ready to formulate concrete proposals. This was combined with pressure from national groups, women's organizations and women in political parties and trade unions, who organized equal pay strikes and invoked Article 119 against governments and employers (van der Vleuten 2007: 72–3).

Beyond the European context, the UN declared 1975 International Women's Year. In June 1975, the first ever global inter-governmental conference specifically organized to address women's issues took place in Mexico. The outcome was the World Plan of Action for the Implementation of the Objectives of International Women's Year, a programme for the advancement of women to be implemented in the forthcoming decade in all countries and all areas (Pietilä 2007: 42). As illustrated below, the UN conference put pressure on the EU to develop its own provisions for equal opportunities.

Defrenne 2

This period also witnessed the ruling in the second *Defrenne* case in 1976. The case dealt with the loss of earnings suffered by Defrenne as a result of a variety of discriminatory practices mentioned above. The arguments for Defrenne rested on the contention that she had an individual right to equal pay based on the direct applicability of Article 119 and on the Belgian Article 14. This time the Court ruled that Article 119 was directly applicable. The Court thus expanded the scope and purpose of Article 119 by stating that the principle created enforceable rights in national courts, regardless of national implementing legislation (Cichowski 2004: 502). Furthermore, it drew a distinction between 'direct and overt' discrimination which could be distinguished using Article 119 alone, and 'indirect and disguised' discrimination which would need further implementation measures (Hoskyns 1996: 92). The judges were influenced by the EU's new emphasis on social policy and by the fact that by the time they made their final ruling, two new directives had been adopted by the Council (see below).

Hoskyns evaluates the significance of the judgement as 'radical' and 'far-reaching'. She writes: 'The decision to find Article 119 directly applicable established a legal base which helped the policy survive in the difficult years to come. It also broke new ground in making European social law directly binding on relations between individuals.' (Hoskyns 1996: 93) The decision enabled Article 119 to become the site for an expansive rights discourse and the driving force behind EU gender equality legislation in the 1970s and 1980s. Furthermore, the transformation of Article 119 had consequences not only for legislative action, but also for the creation of an environment in which the possibility of litigation was opened up. Individuals were provided with new tools to demand rights under EU law before national courts (Cichowski 2004: 502). Vogel-Polsky's test case strategy is also an example of how women can exploit international opportunity structures. While drafters thought they were designing an economic policy with a strict authoritative statement, in fact they were creating a capacity-building policy for women (Cichowski 2002: 229).

Equal Pay Directive

The 1975 Equal Pay Directive extended equal pay to equal pay for work of equal value. The directive clarified the scope of equal pay to include the removal of discrimination in the drawing up of job classification schemes and from laws, regulations or administrative provisions. Employees were given the right to take legal action against their employers and to protection if such action were taken (Pillinger 1992: 86).

A project for a directive on equal pay had been included as a priority item in the 1974 Social Action Programme. The Commission worked on the Equal Pay Directive and was supported by the European Parliament (Pillinger 1992: 86). The UK and France had passed national pieces of legislation on equal pay in 1970 and 1972 and were not opposed to the Community's actions in the field. France demanded the equal pay for work of equal value formulation so that all member states would be bound by the same high standard as France. The UK, Germany and Denmark resisted but France would not give in (van der Vleuten 2007: 87). The UK and Germany finally gave in, assuming that they had achieved concessions, and avoided the need to modify their legislation. The Council approved the directive in February 1975. This was the first time that the Council had approved a binding instrument for the harmonization of national social legislation (Hoskyns 1996: 85–90). The member states were given one year to comply with the provisions.

The Commission succeeded in obtaining member state approval of the directive because of its expert knowledge on equal pay, the *Defrenne 1* case, pressure at national level, support from the pioneer state (France) and the pressure caused by the UN International Women's year (van der Vleuten 2007: 87). Again women were not actively involved in the process which included only very indirect forms of consultation and representation. Nevertheless, the meanings of pay and equal work were defined more extensively, allowing for broader comparisons across jobs and the inclusion of comparable work. The directive also required job classification systems of wage determination (Ostner 2000: 28).

Equal Treatment Directive

The Equal Treatment Directive 1976 sought to establish equality of treatment between women and men with respect to access to employment, training and promotion, and working conditions. It made it illegal for member states to discriminate directly or indirectly against women, particularly on account of their family and marital status (Pillinger 1992: 88).

This was the first directive to be influenced by feminist actors within EU institutions. In 1973 Commissioner Hillery gave Jacqueline Nonon, a French official with expert knowledge on equal opportunities, the responsibility for equal rights policy in the renewed DG V. Nonon formed an ad hoc group of feminist experts to advise the commissioner on equal rights. The group operated under time pressure because Commissioner Hillery wanted the EU to make a contribution to the International Women's Year that involved more than just the Equal Pay Directive. The group believed that women not only needed equal treatment but also special treatment and it proposed a draft directive combining equal treatment (non-discrimination) and equal opportunities (positive action) (van der Vleuten 2007: 88).

At the time, there were no women's policy networks as such and no gender-specific institutional structures. Many women's organizations were already active at the national level but either rejected the mainstream EU institutions or were substantially unaware of the possibilities offered by the supranational level (Ellina 2003: 35). The only women's organization active at the EU level at the time was the Women's Organization for Equality (WOE) but this was essentially a consciousness-raising group founded in 1978 (Hoskyns 1996, 130). Nevertheless, there were active expert women and dedicated individuals including the French sociologist Evelyn Sullerot whose work *History and Sociology of Female Work* (1968) had been influential in the EU. She drew attention to the neglected subject of women's paid and unpaid work, which established her as an authority on the subject. Others included Eliane Vogel-Polsky, the Belgian lawyer, and Emilienne Brunfaut, a trade unionist. Jacqueline Nonon was able to draw on the expertise of these women (Ellina 2003: 34–5, Hoskyns 1996: 26).

The concept of equal treatment soon proved controversial because the Commissioners disagreed on the issue of whether they could stretch EU legislation to cover areas outside the labour market. Furthermore, in contrast to equal pay, equal treatment was a new issue and here the Commission proposal was clearly ahead of national legislation (van der Vleuten 2007: 89). Of the member states, the UK was a pioneer on the issue. The British 1975 Sex Discrimination Act included important features. First, it introduced the concept of indirect discrimination, defining it as: 'where a substantial number of a sex is unable, to their detriment, to comply with an apparently neutral rule, applicable to both sexes, which cannot be shown to be related to job performance' (van der Vleuten 2007: 91–2). Second, the Sex Discrimination Act established the Equal Opportunities Commission (EOC) to oversee the law's implementation (Lovenduski 1995: 114). Third, the Act introduced positive action measures. Under pressure from the women's movement, a clause that allowed positive discrimination in the admission procedures for training and study programmes, but not in job application procedures, was added. The UK was pushing for similar formulations at the EU level.

The Commission proposal contained two very sensitive points: the elimination of protective measures and exemptions for sex-specific professions, and the elimination of unequal treatment in social security and retirement ages. The member states demanded amendments on both issues. Furthermore, Germany did not want a general ban on sex discrimination (Cichowski 2002: 231). It preferred having to deal with unequal treatment and remove discriminatory provisions from its legislation only to the extent that they damaged free movement or competition (van der Vleuten 2007: 95). The Commission refused to give in to pressure on this point. The member states disagreed until the last minute about the scope of the concept of non-discrimination, judicial assistance and the deadline for implementation. The directive ultimately became stronger than the Commission's draft versions because the member states acceded to the British demand to include indirect discrimination (van der Vleuten 2007: 96).

Despite the weakening of the original proposal in some other respects, the directive was a far-reaching agreement. It broadened the principle of equal treatment for women and men to access to employment (including promotion) and vocational training, and to working conditions, and it ruled out all forms of direct and indirect discrimination on grounds of sex, particularly by reference to marital or family status. Section 4 of the directive allowed for positive action measures. The member states had approved these even though they still had few if any rules at the national level in these areas (Ostner 2000: 28, van der Vleuten 2007: 96). Feminists criticised the directive for including a clause permitting unequal treatment between the sexes for 'good reason'. In other words, 'good reason' might at times permit unequal treatment of women and men (Young 2000: 85).

Social Security Directive

The Social Security Directive 1978 provided for the equalization of social security benefits for women and men and covered sickness, disability, retirement, industrial injury and occupational disease and unemployment (Pillinger 1992: 88–9). It was drafted in a changed international and European context where the tide of European gender equality policy had turned. The recession sparked by the oil crisis in the mid-1970s led to a polarization of stronger and weaker economies and to diverging opinions about the aims of joint social policy. Against the background of rapidly increasing unemployment, improving the position of women could even be viewed as undesirable.

Despite their limited enthusiasm for legislating in the field of social security, the member states were obliged to act on the issue in the Equal Treatment Directive. Women's organizations and women in trade unions demanded rapid progress on social security whilst trade unions, employers and governments resisted (Hoskyns 1996). The Commission mandated DG V to draft a directive on equal treatment and social security. The feminist experts were not involved in drawing up this directive and it was prepared by social security experts (van der Vleuten 2007: 76).

By 1977 a draft directive was ready. None of the member states were particularly in favour of a supranational regulation for equal treatment in social security. However, there were significant differences between the member states on the issue. Germany and France expected that they would not have to modify their legislation drastically. The UK and the Netherlands, by contrast, expected that they would have to change their legislation substantially and estimated that reform would be very costly. Between July 1977 and July 1978 the negotiations on the directive ceased entirely because Belgium and Denmark, who held the Presidency, did not want to make room on their agendas for this topic (van der Vleuten 2007: 102). Finally, when the Presidency changed to Germany, which wanted the directive approved under its presidency, the lengthy negotiations ended, with the Council formally enacting the directive on 18 December 1978. The positive impact of the directive was minimized by the long implementation period of six years (Pillinger 1992: 89).

In conclusion, due both to the procedures for decision-making at the time and to the nature of these policy decisions, the three directives were all adopted under unanimity voting that required that all member states agree to pass the legislation. In order to reach consensus among all member states, the resulting legislation sometimes failed to address and clarify some sensitive issues of discrimination and general equality. However, this lack of clarity created an opportunity for legal activists to invoke EU rules against their own national governments. For example, the Equal Treatment Directive states that 'no discrimination whatsoever on grounds of sex' will be allowed under EU law. Scholars have observed that this general 'whatsoever' expression has given opportunities to both litigants and the court to expand the directive's scope. This includes the court decision that found that protection against dismissal for transsexuals fell within the scope of EU equality law (Cichowski 2002: 231).

The enactment of the Equal Treatment Directive also resulted in the creation of a body to oversee the implementation of the directive. This marked the beginnings of the creation of a women's policy machinery at EU level. The 1975 UN Women's Conference in Mexico had recommended the creation of women's policy agencies at national level. In 1976, the Commission acquired two structures dedicated to women: the Equal Opportunities Unit in DG V (then called the Women's Bureau) and the Women's Information Service in DG X. The *Equal Opportunities Unit* was created in 1976 with Nonon as its first head. The Unit had a policy-making role but its position in the Commission's hierarchy was not very high. The personnel were, however, specialists in gender issues. The department was originally assigned to monitor implementation of the Equal Treatment Directive and changes in the European Social Fund (ESF), and to design future polices. Its workload increased steadily with each new policy proposal for directives and other secondary legislation (Ellina 2003: 42).

The Women's Information Service was established in 1976 to disseminate information about women's policy and the EU to women in the member states. To this end, it published a newsletter, *Women of Europe*. Its position in the DG X hierarchy was very low and it had a very small staff. The staff's qualifications were more in the field of communication and information than in the area of women's issues *per se*. Chrystalla Ellina suggests (2003: 43) that had it been adequately staffed and provided with sufficient resources, the service might have influenced women's opinion of the EU and averted some of the negative consequences of national referenda on European integration in the 1990s.

Incremental development in the 1980s

The 1980s were a period of incremental development in EU gender policy. The first part of the decade has been called the 'hard times' and 'cold climate' (Hoskyns 1996a: 18). It was characterized by high unemployment, deregulation, government cuts and a rhetorical emphasis on a 'flexible' workforce (Ostner and Lewis 1995: 164). Margaret Thatcher was the British Prime Minister and her government curtailed social policy development in both the UK and the EU. There were no new directives that would have been of major significance. Rather, this stage in the development of EU gender policy saw the emergence of soft law and a wider women's network. Important steps were, however, taken in implementing directives from the previous decade.

During this period only two out of several proposed directives on equality were adopted, both in 1986, and both of relatively minor importance: one on equality in occupational social security and one on equality between self-employed men and women (the Occupational Social Security Directive and the Self Employed Directive). Both directives were largely symbolic (Cichowski 2002: 231, van der Vleuten 2007: 139).

A number of directives were either rejected or watered down. The Council of Ministers rejected the Commission's draft directives on part-time work (1983), parental leave (1984), social security (1989), widows' pensions (1989), additional benefits for families (1989), retirement age (1989), reversal of the burden of proof (1989), organization of working time (1991) and atypical employment (1991). Draft directives which were watered down into weaker recommendations or announcements were: women's unemployment (1984), equal treatment in taxation (1991), family policies (1991), childcare (1991) and sexual harassment in the workplace (1991) (Young 2000: 86). There was no political will in the member states, with the exception of France, to approve new equal rights policies. The suggested pieces of legislation went against the political ideologies of the centre-right governments in Germany, the Netherlands and the UK. Stagnation in gender policy reflected the general stagnation in the EU from 1979 to 1985 (van der Vleuten 2007: 117–18).

Thus it was not until the late 1980s, when the Council accepted the development of a new social dimension to complement the single market initiative, and the voting system in the Council was modified to permit qualified majority in some areas, that further equality legislation was forthcoming (McCrudden 2003: 4). Then the Single European Act (SEA) 1987 replaced unanimity in the Council of Ministers with qualified majority voting for legislation regarding the single market as well as that concerned with health and safety at work. This removed the national veto power of individual states and provided scope for introducing policies related to the social dimension through majority voting if it could be broadly determined that they were related to health and safety at work, or that social issues could undermine the Single European Act due to the distortion of competition (Pillinger 1992: 124). Chapter 5 analyzes the ways in which this moved gender equality directives forward. For example, the Commission prepared the 1990 proposal for a Pregnancy Directive based on the new health and safety article in order to circumvent British opposition. This and the enactment of the Maastricht Treaty 1992 resulted in significant changes in gender policy (see Chapter 5).

As a result of the watering down of directives into non-binding resolutions and recommendations the period witnessed the use of soft law measures to advance gender equality. 'Soft law' refers to guidelines, recommendations and action plans as opposed to the legally binding directives ('hard law') that were enacted in the 1970s. Included in the soft law measures of the time were the first and second action programmes approved by the Council of Ministers in 1982 and 1986 to promote equal opportunities (Hoskyns 1996: 142). Action programmes are standard EU practice for managing particular policy areas. Drafts of action programmes are developed in the appropriate division of the Commission and then presented, with a budget proposal, to the Council of Ministers for approval (Hoskyns 2000: 45). The aim of the first action programme was to consolidate and extend the achievements that had been made on equal opportunities so far. The second action programme (1986–90), by contrast, reflected the changed circumstances and there was a clear sense that adopting new legislation in the social policy area was increasingly difficult. The legal route was not totally abandoned but there was instead an emphasis on training and education of professionals, support for networking and the adoption of measures that would encourage the 'sharing of family and occupational responsibilities' (Hoskyns 2000: 47–9). The action programmes thus reflect the priorities and tools of gender policies of the time.

The period was also important in terms of the emergence of a larger organization-based community for women's policy. *The European Network of Women* (ENOW) was established in 1983. The Network was a response to the growing interest amongst feminist groups in engaging with EU level policy-making and in creating an EU-wide women's lobby. ENOW was a feminist network that was committed to women at the grass-roots level. It worked with limited resources to put greater pressure on EU institutions to continue with and extend their policy for women and to monitor the implementation of policy at the national level. ENOW began its work by developing a lobby in Brussels, which led to the establishment of a network of women throughout Europe. The network held a series of meetings and conferences in different member states. Its work, however, was hampered by a lack of the resources needed to develop a strong lobby (Pillinger 1992: 72). Both the Commission and the Parliament acquired gender-specific institutional structures during this period, as discussed in more detail in Chapter 4. Within the Commission, DG V's *Advisory Committee on Equal Opportunities* for women and men was established in 1981 (Pillinger 1992: 67), and the European Parliament's ad hoc *Committee on Women's Rights* was set up soon after the first direct elections in 1979, which had resulted in the increase of female representation from 5 to 16 per cent.

Dedicated individuals, newly founded European organizations such as ENOW and institutional structures in DG V and the EP maintained a certain level of attention to gender policy in the 'cold climate' of the 1980s (Ellina 2003: 44, Hoskyns 1996: 140). As the political machinery in Brussels was tightly bound up with interest and lobbying groups, many of whom use professional lobbying organizations or develop their own, the emergence of a women's policy network was increasingly important for advancing gender equality policy (Pillinger 1992: 67).

Implementation of previous legislation

Perhaps the most important development of the period was the implementation of the 1970s directives in the member states, most extensively discussed by Anna van der Vleuten (2007). In most cases, this would not have been achieved without a Commission willing to resort to infringement proceedings in cases of non-implementation. All discriminatory provisions had to be eliminated from national legislation and collective labour agreements and all protective provisions had to be abolished before August 1978 in line with the Equal Treatment Directive. Exceptions were only permitted for positive action measures, professions where the sex of the employee was crucial and provisions for the protection of pregnant women (van der Vleuten 2007: 119).

Whilst progress had been made, not a single government had implemented the directive correctly. In 1983 France had approved the 'Roudy Act', the most far-reaching equal rights legislation in the EU. France therefore believed that it satisfied the requirements of the directives on equal opportunities. The Commission sent a warning (1980) and a reasoned opinion (1981) to France, because women were excluded from certain training programmes and jobs in the public sector. After a new warning (1984) and a new reasoned opinion (1986) to which France did not respond, the Commission took the case to the Court. The French government followed the directive only after the Court ruled that the Commission was correct (van der Vleuten 2007: 120–1). The Commission initiated another infringement procedure against France in 1986 because there were still protective measures in collective agreements. This case culminated in 1999 when the Commission asked the Court to impose a penalty payment of 142, 425 euros per day for the non-implementation of the Court's judgement. Finally, France complied (van der Vleuten 2007: 122).

The Commission brought Germany before the Court in 1983 after having sent warnings and reasoned opinions concerning the Equal Pay Directive and the Equal Treatment Directive. Germany did make minor revisions to its legislation before the court case. It enacted the 'EC Labour Law Adaptation Act – Act Concerning the Equal Treatment of Men and Women in the Workplace' (1980). The act was intended only to satisfy the obligations of the European directives – as indicated by its name – and did not aim to improve the position of working women. The problem, according to the Commission, was that the act did not apply to the public sector, it did not apply to the self-employed, the prohibition of discrimination in personnel advertisements was only a non-mandatory recommendation, and the exceptions to equal treatment were formulated in general terms (van der Vleuten 2007: 122–3). The Court ruled, however, that the German system appeared to work in practice because the Commission could not show that it led to discrimination. In this case, the Commission had underestimated the strength of the German system of constitutional review, and the Court did not dare to compete directly with the German Constitutional Court (van der Vleuten 2007: 124).

The Social Security Directive had to be implemented by the end of 1984. As early as June 1979, DG V had reminded governments that they had agreed to 'gradually' implement the directive. It demanded detailed information about the measures the governments wanted to take. All governments had started to implement equal treatment in social security but there were significant variations. The Dutch case, as discussed by van der Vleuten (2007: 130), is a good example. In the Netherlands the regulations directly affected by the directive concerned unemployment benefits, benefits pursuant to the health legislation, pensions and disability benefits that all discriminated against married women. Women faced multiple discrimination. Disabled men had a right to benefits regardless of whether they had previously had a source of income, while disabled married women only qualified for benefits if they had previously earned an income. Married women did not have a right to unemployment benefit unless they could show that they were the breadwinner, while married men were automatically treated as breadwinners. A married couple received benefits only when the husband turned 65, even if his wife was older than he was (van der Vleuten 2007: 130). The Dutch government combined the obligation to eliminate these discriminatory provisions with its aim to reduce government spending. It amended the regulations by assuming for every type of benefit that there was a family income which could be supplemented with extra payments to the dependent spouse. It ignored the fact that provisions formulated in a sex-neutral fashion could lead to indirect discrimination if in practice they primarily affected persons of a specific sex. The Dutch courts asked the European Court for its interpretation,which then heavily criticised the Dutch government. After a further Commission warning the Dutch government gave in and repaired some forms of discrimination in its social security system (van der Vleuten 2007: 131).

Infringement procedures, in summary, made it impossible for governments to hide behind ignorance about equal rights. The procedure increased 'the costs of non-compliance' and preliminary rulings made it more attractive for governments to amend their legislation rather than risk large numbers of expensive court cases (van der Vleuten 2007: 133). The Court's rulings also gave depth to the equal opportunities directives and strengthened their actual content and impact. This illustrates the power of hard law that sets clear targets, the monitoring of which is relatively easy when compared to some soft law measures.

Positive action

Towards the end of the 1980s steps were taken towards substantive equality as opposed to mere formal equality and anti-discrimination policies. According to many equality advocates, positive action occupies a central position in achieving real and effective equality. Positive action measures embody a different notion of gender equality from anti-discrimination measures as they try to correct the initial disadvantage of women. The application of a compensatory measure means favouring, in cases of equal merit, a woman over a man. Positive actions have been introduced to avoid the strict application of the principle of equal treatment generating further inequality for women (Lombardo 2003: 162). Positive action thus recognizes that equal treatment can reinforce existing inequalities and seeks to create a level playing field. In other words, the emphasis shifts from equality of access to creating conditions more likely to result in equality of outcome by equalizing the starting positions (Rees 1998: 34).

Over the years the EU has supplemented its anti-discrimination legislation with positive action initiatives. For example, in 1984 there was a Council Recommendation 84/635 on the promotion of positive action for women. However, the progress of positive action has been difficult. Positive action measures were initially put in place by using soft law measures. As a result, there was nothing to force member states to act on them (Beveridge, Nott and Stephen 2000: 143). Furthermore, the non-binding formulations created uncertainties and confusions around positive action measures, as illustrated by the *Kalanke* and *Marschall* cases, which represent milestones on the road towards this strategy. Both cases questioned the lack of legal clarity on issues of equal opportunities and expressed the need to introduce new political strategies to overcome structural discrimination against women (Lombardo 2003: 162).

Kalanke

The *Kalanke* ruling in 1995 showed that the notion of equality embedded in a positive action strategy may directly contradict the anti-discrimination notion of equality. The case arose in a public sector (parks department) context in Bremen, Germany, where an equally qualified woman was chosen over Eckhard Kalanke for a job. The local Bremen law on equal treatment stipulated that, in cases of two equally qualified persons, priority should be given to women if they are underrepresented (Young 2000: 89). The German local, regional, and federal labour courts ruled that the Bremen law did not breach the German Basic Law or the Civil Code and that it did not set strict quotas for women. Since it was unclear whether the Bremen law was compatible with European equal treatment, the case was referred to the ECJ. The Court found that 'the European equal treatment legislation defined the principle of equal treatment as meaning that there should be no discrimination whatsoever on grounds of sex. Clearly, national rules such as those in Bremen involved discrimination'. The Court made the argument that national rules that *automatically* give priority to women who are equally qualified in job sectors where they are underrepresented violate the principle of equal treatment. In other words, the ECJ held the regional German law incompatible with the Equal Treatment Directive 1976 (Schiek 1998: 152).

The judgement was possible because of a weakness in the Equal Treatment Directive and the non-binding character of Council Recommendation 84/635/EEC on the promotion of positive action for women. The ruling reduced the scope of the directive and seriously damaged public acceptance of positive action (Stratigaki 2000: 39). The case and the judgement received widespread publicity and media attention and sent shivers through the feminist community; it also created uncertainty within the legal community as to whether EU member states could enact positive action measures to promote equality (Young 2000: 89). Maria Stratigaki (2000: 39) calls this the 'first incidence of the emerging bureaucratic and political opposition to positive action and to the strong alliance on equality created at the EU level'.

Marschall

The *Marschall* case received much less publicity but meant that in 1997, the ECJ made some very fine distinctions between acceptable and unacceptable positive action strategies. A tenured male teacher, Helmut Marschall, challenged a regional German law that gave preference to an equally qualified female candidate in order to create a gender balance in promotions. A technical revision in the law (in the light of the *Kalanke* decision) altered the positive discrimination implicit in earlier law, that the underrepresented group automatically be given preference. Positive action measures were thus flexible and gave the administration some room to manoeuvre (Young 2000: 89). The preferential treatment in this case was therefore acceptable to the ECJ. More importantly, the rationale for the decision presents a departure from earlier rulings since it directly addresses mechanisms of exclusion in employment: that 'men tend to be chosen in preference to women where they have equal qualifications, since they benefit from deep-rooted prejudices and stereotypes as to the role and capacities of women' (Hobson 2000: 101). The decision thus takes into account structural inequalities. Women are excluded from jobs and promotion not only because they do care work in families but because it is assumed that they will interrupt careers more frequently, owing to household or family duties, or that they will be absent from work more frequently because of pregnancy, childbirth, and breast-feeding (Hobson 2000: 101).

The *Kalanke* judgement showed the importance of establishing strong binding instruments, allowing relatively limited scope for interpretations that might adversely affect equality objectives as a means of tackling deeply rooted social problems like the unequal gender division of labour (Stratigaki 2000: 41). The *Marschall* case opened up opportunities for preferential treatment. The new provision of the Amsterdam Treaty (Article 141(4), ex 119) provides that the principle of equal treatment does not prevent the maintenance or adoption of measures providing for specific advantages in order to make it easier for the under-represented sex to pursue a vocational activity or to prevent or compensate for disadvantages in professional careers (McCrudden 2003: 3). It thus further opened the way for positive action measures, although the form in which the concept of positive discrimination is expressed is rather weak (Lombardo 2003: 162). To sum up, this ruling and the insertion of the positive action measures in the Amsterdam Treaty make it clear that member states can still use positive action in certain circumstances to address discrimination.

Feminist critiques

The discussion has shown that EU gender policy has witnessed periods of progress as well as stagnation and setbacks. Feminist scholars have often been highly critical of the EU's abilities to improve the position of women in society (Elman 1996, Ostner and Lewis 1995, Pillinger 1992, Young 2000). This critique has been developed in particular on the basis of EU gender policies up to the end of the 1980s and is thus worth discussing here. The feminist anxieties about the EU included: (i) the *focus* of its policy: it has an excessive focus on the labour market and no binding provisions in other areas (for example childcare or gender violence); (ii) the *tools*: equal opportunities policy resorted to a narrow range of measures that are, furthermore, often poorly implemented and do not tackle structural inequalities; and (iii) the *ideology*: this is based on valuing the market and motherhood.

Feminist social theories highlight that different forms of women's oppression in society – at home, work, schools, and in politics – are interconnected and oppression in one sphere supports and constitutes oppression in another sphere. Thus it is not enough merely to focus on gender inequalities in the labour market. The EU, however, was established to promote economic integration and it is widely agreed that until the Maastricht Treaty in 1993 it treated its people as workers rather than citizens. Thus gender equality was also mainly advanced in relation to the labour market. Feminists argue that the narrow focus on labour market can, in fact, prevent women from entering the labour market: not extending the notion of equal treatment to address women's caring role in the home has repercussions on women's ability to take up employment. Lack of childcare is 'a major obstacle for women's labour market participation'

(Pillinger 1992: 22). In other words, the EU's equal opportunities policy failed to consider the existence of material conditions that prevent women from exercising their rights and from having equal access to the opportunities they are offered (Ostner and Lewis 1995, Lombardo 2003: 161, Hobson 2000: 98). Feminists, by contrast, have long been interested in a broader set of issues including violence against women, reproductive rights and abortion, care, pornography, and women's political representation, and in some cases these have been found to be more pressing concerns than access to the labour market and equal pay.

In addition to the problem of focusing on a narrow sphere of women's oppression, the tools used by the EU have been criticized by feminists as inadequate. As Sonia Mazey suggests: 'While the Equality Directives have been useful in combating individual cases of sex discrimination, they have to date had no significant impact on the sex segregated labour market. In short, the socio-structural causes of sex discrimination lie beyond the reach of the existing Equality Directives' (Mazey 1988: 63). In other words, the tools used by the EU are too narrow. Member states have in many cases not implemented the anti-discrimination directives, which makes their effectiveness questionable. Furthermore, anti-discrimination legislation and equal opportunities polices do not challenge the structural inequalities with their narrow scope (Smart 1989; Kingdom 1991).

Finally, feminist critics have seen the EU's ideological emphasis on the liberalized internal market and the primacy of economics as in contradiction with feminist aims (Rossilli 2000: 1, Young 2000: 86). This explains why social policy at the European level was kept to the minimum, and was regarded not as parallel to, nor as setting a framework for, economic measures, but as subordinate to them (Hoskyns 1996: 52). The EU, it is argued, represents a 'dramatic shift towards a disciplinary neoliberal discourse of capitalism' which shuts the door to more welfare state oriented strategies such as expanding the public sector to create jobs for women (Young 2000: 83). The primacy of economics results in an instrumental conception of women and gender equality: 'The goal of the EU equality policy is to use women as a key resource to create a flexible workforce and promote a more rational management of professional and family responsibilities' (Rossilli 2000: 8).

Some feminist scholars argue that there is a second problematical ideology at work in the EU: that of motherhood. In a series of cases in the area of pregnancy and maternity law, the ECJ has reproduced a particular vision of womanhood that is largely premised on the dominant ideology of motherhood (McGlynn 2000: 34). In this ideology, the mother is the primary carer of young children, mother–child relations are privileged, fatherhood is devalued, and the father is given the limited role of a breadwinner, protector and authority figure, which reproduces stereotypical images of the roles of women and men in families (McGlynn 2000: 34). More precisely, the Court's approach developed through the 'protection of women' principle. When women are considered to be in need of protection, the equal treatment principle need not apply, for instance in cases of pregnancy and maternity, and night work (McGlynn 2000: 35).

For example, in the case of *Commission* v. *Italy* in 1983, the Commission challenged Italian legislation which granted leave to women, and not men, on the occasion of their adoption of a child under six years of age. The Court ruled that the Italian legislation did not conflict with Community law; that the Italian government had been motivated by a 'legitimate concern'; and that the difference in treatment between women and men 'cannot be regarded as discrimination' within the meaning of the Equal Treatment Directive (McGlynn 2000: 36). Also in *Hofmann 1984* the Court ruled in favour of granting women and men different parental rights. The father of a new baby, Mr Hofmann, argued that the German leave that provided an optional period of maternity leave discriminated against fathers. The Court endorsed the German legislation and stated that Community law was not designed to settle questions relating to the 'organisation of the family' or to 'alter the division of responsibility between parents' (Hobson 2000: 96, McGlynn 2000: 36–7). Evelyn Ellis (1998: 379) also concludes that the Court appeared to have lost sight of the objectives of European Community sex equality law and to be operating as a 'drag on the system' at the beginning of the 1990s.

Conclusion

The inclusion of Article 119 in the Treaties of Rome marked the beginning of European policies on women. The negotiators of the Treaties were not concerned about advancing gender equality and it took fifteen more years for an equal opportunities policy to emerge. The early measures to promote equality were anti-discrimination measures. Thus Article 119 and the Equal Pay, Equal Treatment and

Social Security Directives were based on a concept of equality that required women and men to receive equal treatment in the labour market. The benefit of these measures was that they were binding directives although it was clear that the ways in which member states enforce these measures can reduce their effectiveness. The notion of equality was expanded only gradually and positive action emerged as an acceptable tool for advancing gender equality. There was, however, silence with respect to violence against women, pornography, childcare, trafficking in women, sexual harassment, reproduction and abortion – issues on the agenda of second wave feminism and the women's liberation movement. The EU's engagement with some of these issues will be discussed in Chapters 5 and 7.

The EU institutions have played different roles in gender policy. The Commission sometimes took bold initiatives in the field of gender equality, raising issues that were new for member state governments, such as direct and indirect discrimination. At other times, it was rather conservative, avoiding potential conflicts with the Council. Similarly, the Court at times promoted gender equality, starting with the *Defrenne* cases, but in other rulings took a restrictive view, for instance on maternity leave and positive action (*Kalanke*) (van der Vleuten 2007: 11). Overall, the Court extended the impact of European legislation beyond what member states agreed in the Treaty of Rome. Together the Commission and the Court have exerted pressure on the member states to implement the equality directives.

The discussion illustrates not only that it has been difficult to reach consensus in the Council on equal opportunities, but also that member states have resisted implementing the equality directives. Gender policy is constrained by the same mechanisms as other fields in the EU (Liebert 1997: 198). Feminists have however often argued that these problems have been particularly acute in relation to gender. Member states have lacked the political will to implement directives and the Commission has given low priority to monitoring compliance (Young 2000: 78). The following chapters will discuss these issues in more detail.

Chapter 3

Gendering Political Representation in the European Union

The Communications Commissioner Margot Wallström stated in February 2008 that she was fed up with the EU being governed by the 'reign of old men'. 'An inner circle of male decision-makers agree behind closed doors on whom to nominate to EU top jobs' and 'old men choose old men, as always', she said in a widely publicized interview with the Swedish daily *Sydsvenska Dagbladet* (8 February 2008). Whilst many feminists were undoubtedly jubilant at her having spoken out, others may have been disappointed about the realities of the gendered power structures of EU decision-making. Women's political representation both in the European Parliament (31 per cent) and in the Commission (30 per cent) stood at record levels although far from the parity representation of 50–50. The number of women in national governments, by contrast, varied greatly from 5 per cent in Greece to 60 per cent in Finland in 2007, and women continued to be concentrated in some (feminized) ministerial posts. This of course has consequences for the constitution of the Council, where the representation of women is the lowest of all the EU institutions. The ratification of the Treaty of Lisbon created new top jobs in the EU – including that of a permanent president of the Council and a foreign minister – and it is mainly men's names that have been put forward in the media. It is at these highest echelons of power that Wallström's statement seemed to be directed.

Wallström's statement came despite decades of efforts by the Commission and the Parliament to move towards gender balance in decision-making in the EU. This chapter will, first, discuss the policies adopted by the Council, the Commission and the Parliament to promote gender-balanced decision-making. Second, it will focus on the number of women in national parliaments, the European Parliament, national governments, the Commission and the Council of the European Union. An examination of the political representation of women in formal and informal institutions is an important starting point for 'reevaluating the oppressive and/or liberating potential of democratic institutions for them' (Dovi 2007: 299). Political representation is a major although limited way of studying how power is distributed at the EU level.

Yvonne Galligan and Sara Clavero (2008: 5) lament the fact that the scholarship on gender equality in the EU rarely addresses gender issues in relation to political representation and participation (see, however, Freedman 2002, Krook 2002). They suggest that this might be due to the difficulty of applying models that have been developed at national level to a supranational context. The nature of the EU institutions and their political influence do not parallel national ones. First, contrary to national parliaments, the European Parliament shares legislative power with the Council through the co-decision procedure. The Council also retains full legislative power in some policy-making fields (Chapter 4). Second, there is no single government in the EU, but the executive power is dispersed and shared between the Commission, the Council and some independent agencies such as the European Central Bank. Third, the Commission, unlike national governments, is not elected by the European Parliament but chosen by the member states and approved of by the Parliament (Galligan and Clavero 2008: 6). This poses particular challenges for women's political representation. The selection processes remain under the control of national governments and vary from one member state to another.

Feminist scholars have long debated the question: Does it matter whether women are represented in legislative bodies or not (see, for example, Childs 2006 and 2008)? That question is at the core of this chapter: does it make sense to focus on the numbers of women in EU legislative bodies? Anne Phillips (1998) famously identified four arguments to support women's political representation: (i) women politicians act as *role models* for aspiring women candidates; (ii) numerically equal representation of women and men in parliaments is a sign of *justice*; (iii) only women are in a position to represent women's *interests*; and (iv) women's political representation *revitalises democracy* (Phillips 1998). Suzanne Dovi (2007) has recently built upon this and put forward two other arguments: (v) according to the *trust* argument women's political representation is necessary for women to put their confidence in political institutions; and (vi) the *legitimacy* argument contends that the presence of women representatives increases the legitimacy of democratic institutions. Women's presence can thus be justified on its own terms: it is normatively desirable that parliaments reflect the social composition of society and include representatives of both sexes and from ethnic, racial, linguistic and religious minorities. Alternatively, it is possible to highlight the benefits that women's political representation brings in improving the deliberative process, reducing distrust and increasing democratic legitimacy (Mansbridge 1999: 654).

Feminist theories on the concept of gender complicate the debate on women's political representation. Gender theory has moved from studying women (a biologically given sex) to considering gender (socially constructed identities) and then to deconstructing the difference between sex and gender (Butler 1990, Squires 1999). The key challenge for debates on political representation is the recognition of the diversity of women's positions, voices, perspectives and opinions. The category of gender intersects with other grounds of discrimination including race, ethnicity, age, sexual orientation, class and disability, and the concept of intersectionality highlights the perception that the discrimination faced by a black woman is qualitatively different from what would result from merely adding together the impact of discrimination on the basis of gender and race (Crenshaw 1991; see also Chapter 8). As a result, it is now accepted that capturing the diversity of women's experiences into a single category of 'women's interests' is practically impossible. Instead the questions become: which women are represented in the political process and which are not; what happens to the political views of ethnic minority women, lesbians, and disabled women?

Like women's political representation, the representation of ethnic minority women can be justified from different perspectives. Nirmal Puwar (2004) argues that bodily presence – women's bodies, black women's and men's bodies, gay men's bodies – can be quite revolutionary in institutions that have previously been white and male, such as the British Westminster Parliament. She suggests that often even small numbers of these bodies can become amplified and can be seen as representing a threat to the institution. Melanie Hughes (2007), in turn, makes a strong argument for hearing the political voices of minority women: 'if minority women are not politically represented, they risk further marginalization'. Majority women and minority men are not always in a position to represent and articulate the special needs of minority women. The double democratic deficit experienced by white majority women can thus be accentuated in the 'multiple oppressions' or 'double minority' experienced by ethnic minority women (Black 2000, Yuval-Davis 2006). However, identifying and comparing political representation of 'ethnic minorities' can be empirically difficult. What counts as an 'ethnic minority' in one country can be a majority in another country (Hughes 2007: 4).

This chapter looks, first, at the measures taken in the EU to promote gender balance in political representation. Second, it looks at the success of these measures over the decades by focusing on the number of women in the national parliaments and the European Parliament. Third, it provides data on some of the highest glass ceilings that women have faced in terms of political representation, namely their position in the Commission, its preparatory bodies and the Council. The chapter shows that the representation of ethnic minority women is not politicized in the EU despite the fact that their political representation is significantly lower than that of majority women. The conclusion broadens the debate on political representation to the EU judicial bodies and looks at the position of women in the European Court of Justice.

Improving women's political representation in Europe

Measures to increase women's political representation have included soft measures such as public campaigns to change attitudes towards women politicians and funding women candidates' election campaigns, and institutional changes such as reform of electoral systems and internal party rules. Joni Lovenduski (2005: 90–1) differentiates between three available strategies: (i) equality rhetoric (promoting women's participation in different documents and speeches); (ii) equality promotion or positive action (training, financial assistance, setting targets); and (iii) equality guarantees or positive discrimination (quotas). Whilst the effectiveness of quotas depends on their particular requirements and on the sanctions for non-compliance, recent research shows that they are the most effective strategy and can put countries on a 'fast track' to gender parity in political representation (Dahlerup 2006; see also Krook 2009). The rise in the number of women in the parliaments of Latin American and African countries is often cited as a success story. Feminist research thus increasingly highlights the importance and effectiveness of hard law measures in increasing women's political representation.

The EU has embraced the agenda of gender-balanced representation of women in political decision-making since the 1990s. The initial steps to advance equality between women and men were taken in the EU in an all-male environment in the 1950s. As seen in Chapter 2, this continued to be the case until the formulation of the Equal Treatment Directive 1976 when the first feminist actors were included in working groups (Hoskyns 1996: 26). Since then EU thinking around the participation of women in political decision-making has changed dramatically. For example, the European Parliament now argues in one of its key documents in this field that women's inclusion in decision-making 'strengthens democracy, by taking account of the interests of the whole of society, and promotes its proper functioning' and results in 'more efficient use of human resources' (European Parliament 2000: 16). The EU has both been influenced by international developments, such as the 1995 Beijing Platform for Action, and has itself been important in pushing for gender-balanced decision-making internationally (Krook 2002).

Three distinct periods of EU action on women in political decision-making can be identified. In the first period, between 1991 and 1995, the EU adopted the Third Action Programme on Equal Opportunities (1991–5), which led to the establishment of an experts' network, 'Women in Decision-Making' (1992–6). The network played a crucial role in creating a favourable atmosphere and in co-ordinating campaigns and thinking in this field. Other concrete measures included the Athens Declaration in 1992, the Charter of Rome in 1996, and the Council resolution balancing participation of women and men in decision-making in 1995 (Krook 2002, Vogel-Polsky 2000, Hoskyns 2000).

In the second period, from 1996 to 2000, the 1996 Council Recommendation on the promotion of positive action for achieving a gender balance in the decision-making process and the Fourth Framework Programme on Equal Opportunities (1996–2000) were adopted (Lombardo and Meier 2007: 64). The Athens and Rome conferences were followed by the Paris Conference in 1999 on 'Women and Men in Power: a caring society, a dynamic economy, a vision for Europe'. Three years after the adoption of the Council Recommendation, in October 1999, nine indicators were established by the Council for measuring progress in women's participation in power structures. The indicators showed that participation was far from sufficient either at national or at EU level.

The third period started in 2000 with the publication of the

Commission Report (European Commission 2000a). The European Parliament had been actively asking for a report on the issue. The Commission gave a new definition of balanced representation and set 40 per cent as the minimum level of participation of women or men in committees and expert groups. It noted that there was variation on this in member states with the Nordic countries and the United Kingdom targeting 50 per cent participation and most countries considering a participation rate of at least 30 per cent to represent a balance (European Commission 2000a). The new definition was a result of increasing frustration with lack of implementation of the Council Recommendation and Resolution in the member states.

> The draftsperson considers this communication [from some member states] insufficient to establish correctly any progress achieved. Should we then interpret the absence of answers from certain Member States as a non-implementation of the Council Recommendation? ... It is only through precise deadlines and benchmarks that it will be possible to identify Member States, which have not compelled to their obligations, to register global progress and to advance in gender balance. (European Parliament 2000)

The lack of implementation was difficult to document because of the lack of comparable data (Council of the European Union 1999). The Commission therefore launched a European database, 'Women and Men in decision-making: A database with facts and figures', in 2004. The database includes figures on women in politics, covering parliaments, national governments, EU institutions, public administration and the judiciary. Reducing the inequalities between women and men in decision-making was again brought forward as one of the priorities of the Commission's Roadmap for equality between women and men 2006–10. Definitions were widened to cover economic decision-making and the Council has adopted a further set of nine indicators concerning women and men in economic decision-making. One of the key actions in the Roadmap was the establishment in 2007 of an EU network of women in economic and political decision-making positions.

The EU has thus taken several actions in the field over the past two decades. Two criticisms can, however, be directed at its policy. First, it is clear that the EU has mainly used *soft law* to promote gender-balanced decision-making. The tools have included awareness raising

campaigns, collection of comparable data and construction of indicators, and encouraging examples of good practice. The EU
approach thus represents Lovenduski's (2005) first two strategies:
equality rhetoric and equality promotion. The effectiveness of the
strategies is questionable. Whereas hard law provides clear-cut standards in terms of whether a directive is implemented or not in
member states, soft law measures shift from absolute to relative
standards of quality, understanding quality as a matter of technical
measurement as opposed to political judgment or opinion (Verloo
and van der Vleuten 2009). The implementation of the Council
Recommendation and the Resolution in the member states has been
poor and the impact of these strategies limited. In many cases it
becomes a matter of interpretation and definition whether a gender
balance has been achieved. This is further exacerbated by the lack of
comparable data.

   Second, the issue of the political representation of ethnic minority women is absent from the policies, documents and declarations
of the Council, the Commission and the Parliament. Data on ethnic
minority women is not included in the database on women and men
in decision-making and their position is not mentioned in the publicity material produced by the Commission (European Commission
2005a). The debate on ethnic minority women in the EU centres on
asylum-seekers and migrant workers and is focused on their
economic rights in the labour market rather than their political
rights. For example, the Commission report on gender equality does
focus on migrant women but only in terms of their employment
(European Commission 2005b).

Women in the parliaments of the member states and the European Union

As we have seen above, the EU has placed some emphasis on
measures to increase women's political representation in member
states' parliaments. The percentage of women in national parliaments in the current EU-27 countries varies greatly, from Sweden's
near parity of 47.3 per cent to Malta's 9.3 per cent of women (see
Table 3.1). The average in the EU-27 was 23.1 per cent in 2007.
This is slightly higher than the world average, which was 17.5 per
cent for single or lower house of parliament in 2007, but well below
the Commission's target of 40 per cent.

TABLE 3.1   *Percentage of women in the single or lower house of parliament in the current EU-27 member states*

Country	1992	1997	2002	2007
Austria	23.4	26.8	33.9	32.2
Belgium	9.4	12	23.3	34.7
Bulgaria	12.9	10.8	26.3	22.1
Cyprus	5.4	5.4	7.5	14.3
Czech Republic	8.3*	11	12.4	15.5
Denmark	33	33.5	38	36.9
Estonia	12.9	12.9	18.8	21.8
Finland	38.5	33.5	37	42
France	3.7	10.9	12.3	18.5
Germany	20.5	26.3	32.3	31.6
Greece	5.3	6.3	8.7	13.0
Hungary	7.3	11.1	9.8	10.4
Ireland	12	12.1	13.3	13.3
Italy	8.1	11.1	9.8	17.3
Latvia	14**	8	21	19.0
Lithuania	7.6	17.5	10.6	24.8
Luxembourg	13.3	20	16.7	23.3
Malta	1.5	5.8	9.2	9.2
Netherlands	21.3	31.3	34	36.7
Poland	9.8	13	20.2	20.4
Portugal	8.7	13	19.1	21.3
Romania	3.5	7.3	10.7	11.2
Slovakia	14.7***	12.7	19.3	19.3
Slovenia	12.2	7.8	13.3	12.2
Spain	13.4	21.6	28.3	36
Sweden	33.5	41.3	45.3	47.3
United Kingdom	9.2	18.2	17.9	19.7
Average	**13.5**	**16.3**	**20.3**	**23.1**
Average	**13.2 EU-12**	**21.2 EU-15**	**24.7 EU-15**	**23.1 EU-27**

* The figure refers to the former Federal Assembly of Czechoslovakia
** In 1993
*** In 1994
Source: The Inter-parliamentary Union.

The increase in women's representation has been incremental in some countries and rapid in others. In the past 15 years, women's political representation has increased incrementally in Austria, Denmark and Finland. By contrast, it has made more drastic jumps in other countries; in Belgium from 9.4 per cent in 1992 to 34.7 per cent in 2007, in the UK from 9.2 in 1992 to 18.2 in 1997, and in France from 3.7 per cent in 1992 to 18.5 per cent in 2007. These quick advances are the result of the use of legislative gender quotas or political party quotas to promote women into political decision-making posts. The jumps represent the so-called 'fast track to gender balance in politics' (Dahlerup 2006). Thus, for example in the UK, the Labour Party applied all-women shortlists in the 1997 elections, in France the parity law was enacted in 2000 and in Belgium a 1994 and 2002 election law quota decreed that lists must include an equal share of women and men in all elections.

In some European countries the number of women in parliaments has increased only moderately and remains very low, as for instance in Greece (13 per cent), Hungary (10.4 per cent) and Malta (9.2 per cent). Turkey, an aspirant member state, also displays very low levels of women in parliaments. In 1992, the figure of women in the Turkish parliament was 1.8 per cent, in 1997, 2.4 per cent, in 2002 and 2007, 4.4 per cent. Moreover, in many countries the percentage of women has decreased in certain elections. Both tendencies indicate that increase in women's political representation is neither linear nor self-evident.

The history of women's representation in the former communist central and eastern European countries is different from in the so-called West. In the 1970s, many of these countries had 30 per cent quotas for the representation of women in the party-controlled national assemblies. Despite the relatively high numbers of women in the parliaments, women were less well represented in the upper echelons of the parties and the real locus of political power. The fall of communism in 1989 resulted in a dramatic decrease in women's political representation from an average of 26 per cent to a mere 9 per cent in the parliaments of these countries (Galligan, Clavero and Calloni 2007; see also Chiva 2005). By 2005, the percentage of women had increased to an average of 17 per cent, which, however, remained below the European average of 22 per cent and the EU-15 average of 27 per cent.

Ethnic minority women are in many countries significantly less well represented in parliaments than white women. A number of countries, including the UK, Sweden and the Netherlands, have some ethnic minority women MPs. The first black woman MP in the British House of Commons was Diane Abbott (Labour) who was elected in 1987. In 2006, there were 15 ethnic minority MPs, two of whom were women (Women and Equality Unit 2006). Ethnic minorities represented 2.3 per cent of the MPs whilst ethnic minorities make up about 7 per cent of the population of the UK. In Germany in 2007, there were 5 Turkish/Kurdish MPs (0.8 per cent), three of whom were women. 3 per cent of the German population has its origins in Turkey. Many countries, such as Finland, have no ethnic minority women in the parliament. In others, such as the Netherlands and Denmark, the issue has become highly politicized in most recent elections but, as seen above, has not become an EU-wide agenda on gender-balanced representation.

This variation in the number of women in national parliaments has been extensively analyzed in scholarly debates and the factors that either act as barriers or enable women's political participation have been identified. Feminist scholars have traditionally distinguished between supply and demand side factors, the former relating to the availability of women parliamentarians and the latter to their usage (Norris and Lovenduski 2005). The proportion of women in different elites, women's resources including time and money, and their levels of education may result in women being less able than men to contribute to campaigns, finance their own candidacy or take on temporary or poorly paid positions in local or regional governments. The European Parliament emphasizes these factors and refers to women's 'lack of self-confidence based on a purely psychological level' as an issue that needs to be tackled (European Parliament 2000). The focus of scholarly research in Europe has, however, shifted from women's lack of resources or unwillingness to participate in politics (supply side factors) towards institutional and cultural mechanisms of exclusion.

It has been established that women do better in the electoral systems based on proportional representation and multi-member constituencies used by most EU member states than in majority systems and single member constituencies, as in the UK and France. Larger constituencies in proportional representation systems when compared to majority systems are better for women because they can get onto a party's ballot without having to displace a male candidate. Furthermore, in a list system, parties do not look for a single candidate but rather for different candidates appealing to specific sub-sectors of voters. Political parties are important as they choose the candidates. Party ideology plays a role in women's political representation, as it has been shown that parties on the left are more concerned with equality and send more women to parliament (Caul Kittilson 2006).

Cultural ideas about being a woman or a man can affect both the levels of representation and individual women's decision to enter politics. According to the European Parliament: 'Both men and women should assume an equal share of responsibility in the public and private domains, in economic, political and family life' (European Parliament 2000). Cultural ideas can also impact on the electorate's voting behaviour and cultural norms can influence the way that female parliamentarians are able to act in politics and shape perceptions of women's and men's spheres of expertise in politics (Lovenduski 2005). In particular, central and eastern European countries experienced a revival of conservative gender stereotypes after the fall of communism, pushing women into homes and the private sphere (Bretherton 2001, Galligan, Clavero and Calloni 2007). Religion can be used to justify male power: women's subordination can then appear 'divinely approved'. Majority protestant countries have higher percentages of women in parliament than majority catholic countries do and protestant and catholic countries have more women in parliament than orthodox or Muslim countries do (Paxton and Hughes 2007).

Of the EU institutions, the European Parliament (EP) is most gender-equal in terms of balanced representation of women and men. Its importance as the only directly elected and democratic institution of the EU has gradually increased since 1979 when it was directly elected for the first time. Until then the European assembly was composed of delegates from national parliaments. The Common Assembly (1952–8) included one woman out of 78 representatives (1.3 per cent). This increased to three per cent in the Parliament of the Six (1958–72) and to 5.5 per cent in 1978 (Norris and Franklin 1997: 188). These MEPs were nominated by the national parliaments and the responsibility for the low numbers of women rested with the parliamentary parties.

In this context, the 1979 elections, which increased the number of women to 16 per cent, represented a breakthrough. The percentage of women MEPs has been increasing steadily since then to 35.5 per cent in 2009 (see Table 3.2). However, the number of women MEPs elected in the member states varies greatly. For example, currently 62 per cent of the Finnish, 56 per cent of the Swedish, and 50 per cent of the Estonian MEPs are women and five other countries achieve levels above a 40 per cent threshold. Moreover, for countries where women's representation has traditionally been low in the national parliament, it is higher in the European Parliament; for example, in 2009, 44 per cent of the French and 25 per cent of the Irish MEPs (were women (18.7 and 13.3 per cent respectively in the national parliaments). Nevertheless, the Czech Republic and Luxembourg have less than 20 per cent women amongst their MEPs and Malta has none. Two of the 12 Presidents of the parliament have been women (Simone Veil 1979–2 and Nicole Fontaine 1999–2002).

There are various explanations for why there are more women in the European Parliament as opposed to national parliaments. Elizabeth Vallance and Elizabeth Davis (1986) discuss factors relating to institutional circumstances. First, some countries have different electoral systems for the two parliaments. For example, France uses proportional representation in the EP elections but not in national elections. Second, the EP is sometimes considered less important, less attractive and more remote when compared to national politics. Thus, becoming an MEP is not as competitive as becoming a member of the national parliament and women have fared better under these circumstances. Third, the style of politics is sometimes said to be different in the EP compared to some national parliaments. It is, for example, less confrontational than politics in the British Parliament at Westminster. The hours are more structured and committee work involves consensual discussions rather than debates in the chamber. Equally Hilary Footitt's study (2002: 51) found that the women MEPs argued that the European Parliament was more women-friendly than other political bodies.

Fourth, the EP is a relatively new institution when compared to many national parliaments. Thus men's hegemony in national parliaments tends to be more entrenched in the institutional practices and processes. In the first direct elections to the EP in 1979, there were no incumbent MEPs to overcome, and due to lack of interest in the European level of decision-making many of the most experienced men were reluctant to stand. This opened up opportunities for female candidates. A similar trend is apparent in the devolved parliaments of Scotland and Wales, which are both well researched cases (Chaney and Fevre 2002, Mackay 2003).

Other scholars have highlighted factors that relate to activism in

TABLE 3.2 *Percentage of women Members of the European Parliament by country*

Country	1979	1984	1989	1994	1999	2004	2009
Austria					38	38.9	41
Belgium	8	16	16.7	32	32	29.2	36
Bulgaria						(28)*	47
Cyprus						0	33
Czech Republic						20.8	18
Denmark	31	37	37.5	43.8	38	35.7	46
Estonia						33.3	50
Finland					44	35.7	62
France	22	21	22.2	29.8	40	42.3	44
Germany	15	19	32	35.4	36	31.3	37
Greece		8	4.2	16	16	29.2	32
Hungary						37.5	36
Ireland	13	13	6.7	26.7	33	38.5	25
Italy	12	10	12.3	10.3	9	19.2	25
Latvia						22.2	38
Lithuania						38.5	25
Luxembourg	17	17	50	33.3	0	50	17
Malta						0	0
Netherlands	20	28	28	32.2	35	44.4	48
Poland						13	22
Portugal			12.5	8	20	25	36
Romania						(31)*	36
Slovakia						35.7	38
Slovenia						42.9	29
Spain			15	32.8	34	33.3	36
Sweden					45	57.9	56
United Kingdom	14	15	14.8	18.4	24	24.4	33
Average	16	17	19	25.3	30	31	35.5
Female president	Yes	No	No	No	Yes	No	No

* Bulgaria and Romania had elections later than the other member states.
Sources: The Interparliamentary Union, European Parliament website; Vallance and Davies 1986, p. 7, for 1979 and 1984.

women's policy networks (Krook 2002, Hoskyns and Rai 1998, Lombardo and Meier 2007: 63). Here women's activism and lobbying at the EU level has played a role in increasing women's representation in the Parliament. The European Network of Experts on Women in Decision-Making was created in 1992 to assist the Commission on the issue of women's representation. It ran successful campaigns and put forward new initiatives to increase the numbers of women in the European Parliament. Balanced representation was a high-profile issue in the 1994 elections in particular and one of the campaign slogans asked: 'Why does 81 per cent of Parliament have to shave each morning?' The European Parliament's Committee on Women's Rights published working documents and brochures to promote women in decision-making and the European Women's Lobby (EWL) similarly ran campaigns and drafted electoral strategies and recommendations (Gréboval 2004). However, it must be noted that these factors have been studied in relation to the old rather than new member states and they might be different in the case of the central and eastern European countries. The EU exerted some pressure on these countries to adopt a gender mainstreaming approach when they joined the Union (Velluti 2005).

Ethnic minority women are less well represented in the European Parliament than majority women. The numbers here reflect the difficulties of bringing the differences within the category of women into the political representation discourse. In 2007, there were just 9 non-white MEPs (1.1 per cent). If those of Turkish/Kurdish descent are included, the figure rises to 13, and to 15 with those of Roma origin. Five UK MEPs (6 per cent) were of non-white background and one of them was a woman. Three German MEPs (3 per cent) were of Turkish/Kurdish descent and one of them was a woman. Three French MEPs (3.8 per cent) were non-white. One of the Dutch MEPs (3.7 per cent) was of Turkish background and a woman, Emine Bozkurt (Labour). In 2004, she was the first MEP to be elected from the Netherlands with an ethnic minority heritage. Belgium also had one non-white MEP (4.2 per cent). None of the other 21 EU member states (for Hungary see below) had any non-white MEPs despite significant ethnic minority populations in countries such as Italy and Spain (*The Guardian*, 14 February 2007).

The eight million Roma form the biggest homogeneous ethnic minority in the EU. The first Roma MEP was elected from Spain in 1994. In 2007, two MEPs, both from Hungary, were from a Roma ethnic background, and both of them were women. Both faced discrimination in the parliament based on their ethnic origin. Livia Jaroka's nomination for a parliamentary award in 2006 prompted discriminatory remarks. Viktoria Mohasci, in turn, described her experiences in an interview: 'If I speak of how Roma kids in schools are not getting as many qualifications, most people smile and say the Roma produce these kids – they are to blame' (*The Guardian*, 14 February 2007). Indeed, the far right outnumbered the non-white MEPs in the European Parliament: the new Identity, Tradition and Sovereignty parliamentary group had 19 members in 2007 (the group ceased to exist later in the year). There are no figures for non-white parliamentary officials – civil servants, administrators and other staff working for the parliament, commission and other bodies – as this is not recorded. Gathering data on ethnic/racial background is illegal in a number of member states because of fears of racial profiling and racism, but it could provide a way of making the position of ethnic minorities in these countries visible.

Since 1952, members have sat not in national groups but in the European Parliament's party groups, created to reflect shared political affiliation. These are loosely co-ordinated umbrella groups linking representatives from like-minded parties. They have very few formal structures, no internal party discipline and little internal cohesion (Pedersen 1996). In 2009, the Greens and the European Free Alliance (G/FRA) had a female majority for the first time (54.5 per cent), and the Group of the Alliance of Liberals and Democrats (ALDE) and the Progressive Alliance of Socialists and Democrats in the European Parliament both had over 40 per cent of women. The conservative groups such as the newly formed Group of European Conservatives and Reformists (ECR) and the Europe of Freedom and Democracy Group (EFD) had lower figures, 12.7 and 15.6 per cent respectively. The representation of women in the biggest party group of the European Parliament, the European People's Party/European Democrats (EPP-ED), was 33.6 percent in 2009, showing an increase from 24.5 per cent in 2007 (see Table 3.3). A familiar distinction between the parties of the right, on one hand, and left and green parties, on the other, emerges when the data is segregated according to party groups, with parties on the left having more women in their ranks. All the presidents of the political groups were men in 2009 with the exception of the Greens/EFA group which had a woman Co-President.

TABLE 3.3   *Percentage of women in the European Parliament's party groups*

Groups*	1994	1999	2004	2009
EPP-ED	22.2	26.7	24.5	33.6
S&D/PES	31.5	37.6	40.3	40.2
ALDE	31.7	32.7	38.5	45.2
ECR				12.7
G / EFA	50.0**	43.5	47.6	54.5
GUE/NGL	29.4***	35.7	29.3	28.5
EFD				15.6
European Parliament	**25.4**	**30**	**31**	**35.5**

*Abbreviations and the distribution of seats in 2009: EPP-ED – European People's Party / European Democrats (265 seats, 36%), S&D/PES – The Group of the Progressive Alliance of Socalists and Democrats (184 seats, 25 %), ALDE – Alliance of Liberals and Democrats for Europe (84 seats, 11.4%), ECR – European Conservative and Reformists (55 seats, 7.5%), G/EFA – Greens / European Free Alliance (55 seats, 7.5%), GUE/NGL – European United Left – Nordic Green Left (35 seats, 4.7%), EFD – Europe of Freedom and Democracy (32 seats, 4%).
** The figure refers to the Green Group (GG).
*** The figure refers to Confederal Group of the European United Left (CEUL).
Source: The European Database: Women in Decision-making, European Parliament.

The European parliament has twenty policy committees, whose political composition reflects that of the Parliament as a whole. The committees examine all legislative proposals before they return to the plenary session for a vote. A scrutiny of their gender composition answers questions about where women are in the parliamentary institutions of the EU. One of the committees is the Women's Rights and Gender Equality Committee (FEMM) (see Chapter 4). Only four other committees were chaired by a woman in 2007, leaving 15 of the committees to be chaired by a man (see Table 3.4). During the previous parliamentary term (1999–2004) only four out of 17 committees were chaired by a woman. Women dominate the Women's Rights Committee (95 per cent) and were well represented on the Internal Market and Consumption (52.3 per cent), Environment (48.5 per cent), Climate Change (40 per cent) and Human Rights (40 per cent) Committees in 2004–9. Three of these

TABLE 3.4   *Percentage of women in the Committees of the European Parliament during the parliamentary terms 1999–2004 and 2004–9*

Committee	1999–2004		2004–9	
	Chair-women	% of women	Chair-woman	% woman
Foreign Affairs		16.9		20.9
Development		25.7		30.6
International Trade				24.2
Budgets		24.4		26
Budgetary Control		23.8		20
Economic and Monetary Affairs	x	26.7	x	23.5
Employment and Social Affairs		38.9		34.6
Environment, Public Health and Food Safety	x	54.2		48.5
Industry, Research and Energy		30.0	x	38.9
Internal Market and Consumer Protection			x	52.3
Transport and Tourism				12
Regional Development		18.6		28
Agriculture and Rural Development		23.7		25.5
Fisheries		25.0		24.3
Culture and Education		42.9		39.5
Legal Affairs	x	28.6		17.9
Civil Liberties, Justice and Home Affairs		27.9		41.2
Constitutional Affairs		23.3		17.2
Women's Rights and Gender Equality	x	89.5	x	95
Petitions		30.0		31.6
Human Rights			x	40
Security and Defence				16.7
Climate Change				40

Source: The European Database: Women in Decision-making, European Parliament website.

were new committees, creating new opportunities for women's participation. Women were less well represented on the Transport and Tourism, Legal Affairs, Constitutional Affairs and Security and Defence Committees where they constituted less than 20 per cent of the committee membership. Clearly, committee work continues to be divided on the basis of gender.

Women in cabinets in the member states

Mapping the number of women in cabinets is more difficult than finding out about the percentage of women in parliaments. Sizes of governments vary greatly and they include ministers with portfolios and their deputies. Governments are often reshuffled. Table 3.5 gives, however, some indication of the position of women in member states' cabinets. These are important to a study of the representation of women in the EU, as cabinet members represent their countries in the Council of Ministers meetings and direct the work of the civil servants in the working groups that prepare for the Permanent Representatives Committee, Coreper.

In 2007, the percentage of women in cabinets was highest in Finland where women constituted 60 per cent of the centre-right government. Austria, France, Spain and Sweden each had over 40 per cent women in their cabinets. By contrast, a number of countries, including Estonia, Greece, Portugal, Slovakia and Slovenia, had less than 10 per cent women in their cabinets, and Cyprus and the Czech Republic had no women in their cabinets in 2002. The EU average was 20 per cent in 2002 and 23.4 per cent in 2007. This was higher than the world average which in 1998 was 8.7 per cent (Reynolds 1999: 561). Some figures exist for ethnic minority women in cabinets. For example, in the UK there was one woman from an ethnic minority in a cabinet of 21 ministers in 2004, as there was in Sweden in 2007.

There is clearly more variation between countries in the number of women in cabinets than women in parliaments (Siaroff 2000). There is also more variation within individual countries over time. In other words, the percentage of women in cabinets is very volatile and fluctuates significantly depending on the views and practices of particular parties. For example, in Spain in 2002 the conservative government had 21 per cent women and this increased to 41 per cent under the left-wing government in 2007. In Germany, 43 per cent of the ministers were women under the social democratic

TABLE 3.5   *Percentage of women in cabinets in EU-27 member states*

Country	2002	2007
Austria	25	50
Belgium	24	19
Bulgaria	19	25
Cyprus	0	18
Czech Republic	0	11
Denmark	28	31
Estonia	19	7
Finland	39	60
France	21	44
Germany	43	26
Greece	12	5
Hungary	6	15
Ireland	13	20
Italy	8	23
Latvia	5	30
Lithuania	23	21
Luxembourg	29	20
Malta	7	15
Netherlands	31	31
Poland	21	22
Portugal	14	9
Romania	20	13
Slovakia	10	6
Slovenia	20	6
Spain	21	41
Sweden	45	41
United Kingdom	30	24
Average	**20**	**23**

Sources: The European Database: Women in Decision-making (2007 figures); The Council of Europe: Women in Politics in the Council of Europe Member States, 2002(2002 figures).

government in 2002, but 26 per cent were women under the conservative government in 2007. In France and in Finland, by contrast, governments of the right appointed significant numbers of women to the cabinet in 2007.

Less research has been conducted on women in cabinets than on women in parliaments. In one of the rare studies, Rebecca Davis differentiates between specialist and generalist recruitment norms that impact on the number of women in cabinets (Davis 1997). The Netherlands is an example of a specialist system where ministers are selected because of their expertise in a particular policy area and may come from outside the parliament. In Ireland and the UK ministers almost always come from parliament and are considered generalists who can move from portfolio to portfolio. One of Davis's findings is that women are much less likely to be selected for cabinets in generalist systems, where holding positions in male-dominated party committees and other stepping-stones are crucial factors.

Some attention has also been paid to the tendency to place women in the softer socio-cultural ministerial positions rather than in the harder and politically more prestigious areas such as economic planning, national security and foreign affairs (Reynolds 1999). The Council confirmed this trend and recorded that when cabinet ministers were considered, the women in the Finnish Government were the only ones who held portfolios in all areas of the state functions in 1999 (Council of the European Union 1999: 16). In the most typical case a majority (Austria, Denmark, Finland, Germany, and the Netherlands) or half (Sweden, Portugal and Greece) of the women ministers dealt with socio-cultural matters while the rest of the women ministers held other kinds of portfolios. This, however, was not the case for all member states or for the Commission, where women ministers were also found in fields other than the socio-cultural.

Women in the European Commission

The most recent European Commission (2004–9) consisted of 26 commissioners and the President. Member states appoint commissioners independently in a highly politicized process. The first woman commissioner was appointed in 1989. This means that between 1958 and 1989 there were no female commissioners. In the past fifteen years there has been a significant increase in the percentage of female commissioners from 6 to 30 per cent (see Table 3.6). There have been 11 male presidents of the commission and no women.

TABLE 3.6 *Women in the European Commission*

European Commission	1989	1993	1995	1999	2004
Members	17	17	20	20	27
Women	2	1	5	5	8
Women as %	12	6	25	25	30
Women presidents	No	No	No	No	No

Source: The European Database: Women in Decision-making, European Parliament website.

To date there has been little or no academic research into the gendered dimensions of commissioner appointment. There was an increase in the number of female commissioners in 1995 when Sweden, Finland and Austria became members. Their membership was welcomed by feminist activists who looked for support from the Nordic countries, which were known for their high levels of gender equality. Sweden, indeed, appointed Anita Gradin as its commissioner, and she was committed to gender equality. Other countries have previously or currently appointed a female commissioner as follows: Austria (1), Bulgaria (1), Denmark (1) France (3), Germany (4), Greece (2), Italy (1), Lithuania (1), Luxembourg (2), the Netherlands (1), Poland (1) and Sweden (2). Fifteen member states have never appointed a female commissioner. The findings are only indicative, as the old member states have of course had more chances to appoint female commissioners. New member states such as Bulgaria, Lithuania and Poland have had only one opportunity to nominate commissioners and have put forward women in these instances. The 2009 European Parliamentary elections politicized the commissioner selection process in some member states, and there were political demands that countries nominate both a male and a female candidate to make it possible for the chair of the commission to select a gender balance.

The Commission services are organized into Directorates-General (DGs) and general and internal services. The Commission's most senior official is the Secretary-General. Of the five Secretaries General in the history of the Commission one has been a woman,

Catherine Day, who is Irish and was appointed in 2005. Most DGs are concerned with policy sectors such as trade, environment or competition. Each Directorate-General is headed by a Director-General. In 2007, 4 DGs out of 41 (9.8 per cent) were headed by a woman. They were the Education and Culture DG, the Office for Official Publications, the Secretariat General and the Office for Administration and Payment of Individual Entitlements.

The Commission attempts to make what changes it can within its own mandate. To make more progress in achieving greater gender balance within its own committees and expert groups it has adopted a decision relating to gender balance within the expert groups and committees established by it (European Commission 2000b: 34). In this decision, it proposed that both existing and new committees and expert groups should be gender-balanced. However, in considering how to increase the gender balance in its expert groups and committees, the Commission was faced with the problem that whilst it has the formal power of appointment to such groups and committees, nominations for members usually come via the member states. Frequently member states merely pass on to the Commission nominations from the social partners, NGOs and professional bodies. Thus, while the Commission can try and appoint members to expert groups and committees in order to achieve a gender balance, its ability to appoint members to achieve this balance is severely limited if there is no gender balance among the nominees put forward. The Commission has called on the member states and all bodies and organizations responsible for proposing candidates to put forward the names of men and women in sufficient numbers to allow it to appoint members so that expert groups and committees are gender-balanced (European Commission 2000b).

Women in the European Council and the Council of the European Union

The European Council and the Council of the European Union represent the highest glass ceiling for gender-balanced decision-making in the EU. The European Council was created in 1974 and it brings together heads of state or government and the President of the Commission. They are assisted by the ministers for foreign affairs and a member of the Commission. When the European Council deals with questions linked to economic and monetary union, finance ministers are invited. The European Council meetings thus include a limited number of political figures, headed by the chief executives of all member states, meeting in a closed room with no assistants. Before the Lisbon Treaty the European Council was not an institution of the Union but exercised significant powers without any legal basis in the treaties. The European Council was thus not an institution in legal terms but was, rather, a locus of power. In the European Council the role of the heads of the state and prime ministers is crucial. The EU member states have had very few women as heads of state to date. Only Finland, Ireland and Latvia had had female presidents by 2007. The UK, France, Finland and Germany have had a female Prime Minister – two of these, France and Finland, for less than a year by 2007.

The ministers of the member states meet within the Council of the European Union. Depending on the issue on the agenda, each country is represented by the minister responsible for that subject, for example finance, social affairs, transport or agriculture. The Council meets in nine different configurations depending on the subjects under discussion. For example, the General Affairs and External Relations configuration is made up of foreign affairs ministers, the Justice and Home Affairs configuration of justice and home affairs ministers and so on.

The composition of the Council depends on the ministerial appointments within the member states. The key ministries – prime minister, foreign and finance ministers – continue to be very male-dominated in the 27 member states. In 2007, the German Chancellor Angela Merkel was the only female prime minister in the EU (3.7 per cent). Four countries, Austria, Greece, Hungary and Poland, had female foreign ministers (14.8 per cent) but none of the member states had female finance ministers. The portfolio of foreign minister has also previously been held by women in, for example, Finland, Luxembourg, Sweden and the UK.

All the work of the Council is prepared or co-ordinated by the Permanent Representatives Committee (Coreper), made up of the permanent representatives of the member states working in Brussels (ambassadors) and their assistants. The work of this committee is itself prepared by some 250 committees and working groups consisting of delegates from the member states. Coreper continues to be male-dominated. In 2007, only Luxembourg had a woman as the permanent ambassador to the EU in Coreper II, making women's representation only 3.7 per cent. Six countries (Czech Republic, Finland, Latvia, Slovenia, Sweden and the UK) had a female deputy ambassador in Coreper I, bringing women's representation up to 22.2 per cent in this body.

The General Secretariat of the Council of the European Union, better known as *Council Secretariat*, assists the Council of the European Union and the EU Presidency. It is a relatively small and officially politically neutral body. It is headed by a Secretary-General who combines this role with that of the High Representative for the common foreign and security policy. A Deputy Secretary-General is responsible for the day-to-day running of the Secretariat. Both are appointed by the Council for five years and were both men, Javier Solana and Pierre de Boissieu (1999–2004, 2004–9).

To sum up, an analysis of the number of women in the highest echelons of power in the EU, that is the Council and its preparatory bodies, illustrates that some of the key locations of power continue to be very male-dominated. Gender segregation continues to take place as regards the delegation of sectors to women and to men. In general women do better in newer institutions, where male dominance is not entrenched.

Conclusion

This chapter has focused primarily on gendering political representation and analysing parliaments, governments, the Commission and the Council. Current feminist debates on representation highlight that representation also occurs in extra-parliamentary arenas such as courts (Celis, Childs, Krook and Kantola 2008, Squires 2008a). Despite strong denials of the political role of the courts, feminist scholars argue that courts are important representative institutions where gender-sensitive analysis should take place, for example in cases of domestic violence, rape, divorce or child custody (Chappell 2003, Kenney 2002). To take into account these theoretical insights on women's representation and to broaden the question of representation beyond political bodies, this chapter concludes with a focus on the European courts.

In Europe, the European Court of Justice forms the core of the autonomous legal system whose purpose is to ensure that the obligations undertaken by the member states are fulfilled, and that the institutions exercise their respective powers without encroaching on those of the others or those of the member states. The Court also ensures that the rights of individuals and undertakings (firms and other economic and social actors) are respected, and that the treaties and the laws made under their authority are applied uniformly. Partly to compensate for the existence of only one round of judicial review and the lack of an appeals system, the ECJ includes Advocates General (8 in 2007), as well as judges, who provide an additional level of judicial review but have no power to resolve a case (Kennedy 2006: 127). Judges are appointed by member states through an internal selection procedure that is usually secretive and attracts little public attention (Kenney 2002: 259–60).

When looking at the number of women and men judges it is evident that the Court is and has traditionally been very male-dominated. Of the 82 judges of the Court, 5 (6 per cent) have been or are women. The first woman judge, Fidelma O'Kelly Macken, was appointed in 1999, and another woman judge, Ninon Colneric, came shortly after her (Kenney 2002: 261). Currently, there are 3 women out of 27 judges in the Court, constituting 11 per cent of the total. Of the 33 Advocates General (AGs), 5 have been or are women (15 per cent). The first female AG, Simone Rozès, was appointed in 1981. The next female AG, Christine Stix-Hackl, was not appointed until 16 years later in 2000. Currently, there are 3 female AGs in the Court out of 8 AGs (38 per cent). Yet Sally Kenney (2002: 260, 266) notes that non-merit factors have always been part of judicial appointments in the EU. The question thus becomes: what factors need representing, which, in turn, opens up discursive space for arguments about gender-balanced representation in the Court.

In conclusion then, whilst women's political representation in member states' parliaments has increased over the past 15 years, pockets of under-representation remain. Women's political representation varies greatly between member states, and the EU record in promoting gender-balanced decision-making remains uneven. The number of women in national governments varies, however, and women are concentrated in particular ministerial posts. This has consequences for the constitution of the European Council and the Council of the European Union, where the representation of women is at its lowest. The European and the national levels are thus closely linked and the national level shapes women's political representation at the EU level. The Commission's hands have been tied on many occassions when it has attempted to promote gender balance in decision-making.

Furthermore, the EU has resorted to soft law in promoting

women in political decision-making. Soft law measures often rely on comparable data and this continues to be a problem for the Union in the field of gender-balanced decision-making. Currently, the European Parliament and its Women's Rights Committee are exploring the use of quotas in different member states, which signals an interest in exploring hard law measures (Lovenduski's 'equality guarantees') to increase women's representation. The European Women's Lobby also continues to lobby for 50–50 representation ('parity'). These developments are, however, likely to remain contentious given the diverse traditions of political representation in the member states. The EU debates on women and men in decision-making are silent about the position of ethnic minority women.

Chapter 4

Policy-Making Processes, Actors and Institutions in the EU from a Gender Perspective

The European Union operates within a complex setting of transnational actors, institutions and policy-making processes. The aim of this chapter is to provide an overview of the policy-making processes in the EU and evaluate their strengths and weaknesses from a gender perspective. This chapter therefore tackles some basic questions involved in the formulation of gender policy: What opportunities do the EU policy-making processes provide for promoting gender equality? With what political tools is gender equality being advanced and what challenges are there in the process? What role do civil society organizations play in these policy-making processes?

The chapter starts by mapping three broad policy-making mechanisms in the EU: the so-called classic Community method; the intergovernmental method; and the co-ordination method. The roles of the EU institutions and member states vary according to the policy-making process as do the 'policy outputs', from binding legislation to softer co-ordination policies. As a result, each policy-making process provides different opportunities and challenges for gender policy. The increased powers of the European Parliament in the Community method enhance the chances for progressive gender policy in the EU. The intergovernmental and co-ordination methods, by contrast, favour bureaucratic rather than democratic and political decision-making and entail more challenges for the representation of a gender perspective.

The chapter also focuses on women's policy agencies at the EU level. 'Women's policy agency' is a notion generally used to describe any state-based agency, at all levels of government or in any type of organ, that has been officially assigned the responsibly for promoting the advancement of women and gender equality (Mazur and

McBride 2008: 256). These bodies are called 'state feminist' in cases where they represent the concerns of, and provide access and voice to, women's movements in state policy-making (Lovenduski 2008: 176). Such bodies can now be found at the transnational EU level, where the European Parliament and the Commission have established a wide array of women's policy agencies that form key avenues of influencing gender policy. Finally, the chapter discusses the role of civil society actors in EU gender policy. The European Commission has played a key role in establishing a centralized voice to represent women's concerns in EU level policy-making, namely the European Women's Lobby (EWL). The chapter concludes by illustrating how this complex set of actors and institutions work together to enact European gender policy.

Policy-making processes and gender in the EU

EU policy-making is a complex transnational process in which politicians, officials and interested groups interact to shape policy outcomes. One way to characterize the process 'from a proposal to a decision' is to differentiate between three policy-making processes: the classic Community method, the intergovernmental method and the co-ordination method (see Stubb, Wallace and Peterson 2003, Wallace 2005). These processes are assessed from a gender perspective throughout the book. This section gives an overview of their strengths and weaknesses from a gender perspective and asks what avenues they provide for advancing gender equality.

The Community method

The classic Community method gives a significant role to the EU institutions and is applied in cases where powers are clearly assigned to the EU (see also Chapter 1). In this process, the Commission has a monopoly over the right to take the initiative, and it tables a formal proposal to the Council and, in most cases, to the Parliament. The role of the Commission is also enhanced by its powers to broker policy compromises and supervise policy execution. The Council of Ministers takes the final decision after consulting other EU institutions. The Parliament's powers vary between policy sectors. Under the *co-decision procedure*, under which most EU legislation now comes, the Parliament is a political and legal equal of the Council. This means that the Parliament and the

Council must enter into direct negotiations if they cannot agree on a proposal. If these negotiations fail, the proposal fails. The co-decision procedure hence gives the Parliament the power to veto any legislation that comes under this procedure. Under the *consultation procedure*, used only for a few policies today, the Commission submits a proposal to the Council, which then seeks the opinion of the Parliament but is not obliged to pay attention to it. The role of the European Court of Justice (ECJ) is to resolve legal disputes and to reinforce the power of the EU institutions and law. Lobbies and interest groups seek to influence EU policy and provide expertise to the different institutions during the process. A successful policy output from this process is binding hard law in the form of regulations (which are binding in their entirety and directly applicable in all member states); directives (which bind member states as to the results to be achieved, have to be transposed into the national legal framework and thus leave margin for manoeuvre as to the form and means of implementation); or decisions (which are fully binding on those to whom they are addressed) (Hix 2005, Stubb, Wallace and Peterson 2003, Wallace 2005.)

The Community method provides different opportunities for gender policy and gender advocates depending on whether the co-decision procedure or the consultation procedure is used. Box 4.1 illustrates how the co-decision procedure worked for a programme directly related to gender. The Daphne Programme, which was adopted by the Council and the Parliament in 2000 after a Commission proposal in 1998, is an EU Action Programme providing funding for projects on violence against women and children (see Chapter 7). The Commission initially proposed Article 235 EC (human rights) as the legal basis for the Daphne programme. This would have required unanimity in the Council and come under the consultation procedure, thus giving a minor role to the Parliament. The Legal Service recommended a new basis – Article 129 EC (public health) – which came under the co-decision procedure and enhanced the role of the Parliament. As a result, the Parliament, the Council and the Commission had to engage in complex negotiations, and the Commission and eventually the Council had to take into account the Parliament's amendment proposals (Locher 2007: 276–80). The Parliament managed to lobby for some specific formulations in the Daphne programme, such as the central role given to civil society organizations in the fight against violence against women (see Chapter 7 for a discussion).

Box 4.1   The Daphne programme under the co-decision procedure

1. The Commission Communication on violence against children, young persons and women and the proposal for a Council Decision on an Action Programme (Daphne) (20 May 1998).
2. The first reading of Daphne in the Parliament.
3. Amended Commission proposal on Daphne.
4. Common position of the Council on Daphne.
5. Commission Communication on the common position on the Council.
6. Second reading on Daphne in the Parliament.
7. Commission opinion on Parliament's amendments.
8. Decision of the European Parliament and the Council adopting Daphne (24 January 2000).

Source: Locher 2007: 280–1.

The first binding gender directive enacted under the co-decision procedure in 2002 was the Equal Treatment in Employment Directive (2002/73/EC), which amended and updated equal treatment provisions. The directive was based on Article 141 EC, which meant that it was subject to qualified majority voting and not unanimity in the Council. Again, the important role that the policy-making process gave to the Parliament enhanced the contents of the directive (see Chapter 5 for a discussion; see also Clavero and Galligan 2009: 105, van der Vleuten 2007: 161).

Hence the Parliament's role in the policy-making process is crucial from a gender perspective. Its Committee on Women's Rights and Gender Equality (FEMM), discussed in more detail below, can appoint *rapporteurs* who have considerable expertise on gender issues and whose reports can shape the plenary debate in the Parliament. As a consequence, the Parliament often proposes significant amendments to Commission proposals. For example, in the case of the Daphne programme, at its first reading the Parliament proposed 36 amendments and the Commission accepted the majority of these in full or in part or with minor revisions. The Commission also accepted all the additional amendments that the Parliament made after the second reading (Locher 2007: 283–4).

In contrast to the Equal Treatment Directive 2002, the Goods and Services Directive 2004 came under the *consultation* procedure of the Community method. Its legal basis was in Article 13 EC introduced in the Treaty of Amsterdam 1997 (see Chapter 1). The legal basis meant that the directive was subject to unanimity voting in the Council. The role of the Parliament was very limited. As a result, women's organizations and gender advocates were limited in their ability to influence the negotiations and the contents of the directive (Clavero and Galligan 2009: 106). Shortly after the directive was announced, the European Women's Lobby (EWL) began to lobby for a widening of the application of the directive to areas hitherto not covered by EU gender equality legislation. The lobby's demands included issues such as parity participation in decision-making, violence against women, and the reconciliation of family and working life. These claims, however, found little support in the Council and were excluded from the final outcome (Masselot 2007: 153–4).

It is evident then that the co-decision procedure opens avenues for gender through the powers of the Parliament, while the consultation procedure tends to close them because of the limited powers of the Parliament. The former results in more transparency and openness in the policy-making process, for example via the parliamentary hearings that are open to the public, hence in more opportunities for gender advocates to lobby. Catherine Hoskyns (1999: 81) suggests that such opportunities were missing in the 1990s and lobbying on gender policy was redirected to the national level. The discussion below illustrates the trend in the 2000s towards strong transnational lobbying rather than national lobbying based on a transnational dialogue in gender policy and transnational gender interest construction.

The intergovernmental method

The intergovernmental method is used in policy co-operation that depends mainly on exchanges between national policy makers with little or no involvement by the EU institutions. This includes policy areas that, on one hand, are very sensitive issues for member state sovereignty, such as fiscal or foreign policy, but where, on the other hand, there may be benefits from co-operation. When the intergovernmental method is applied, the member states take the lead and the European Council sets the direction of policy. The EU institutions play a minor role: the Commission has no formal role, the Parliament has only a consultative voice and the Court has little or no jurisdiction. Decision-making can be opaque to national parliaments, civil society organizations and the public. The proceedings lack transparency, democratic accountability, legal clarity and judicial control. The method may, however, build confidence among member states and result in future co-operation at EU level. For example, in the field of justice and home affairs both intergovernmental consultation and pressure of events such as immigration and terrorism have increased common measures and subjected the field to co-ordination measures. Accordingly, visa, immigration and asylum policy-making has slowly moved towards the Community method. The intergovernmental method has also created and empowered a range of new actors in the EU, such as the European Central Bank and Europol. Unlike the Community method, the policy outputfrom the intergovernmental method is light co-operation and informal regimes that do not commit the member states to too much. Legal instruments, such as strategies, joint action and common positions are used in the area of the Common Foreign and Security Policy (CFSP), and decisions, framework decisions, joint positions and conventions in the area of Justice and Home Affairs (JHA) (Denza 2002, Stubb, Wallace and Peterson 2003, Wallace, Wallace and Pollack 2005).

Trafficking in women is an example of a gender policy area that at first came under the intergovernmental method. The Maastricht Treaty 1992 established the so-called 'third pillar' enabling member state co-operation in Justice and Home Affairs (JHA) on the basis of the intergovernmental method. (After the Amsterdam Treaty the third pillar was divided into two and the part remaining within the scope of the intergovernmental method is called Provisions on Police and Judicial Cooperation in Criminal Matters.) This created the Task Force JHA and ever closer co-operation in the field through committees and working groups. This co-operation came to include trafficking in women.

Before trafficking in women could be seen as an issue that required EU-wide co-operation measures it needed to be politicized at EU level. Here the different gender advocates played a crucial role. The issue was first put on the agenda through high-level conferences in the mid-1990s. For example, the Swedish Commissioner Anita Gradin hosted a pivotal conference in Vienna in 1996 on trafficking in women. Representatives of member state governments, international NGOs and experts were present, and the key aim was to present the scale of the problem of trafficking in women, with figures supplied by an official EU report. This forced the EU to recognize its responsibility on the issue. The emergence of trafficking in women as a policy issue was accelerated though the paedophile and sexual violence scandals that took place in Belgium around the same time and led to a Europe-wide outcry against violence against children and women (Locher 2007: 226–37).

The Council established a *co-ordination office* for measures against trafficking in women within the Task Force Justice and Home Affairs and trafficking in women was included in the Europol mandate in 1996. An informal meeting of the EU Justice and Home Affairs Ministers took place in 1996 and they started to discuss trafficking in women and child abuse. As a result, a *resolution* of 14 October 1996 laid down the priorities for co-operation in the fields of Justice and Home Affairs and included the fight against trafficking in human beings (Locher 2007: 238). The Council also launched the Stop programme, the first *Community Action Programme* for Combating Trafficking in Human Beings and the Sexual Exploitation of Children (1996–2000). It was prepared in the Justice and Home Affairs working groups after Anita Gradin made a successful argument that its legal basis was to be found in this third pillar co-operation. It encountered no serious resistance in the Council because of the pressure created by the Belgian scandals. Moreover, Gradin and national NGOs had done some serious lobbying work and the Council negotiations were chaired by the Irish Minster of Justice Nora Owen, who was committed to the issue (Locher 2007: 242–3) .Chapter 7 discusses EU policy on trafficking in women further and illustrates how these actions were later followed by a Council Joint Action, the Daphne Initiative and the Daphne Programme. The case is thus a good example of how member state co-operation through the intergovernmental method can subsequently result in more formalized and EU-led policy and binding measures.

Note that the intergovernmental method did not mean that the other EU institutions were passive on the issue. For example, the Parliament issued a resolution that made reference to women's rights and forced labour (Resolution on Human Rights in the World in 1995–6 and the Union's Human Rights Policy), and a report (Eriksson report) and debated the issue in parliamentary hearings addressing sexual violence against women in trafficking cases (Locher 2007: 228). The Commission communication to the Council and Parliament on trafficking in women (20 November 1996) was a soft law measure, but what is remarkable is that it came from the Commission and not from the Parliament as had previously been the case. Its aim was to initiate a broad policy debate and it contained radical and progressive language about women's bodily rights. Because of this language, the communication encountered opposition and depended heavily on the support of femocrats and feminist politicians in the Council (Locher 2007: 239–41).

To summarize, the intergovernmental method can result in gains in gender policy although the avenues for advancing gender concerns may be less formalized, open and accessible than under the Community method. The intergovernmental method requires high level lobbying in the Council and feminist successes are shaped by the presence of friendly individuals in the Council and the Commission. Overcoming national differences in gender norms and policies can be a particular challenge. The way in which trafficking in women became politicized as an issue that required EU-wide co-operation showed the need for an exceptional sense of crisis, as created in this case by the Belgian scandals.

The co-ordination method

Finally, *the co-ordination method*, the third EU policy-making process discussed here, is based on shared powers between the EU and the member states. The co-ordination method is used to co-ordinate national policies more effectively with EU policies, whilst avoiding legally binding EU directives or regulations. Hence, the aim is not to find 'one size fits all' EU solutions to policy problems, but rather that member states learn from one another through the exchange of best practices. The soft co-ordination method extends the EU's reach beyond its formal competencies. The role of the Commission is to facilitate networks of national experts, to issue proposals and to evaluate member state performance, although it is less powerful than in the Community method (Büchs 2007: 29). High level groups in the Council compare national approaches and encourage peer review of national policies. The Parliament does not play a formal role or possess the right to co-decision but there can be dialogue with its specialist committees and it can issue opinions (Büchs 2007: 29). Independent experts play a role as promoters of new policy ideas and techniques. Policy output comes in the form of soft rules and policy recommendations (Stubb, Wallace and Peterson 2003: 143).

The first and most developed example of the Open Method of Co-ordination (OMC) was the European Employment Strategy (EES), initially launched in 1997. The OMC represents a new governance model that differs radically from the top-down, rule-based, centralized approaches discussed above (see Box 4.2). The policy-making process is evaluated in Chapters 5 and 6 in relation to childcare policy, gender mainstreaming and employment policy. Whilst the method has extended EU policy to areas such as childcare, its challenges from a gender perspective include the lack of democratic channels for participation and the minimal opportunities that civil society organizations have to participate in the process. For example, the key NGO in social policy, the Platform for European Social NGOs, was excluded from the process leading up to Commission Communication 2003 on OMC (Cullen 2009: 147). The softness of its policy tools, in turn, means that the goals are not easily achieved, and due to the vagueness of the standards it is easy for member states to create an impression of progress in gender policy (see Chapters 5 and 6).

Box 4.2   The Open Method of Co-ordination

1. Joint definitions by the member states of initial objectives, indicators, and in some cases guidelines.
2. Member states draw up national reports or action plans that assess performance in light of the objectives and metrics, and propose reforms accordingly.
3. These reports are peer reviewed by other member states and include mutual criticism and exchange of good practice, backed up by recommendations in some cases.
4. Member states re-elaborate their plans and, at less frequent intervals, the broader objectives and metrics in the light of the experience gained in their implementation.

(See Büchs 2007: 28, Scharpf 2002: 625, Trubek and Trubek 2005: 347–8.)

Women's policy agencies in the EU

Political representation of women in parliaments and governments, discussed in Chapter 3, is an important but limited way of ensuring that gender issues are represented in the policy-making process. Effective representation of gender concerns additionally requires that women's policy agencies and women's movements work together to ensure that a diversity of views on women's concerns are included in policy-making. In combination, the two 'provide more effective avenues of expression for women' than do individual women legislators (Weldon 2002: 1153). Whilst both the women's movements and the women's policy agencies have been studied extensively at the national level (see Mazur 2001, McBride Stetson 2001, Outshoorn 2004, Lovenduski 2005a and 2008, Haussman and Sauer 2007, Outshoorn and Kantola 2007), a women's policy network has also emerged at EU level. A few decades ago this network consisted mainly of dedicated individuals (Hoskyns 1996), but it is now highly institutionalized and includes formal organizations and agencies (Woodward and Hubert 2007).

Like women's policy agencies in the nation states, those in the EU have varied characteristics. Features that impact on the operation of these agencies include status, location, resources, questions about accountability and relationship to the women's movement. Notably it is the Parliament and the Commission rather than the Council that have established these bodies (see pp. 223 ff). The Council has an Employment Social Affairs Council and informal meetings of ministers responsible for equal opportunities and gender equality.

Of these agencies, the European Parliament's *Committee on Women's Rights and Gender Equality* (FEMM) is the most visible to the general public. It was set up as the ad hoc *Committee on Women's Rights* soon after the first direct elections of the European Parliament in 1979, which resulted in the increase of women's representation from 5 per cent to 16 per cent. Simone Veil's election as the Parliament's President, combined with the increasing presence of female MEPs, created a favourable environment for the creation of the committee. It was chaired by Yvette Roudy and its remit was to analyze the situation of women within the European Community. The committee's work led to the adoption of a resolution on 'the situation of women in the European Community'. In June 1981 the Parliament set up a committee of inquiry to monitor the achievement of the objectives set by the resolution. This committee proposed, in a resolution adopted in January 1984, setting up a permanent committee.

Like other parliamentary committees, FEMM is made up of representatives from all political groups within the Parliament. Overall the Committee has become a strong actor in gender policy (Ellina 2003: 46) and has been called 'the foremost place of activism for feminist politicians serving in the Parliament' (Locher 2007: 219). Its tasks include developing and implementing women's rights policy in the EU and evaluating policies and programs that concern women. It is in charge of monitoring and implementing international agreements and conventions concerning women's rights.

To carry out these tasks the committee has at its disposal the tools and powers of the Parliament's increasingly powerful committee system. The Parliament refers Commission proposals that deal with gender, women's rights or equality to the Women's Rights Committee (FEMM) for legislative processing. The committee then appoints a *rapporteur* from amongst its members whose task is to draw up a draft report on the legislative proposal. The *rapporteurs* in the FEMM have often been experts on the relevant topic, which has greatly enhanced the contents of the reports and influenced both policy and discourse on the topic. Examples include the Eriksson report of 1996 (report on the need to establish an EU-wide campaign for zero tolerance of violence against women) which for the first time explicitly made the link between violence and trafficking in the context of the EU (Locher 2007: 254; see also Chapter 7). Background work for the reports is often carried out by committee personnel who seek to accommodate the views of the political party groups but also to consult civil society organizations and other experts on the topic. The committee votes on the draft report and suggests amendments to it. The report and the committee stance on it form the basis of the Parliamentary debate on the topic. In addition, the committee can be asked to issue opinions on legislative proposals that are dealt with in some other committees. The committee also reviews the annual report of the Commission on its actions for gender equality.

Using these powers the Committee on Women's Rights and Gender Equality has sought to strengthen the provisions for equal opportunities and non-discrimination in EU legislation. It has emphasized the importance of implementing gender mainstreaming, positive action and the Beijing Platform for Action (1995). In the context of the 1998 employment guidelines, it worked to make equal opportunities one of the pillars of the new employment strategy (see Chapter 7). It also worked on the Equal Treatment Directive 2002 and the Goods and Services Directive 2004, and on the issues of trafficking of women and children and violence against women (see Chapters 5 and 7; see also Locher 2007: 254–5, Schmidt 2005: 159, Woodward and Hubert 2007: 14).

In terms of co-operation with other gender policy actors, the committee has generally been in agreement with the views and advice of the Commission's Advisory Committee on Equal Opportunities for Women and Men (see below). It has also supported the European Women's Lobby, often arguing against reductions in funding proposed by the European Parliament's Committee on Budgets, and opposing the positions adopted by the Council of Ministers (Stratigaki 2000: 33). The committee itself has twice been threatened with dissolution, in 1998 and 2000. The former Chairperson of the Women's Rights Committee, Heidi Hautala, writes that when she was the newly elected chair of the committee, she was astounded to learn that some senior male officials and MEPs had suggested abolishing the committee because 'its 18-years existence must have been enough to achieve the goal of equal rights between women and men' (Hautala 1999: 23). The timing coincides with a similar trend in some member states, such as the Netherlands, Austria and Germany, where women's policy agencies were either dismantled or faced the threat of it (Outshoorn and Kantola 2007). The trend is partly explained by the emergence of gender mainstreaming as a gender policy tool (Chapter 6). When advancing gender equality becomes everyone's responsibility, it is possible to argue against special bodies dedicated to it. Furthermore, the idea that dealing with only one form of equality (be it gender, disability, race and ethnicity) is old-fashioned may result in similar attempts. Chapter 8 illustrates that the EU puts pressure on member states to move towards integrated or single equality bodies that bring different discrimination policies under one roof. This is changing the institutional landscape of women's policy agencies both in the member states and possibly, in the future, in the EU too, as illustrated by the debate on the European Institute for Gender Equality (EIGE) discussed below (see also Kantola 2010a, Lombardo and Verloo 2009).

The European Commission has an even wider range of bodies that count as women's policy agencies than the Parliament (see pp. 223 ff). The establishment of some of these dates back to the 1970s and 1980s (Chapter 2), whilst others are very recent. The Commission brought together various national equality representatives and formed the Standing Liaison Group, which was institutionalized in 1982 as the Advisory Committee on Equal Opportunities for Men and Women (Hoskyns 1996: 125–6). It consists of 40 members with 3-year renewable terms and includes representatives of member states' national equality bodies and, since 1995, the social partners and representatives from the European Women's Lobby as observers. It has a *political-advisory function* in that it assists the Commission in drawing up and implementing its policy on gender equality. It also plays an important role in managing multilevel governance within the EU policy process and in building consensus among a diversity of actors on gender issues (Laatikainen 2001: 83, Stratigaki 2000: 33). One of the first achievements of the committee was a proposal that eventually became the Commission's First Action Programme on Equal Opportunities (Cichowski 2007: 191).

The composition of the committee has indeed been crucial in forming a European women's constituency and in co-ordinating the pressures exerted on political decision makers at national level (Stratigaki 2000: 33). Co-operation has resulted in mutual strengthening of roles in equality policy. The frequency of meetings and the substance of debates depend on the extent of the commitment of the head of the unit and the president of the Advisory Committee. The committee itself has benefited from the networks of experts that have also enabled national monitoring at EU level and nationally in the member states (Pillinger 1992: 68).

Within the Employment, Social Affairs and Equal Opportunities Directorate-General (DG), two units deal with gender equality issues: the 'Equal Opportunities for Women and Men: Strategy and Programme' Unit (established in 1976) and the 'Equality of Treatment between Women and Men: Legal Questions' Unit (established in 1983). The unit dealing with strategy and programme has *executive-administrative functions*. It co-ordinates gender mainstreaming and assists other services of the Commission to gender mainstream their policies. The unit also prepared the Roadmap for equality between women and men 2006–10 and it submits a report on equality between women and men to the European Council each spring. The unit dealing with legal questions has *law-enforcement functions*. It ensures the transposition and implementation of

Community legislation and initiates new legislative proposals if necessary. The units keep in close touch with the Parliament's Committee on Women's Rights and maintain contacts with the European Committee for Equality between Women and Men of the Council of Europe and the Commission on the Status of Women of the United Nations Economic and Social Council.

The Commission has also created a number of gender-specific expert networks. The first one was DG Employment's Legal Experts Network on the Application of the Equality Directives. The network consisted of legal experts from member states' trade unions, academia and legal professions. It provided in-depth national updates on the implementation of EU equality laws and special reports to the Commission, as well as suggestions for new EU policy in the field of equal opportunities. Although this network was created by the Commission, its activities have taken on a life of their own and have facilitated the expansion of EU law in the field of equal opportunities (Cichowski 2007:192).

The Commission's Third Action Programme on Equal Opportunities in 1990 established a total of nine networks that covered issues from childcare to positive action in enterprises. The funding of such networks came under scrutiny in 1995 and, in 1998, the ECJ issued a ruling in a case brought by the UK government against the Commission arguing that the Commission had overstepped its competence by funding 86 projects focusing on social exclusion. As a result only the original two networks (Legal Experts and Women in the Labour Market) continued to receive funding in the subsequent Fourth Action Programme (Cichowski 2007: 203). Some new ones have also been created, such as the WES network composed of government representatives responsible for the promotion of women's entrepreneurship. Its aim is to raise the profile of women entrepreneurs and to create a climate that is favourable to increasing the number of women entrepreneurs and the size of existing women-led businesses (WES 2005: 3).

In addition to these formal bodies, the Commission has a number of other networks. For example, the High Level Group for Gender Mainstreaming is an informal forum for discussion and exchange of information about gender mainstreaming set up by the Commission in 2002. It consists of representatives of member states' women's policy agencies and meets twice a year. It supports and assists the Commission in identifying relevant policy areas and in preparing the annual report to the Council. It provides a single access point for the member states' women's policy agencies to EU level policy-making (see also Chapter 6).

This complex set of women's policy agencies in the Parliament and the Commission was extended in 2009 with the creation of the European Institute for Gender Equality (EIGE), based in Vilnius, Lithuania, first established by a Commission regulation in 2006. The overall objective of the Institute is to contribute to and strengthen the promotion of gender equality, including gender mainstreaming, in all EU and national policies, to fight against gender discrimination, and to raise EU citizens' awareness of gender equality by providing 'technical assistance' to the EU institutions, in particular the Commission, and the authorities of the member states. In contrast to the agencies discussed above, the Institute will have the task of collecting, analyzing and disseminating knowledge and information on gender equality in Europe. Gender mainstreaming extended to various policy fields has generated this demand for information (Chapter 6). Interestingly, gender mainstreaming does not have purely negative repercussions for women's policy agencies, as suggested above in relation to attempts to dismantle the Women's Rights Committee of the Parliament. Gender mainstreaming also increases the demand for 'gender expertise' (Woehl 2008) and thus facilitated the creation of the Gender Institute whose main task is to provide information to the Commission to aid policy-making.

The parliamentary debate on the creation of the institute shows that establishing an institute dedicated to gender equality became a contested issue (Lombardo and Verloo 2009). The favourable political climate in which the institute had first been put forward had changed by the beginning of the 2000s to one that was less sympathetic to gender equality, especially after the 2004 enlargement (Zippel 2008, Hubert and Stratigaki 2007). The pressures to move towards 'more efficient' one-stop equality bodies that deal with all six strands mentioned in the Amsterdam Treaty (gender, race and ethnicity, disability, religion and belief, age, sexual orientation), instead of focusing on one, were starting to affect the establishment of the institute (Chapter 8; see also Kantola and Nousiainen 2009). Arguments were put forward that the newly established Fundamental Rights Agency (FRA) would be able to deal with gender equality as it was already mandated to tackle multiple discrimination (Lombardo and Verloo 2009).

Feminist commentators have been somewhat cautious about the mandate and the tasks of the Institute. The form of knowledge that the Commission wishes the Institute to provide and disseminate is very technical and is based on the values of 'objectivity, reliability and comparability' (Zippel 2008). In evidence-based policy-making more generally, the role of external actors, such as women's movement organizations and women's policy agencies, is to supply technical knowledge relevant to policies rather than to envision political alternatives or new agendas. The tendency is symptomatic of the managerial dynamics of neo-liberal governance, focusing on the growth of consultancy services, which can have very depoliticizing effects on activists and agencies (Kantola and Squires 2008). This illustrates how the women's policy agencies in the EU, like those in the member states, are embedded in the broader changes in patterns of governance and the New Public Management (NPM) form of governance (Chapter 6; see also Kantola 2010a).

Civil society groups lobbying for gender equality in the EU

Women's policy agencies, such as those discussed above, work together with women's movement actors to exert pressure on policy makers. The EU level trajectory of the emergence and establishment of women's organizations is rather different from the national level. Within the member states most women's movements grew independently from the state in the 1960s and 1970s. Whilst their autonomy has since been compromised by state funding and amalgamation with state bodies, distinct feminist ways of operating continue to be of significant value to women's movements in a number of countries (Kantola 2006). In the EU, by contrast, the European Commission has played a central role in the construction of European civil society (Greenwood 1997 and 2004). Both the Commission and the Parliament have created, sustained and institutionalized certain policy actors in Europe.

Broadly speaking, NGOs at EU level can be divided into three categories on the basis of the ways they first appeared on the EU agenda. First, large national or even international NGO organizations have opened a Brussels office. Most of the groups established between 1950 and 1980 were trade unions and had little involvement with women's issues (Cichowski 2007: 177). For example the European Trade Union Confederation (ETUC), established in 1973, showed weak commitment to equal opportunities for women for a long time (Cockburn 1995 and 1996). An exception to this initial trend was the conservative European Union of Women (EUW) established in 1953. The group members were from elected positions and from the Christian Democratic or Conservative political parties. Its aim was to encourage more women to take part in politics but this was effected in the context of 'Christian spiritual and moral values' (Cichowski 2007: 177). Others, such as the Committee of Agricultural Organizations in the EU (COPA) and Public Service International (IPS) had women's committees (Cichowski 2007: 177–8).

Second, networks were either created in or moved to Brussels because they realized the increased importance of the EU and needed to find ways to influence EU affairs. For example, the feminist network Women in Development Europe (WIDE) was initially based in Dublin but in 1993 moved its office to Brussels, so that it could more effectively carry out its lobbying and advocacy work within the EU (Moghadam 2000: 69). Equally the European Women Lawyers Association (EWLA) was founded in 2000 as a response to the male dominance of European jurisdiction discussed in Chapter 3 and has become increasingly influential (Kenney 2002: 265).

Finally, a number of actors were set up in the 1990s with the help of the Commission, including, for example, the European Women's Lobby (EWL), European Network Against Racism (ENAR), European Disability Forum (EDF) and the Platform of European Social NGOs. This trend has continued in the 2000s with the Commission funding the creation of the European Platform of Women Scientists (EPWS) which promotes the work of and networking among women scientists in Europe. The NGOs and the Commission have differing opinions on which of them should take credit for the new organization, each claiming the credit for themselves (Cullen 1999).

The Commission has played a key role in facilitating, regularizing and institutionalizing a European 'NGO structure'. Of the EU decision-making bodies, the Commission has both been the most open to lobbying and has also needed the expert information provided by NGOs for a number of different institutional reasons. First, it lacks the resources for detailed preparation of policies and thus the relatively small number of EU civil servants are keen to draw on expert knowledge. Second, consultation with civil society actors 'accords legitimacy to the Commission, whose position as an unelected body formally charged with policy initiation is, at least, ambiguous'

(Bretherton and Sperling 1996: 490, Schmidt 2005: 140). Third, civil society has been an attractive partner also in terms of 'privatization of governance', in which civil society acts as a partner in governance and also as a service provider. The NGOs are thus required to act as 'cheerleaders for the EU projects, representatives of and service providers to their national constitutents, and policy advisors' (Cullen 2009: 149). The roles can, however, be incompatible and create challenges for the NGOs, as we shall see below.

Contacts between the Commission and civil society are either formalized in advisory committees or groups of experts, as described above, or conducted on an ad hoc basis (Watson and Shackleton 2003: 99). Commission tools for involving civil society actors in policy-making include public hearings and consultative Green and White Papers that actively solicit input from outside interests. Aspects of 'civil dialogue' between the Commission and NGOs include NGOs taking part in bi-annual meetings with Commission officials, engaging with the Commission through policy-related meetings, and participating in information meetings or seminars, workshops and roundtables. Organizations can also submit online policy proposals or engage in bilateral meetings with Commission officials for more direct influence (Cullen 2009: 145).

The Commission has, however, been criticized for its top-down approach to civil society, and particularly for emphasizing the needs of the Commission and the EU rather than those of civil society (Armstrong 2001: 8, Greenwood 2004). In general, EU officials have resisted formalizing NGO consultation, which has meant that the NGOs work in 'a fluid, informal and semi-corporatist context, which privileges large and well-resourced organizations employing insider tactics' (Cullen 2009: 140). The Commission displays a distinct preference for dealing with pan-European associations rather than with representatives of national or individual organizations. For example, a range of civil society organizations working on equality and discrimination issued opinions on the Commission Green Paper on 'Equality and non-discrimination in an enlarged European Union 2004'. Again, the organizations which were already recognized by the Commission and had resources were the most successful in their participation in the process, casting some doubt on its deliberative character and legitimacy from the point of view of other, more diverse and dispersed groups (Rolandsen Agustin 2008). Access to Commission policy-making provided by the different forms of civil dialogue does not always amount to actual influence on the policy. Instead, consultation may require significant resources from NGOs in terms of preparing statements and policy submissions and attending meetings, and this may divert attention away from other tasks (Cullen 2009: 146).

In contrast to the Commission preference for a unified voice for particular groups, there is great fragmentation in women's movements in Europe today. Rather than being unitary and general, the work of these NGOs and networks is often differentiated and issue-specific. In one study, Wiercx and Woodward (2004) identified 90 formal organizations of women working at the European level with an inter- or transnational membership. These included professional, political and church based organizations, and women's interest groups around the environment, peace and feminism itself. This indicates both the plurality of women's concerns and feminisms in Europe (Bull, Diamond and Marsh 2000) and the difficulty of establishing who exactly represents women's concerns and voices and which part of the women's movements to listen to in consultation processes (Squires 2007).

The contexts where the European women's movements operate continue to differ both in the West and the former communist countries. In a number of western European countries, women's movements have become highly institutionalized and movement actors have been able to consolidate their positions and act as partners in policy-making, while in others the women's movement is in decline, a development that has taken place simultaneously with the weakening of women's policy machineries (Outshoorn and Kantola 2007: 281). In the central and eastern European countries, women's civil society organizations witnessed significant growth in the post-communist times of the 1990s (see Forest 2006, Einhorn 2006, Hašková 2005, Roth 2007 and 2008; Sloat 2005). Initially, there was less focus on the more political forms of mobilization, which had some negative repercussions on the ability of the organizations to influence policy-making (Sloat 2005: 440, Einhorn 2000: 118). Instead the organizations took on some of the welfare functions abandoned by the state, resulting in a 'civil society trap' based on the idealization of civil society after the fall of communism (Einhorn and Sever 2003).

Despite the diversity of women's organizations in Europe today, the European Women's Lobby (EWL) has become the main formal pan-European organization representing women's concerns and voice in the EU. It is an example of an organization funded by the

Commission and one that occupies a privileged position in EU policy-making processes in terms of access and voice. Challenges from a gender perspective include questions of (i) autonomy versus dependence; (ii) 'transnational interest formation'; (iii) access and influence; and (iv) fair representation.

Debates about the European Women's Lobby's *autonomy* from and *dependence* on the Commission date back to its establishment in 1990. There are differing interpretations about the roles that the Commission and the women's organizations played in the process, with some emphasizing the role of the Commission in establishing the Lobby (Schmidt 2005: 152), and others attributing a role to the national women's organizations that perceived European level co-operation as crucial for the advancement of their national agendas (Helfferich and Kolb 2001: 148; see also De Groote 1992). In both social movement and feminist theory, a movement's autonomy is seen to enable societal critique and financial dependence on the state to compromise it. Currently, 80 per cent of the EWL budget comes from the European Commission, and it has to acquire 20 per cent co-financing from elsewhere, mainly through project funding from different European bodies. When compared to other European NGOs, the Lobby is privileged as it receives Commission funding for its basic functions and not just for specific projects supporting Commission policy initiatives (Cullen 2009). However, the share of co-financing increases annually, ensuring it is a challenge to the Lobby. The Lobby is also motivated to raise more funds from elsewhere to become less dependent on the Commission and make its existence less dependent on 'friendly individuals' in the Parliament and the Commission (Helfferich and Kolb 2001: 148).

The 2009 policy priority and activity areas of the EWL were divided between EU priorities and traditional and emerging women's movement concerns. Issues such as women in decision-making, European gender equality policies and legislation, women's employment and economic independence, women's human rights in the world, women and migration, immigration and asylum, and violence against women parallel the EU gender policy priorities found in hard law and soft law documents (Chapter 1). Of these, women in decision-making, European gender equality policy and legislation, migration and immigration, and violence against women have been long-term lobbying priorities of the EWL. EU funding was also available for projects on migrant women and violence thus supporting their position as priority areas. A focus on gender stereotypes in society, media and education and prioritizing a focus on women's health (including abortion) are themes that the Lobby seeks to put on the EU agenda.

Successful lobbying in the EU requires the construction of common interests and shared goals as the Commission prioritizes input from umbrella organizations like the EWL. The EWL has adopted a professional approach to lobbying based on a *'transnational interest formation'* (Helfferich and Kolb 2001: 149, Stratigaki 2000: 35). The EWL policies and agreed stance on a specific topic are finalized and put down in 'position papers'. Some issues such as abortion and prostitution have been very contentious and some, such as positive action, have resulted in a shared agreement (Cichowski 2007: 201).

Barbara Helfferich and Felix Kolb (2001: 149–50) identify three factors that shape 'transnational interest formation' in the EWL. First, the EWL has to mediate between differing national conceptions of gender equality. Some of its members, like the National Council of German Women (*Deutsche Frauenrat*), are centralized conservative organizations; others, like the Greek women's organizations, loose and decentralized lobbies. Second, relations between national governments and women's organizations play a role. For example, the National Council of German Women is funded by the German government, which has prevented the Council from taking positions independently of the government. Other organizations have less funding, more insecurity and efficiency problems, but have been freer to put forward new and innovative ideas. Third, the structures of national and European organizations that are members of the lobby are very different. Some are individual membership organizations, others umbrella organizations with associations as members. This has resulted in debates about representation and voice in EWL decision-making and 'transnational interest formation', where each organization has one representative irrespective of its size (Helfferich and Kolb 2001: 149–50).

An example of a successful 'transnational interest formation' by the EWL is the inclusion of a gender perspective in the Amsterdam Treaty 1997 (see Helfferich and Kolb 2001: 149–50). The limitation of gender equality policy to the labour market in Article 119 of the Treaty of Rome was identified as a major shortcoming and the need for a broader legal base was recognized. A shared goal was to extend gender equality provisions beyond the narrow frame of the labour market. This resulted in a well co-ordinated campaign that relied on expert hearings, detailed proposals on the treaty, co-operation with national level women's organizations and European level lobbying where the EWL's strategic action was crucial. For example, in 1995, the EU established 'The Group of Wise Men' to advise the member states on treaty revisions. The group did not include any women except for one observer from the European Parliament. In response, the EWL established a shadow 'Wise Women's Group' that included legal and women's organization experts from the member states. On the basis of the work done in this group, the EWL was able to develop its position on the treaty and put forward detailed proposals. It was much better prepared than other similar lobbies. Furthermore, the EWL fostered sustained contact with national member groups and motivated national organizations to undertake lobbying of their MEPs and national governments. This involved co-ordinated transfer of knowledge to the national level (Helfferich and Kolb 2001: 145; see also Hoskyns 2001: 45). While the final outcome did not incorporate all of the EWL's demands, it was nevertheless regarded as a success (see Chapters 1 and 8).

In terms of *access and influence* in the EU policy-making process, the Lobby has some formalized contacts with the decision-making institutions. The EWL has observer status on the European Parliament's Women's Rights Committee and the Commission's Advisory Committee on Equal Opportunities, and it works in close co-operation with the Equal Opportunities Unit and with politicians from all parties at European level (Laatikainen 2001: 83). On a more informal level, it takes part in meetings with Commission officials, engages with the Commission through policy-related meetings, participates in information meetings or seminars, workshops and roundtables (cf. Cullen 2009: 145).

Such access does not always amount to actual influence. The EWL experiences failures and setbacks when trying to promote gender equality in the EU. One of the unsuccessful campaigns was on the EU constitution drafted by the Convention on the Future of Europe. The EWL sent out letters to decision makers highlighting the need for equal participation of women and men in the autumn of 2001. It also launched an official campaign, 'Put your weight behind equality in Europe', based on a postcard petition (Gréboval 2004: 8). Despite the lobbying, only two of the 12 members of the Presidium of the Convention were women. The president and the two vice-presidents were men (Chapter 10). This illustrates that even if the EWL succeeds in forming a shared transnational interest among its constituents and lobbies for its inclusion in EU policy, some policy-making environments remain closed and hostile.

Similarly, lobbying for parity democracy to be included in the Goods and Services Directive 2004 failed. At the 2002 EWL General Assembly, several motions were approved on the need to lobby for the introduction of parity democracy in the EU. The scope of the new directive adopted in December 2004, however, concerned only equal treatment of women and men in goods and services and the issue of women in decision-making was not included (see above and Chapter 1). Cécile Gréboval (2004: 9), the policy co-ordinator of the EWL, argues that 'the different strategies employed by the EWL to date have failed, mainly because of a lack of political will and a lack of support for gender equality in decision-making at the European level'. Both examples show that the issue of political representation in the EU is a difficult policy area and environment for advancing gender equality (see Chapter 3).

Finally, the position of the EWL raises questions about *representation and voice*. Each member state has a national co-ordination for Women's NGOs for EWL. In 2004, the number of national co-ordinations increased from 18 to 25 when new national co-ordinations joined from the new member states and Turkey. The 2008 Annual Meeting was historic in that it accepted the national co-ordinations from Cyprus and Poland, thus making the EWL representative of all member states (and Croatia, Macedonia and Turkey). The cases of Cyprus and Poland are illustrative of the way in which the EWL membership motivates national women's movements to form broad national umbrella organizations so as to be eligible to join the EWL. The impetus for this activity came clearly from above and is reflected in the names of these organizations, which parallel the name of the European Women's Lobby: The Polish Women's Lobby and the Cyprus EWL Co-ordination. These coalitions or co-ordinations can also break down easily as happened in Poland and Latvia in 2007 and 2008. In addition to national co-ordinations, 23 large European networks are members of the EWL, including for example the International Alliance of Women and the women's section of the European Trade Union Confederation (ETUC).

A combination of the EWL attempting to represent diverse interests and the Commission preferring to listen to one centralized voice has resulted in the Commission discouraging women's groups from operating autonomously from the EWL (Cichowski 2007: 201). This emphasis on the EWL as a formal access point raises questions about whose voice is heard and whose is not, and which parts of the women's movement are represented and which are not in EU level policy-making.

One particularly sensitive issue is the representation of black and ethnic minority women in the EWL. Traditionally, their representation has been poor in the EWL and the board continues to be white although its member organizations now include minority women's organizations, such as the Federation of Kale, Manouche, Romany and Sinte Women (since 2008), and the Lobby places policy emphasis on immigrant and minority women in its work programme. Only two women out of the 70 who attended its inaugural meeting in September 1990 were ethnic minority women (Hoskyns 1996: 186). The first attempt to address the concerns of black and ethnic minority women was the drafting of the report *Confronting the Fortress* in 1993. The report was written by a mixed group of black and white women who worked together uneasily (Hoskyns 1996: 187–8). The report focused on the better involvement of black and ethnic minority women in the EWL and recommended developing more open and democratic structures and taking up the issues of racism and immigration. The report was contentious within the lobby and was adopted by a narrow margin at its General Assembly in 1993 (Hoskyns 1996: 188).

The EWL has also been criticized for its slowness in including women's organizations from the new member states from central and eastern Europe in the 2000s. The first general conference about enlargement was held in 2003 and in that year the EWL extended its network to NGOs in the accession countries (Roth 2007: 472). The fact that the lobby promotes the participation of umbrella organizations rather than individual subscriptions may also have delayed co-operation with Eastern NGOs which remained weak and acted separately (Forest 2006: 179). Before May 2004, when ten new member states joined the EU, only Hungary and Latvia had established EWL national co-ordinations. The Czech Women's Union was only an associate member. Some commentators have described EWL's attitude as 'cautious' towards these organizations because of differing views on gender equality (Forest 2006: 179). For example, the Karat Coalition, a regional co-operation body among women's NGOs in the CEECs, was very involved with questions of EU enlargement (Forest 2006: 179) but rather than joining the EWL it decided to develop its own agenda and collaborate with the lobby (Roth 2007: 472). For women in the East, the EWL's lack of knowledge about women's situation in the former communist countries was 'shocking' and they were disappointed at its lack of action during the accession process (Roth 2007: 472). EWL addressed Eastern enlargement mainly through the dangers of trafficking, migration and prostitution. Burning issues for the CEECs' women's organizations, such as women's health and reproductive rights, abortion in particular, were non-issues for the EWL (Fuchs and Payer 2007: 173). This resulted in a belief that the EWL did not represent the concerns of the women's organizations in the new member states (Hašková and Křížková 2008: 168).

Co-operation and contestation in 'velvet triangles'

Such a complex set of women's policy agencies and organizations raises a number of questions. How do these institutions and actors work together in EU gender policy? Are they effective and successful in promoting gender equality? Alison Woodward (2003) uses the notion 'velvet triangle' to describe the partially institutionalized forms of co-operation in gender policy in the EU. The velvet triangle consists of: first, femocrats ('state feminists') in the Commission and the Parliament, second, gender experts in academia or consultancies, and third, the established women's movement and organizations. The formal and informal contacts and collaboration between these actors make it possible for them to effectively advance issues commonly perceived as important for women or for gender equality. Personal ties, common biographies and career mobility between both individuals and representatives of movements and institutions in the area of European gender policy ensure policy success (Woodward 2003: 85; see also Holli 2008).

Two empirical case studies, one on trafficking in women (Locher 2007) and another on job training (Laatikainen 2001) illustrate how these velvet triangles work in practice in the EU and what opportunities and challenges are involved. Birgit Locher's study on trafficking in women shows that a wide range of both national and pan-European NGOs were involved. National ones included, for example, the Dutch Foundation Against Trafficking in Women and pan-European ones the European Network Against Trafficking in Women and the European Women's Lobby. One factor that was a challenge for NGO co-operation in this field was polarized views on prostitution (for a discussion see Chapter 7; see also Locher 2007: 217). For example, the Dutch STV adopted an anti-abolitionist stance whilst the EWL defined prostitution as always an involuntary activity. The lack of a common position hindered effective lobbying and networking in the field and is part of the reason why the NGOs were not effectively included in the policy-making process.

This was compensated for by the activities by the other actors in the velvet triangle, namely feminist politicians and women's policy agencies. The Parliament's Women's Rights Committee (FEMM) and the Civil Rights Committee were both active and committed; women MEPs initiated policy papers on trafficking in the Parliament in the 1990s. Feminist politicians who had considerable expertise and involvement in the issue were appointed as *rapporteurs* of FEMM. Also decisive was the appointment of Anita Gradin in 1995 as the Commissioner of Justice and Home Affairs; she has been described as 'a major driving force' and 'committed to advance the issue of trafficking in women' (Locher 2007: 220). These actors brought in feminist experts on the topic who provided knowledge, served on various advisory committees of the Commission, and were called upon as experts to report on trafficking (Locher 2007: 221–2).

The velvet triangle in this case was based on effective links and close co-operation between these groups. A number of individuals had double roles in many organizations working on the issue. Furthermore, Gradin worked to establish close links between women MEPs in the Parliament and the Commission, and in the Council she was helped by her Swedish colleagues (Locher 2007: 223). Hence the commitment of feminist actors within the Commission was crucial.

Katie Laatikainen (2001) has studied these questions in relation to women's movements' and women's policy agencies' impact on EU job training policy. Her case study illustrates a number of points. First, whilst the co-decision procedure has enhanced the role of the European Parliament and afforded women's groups greater access and voice in the process, the pre-eminent role of the European Council remains a source of frustration. It is both impervious to European level lobbyists and too far removed from the national context to be influenced by national women's lobbies (Laatikainen 2001: 79, 87–8).

Second, in this case there was a split between the women's policy agencies (the Equal Opportunities Unit, EOU) and the women's organizations (the EWL) on the issue of gender mainstreaming in job training. The EOU was supportive of the

Commission's mainstreaming approach which characterized the reform process (known as Agenda 2000). However, gender mainstreaming in this context meant dismantling women-specific programmes such as New Opportunities for Women (NOW), established in 1991, whicht sought to reduce unemployment among women and to improve the position of women already in the workforce through training opportunities (Laatikainen 2001: 84). Although the representatives of the women's movement supported gender mainstreaming, they were critical of the decision to abandon positive, gender-specific training programmes.

The objectives of the EOU and the EWL as well as the two other women's policy agencies in the EU, the Advisory Committee and the Women's Rights Committee, diverged in the debate over Agenda 2000. The EOU promoted the idea of flexibility and of selling the equal opportunities approach with an emphasis on that. The EOU thus bought into the dominant, liberal discourse of the Commission on employment (Laatikainen 2001: 101). So although the EOU contributed to gendering the debate on Agenda 2000, it pursued a quite non-feminist policy line throughout the discussions. Unlike the EOU, the Advisory Committee, the Parliamentary Women's Rights Committee and the EWL were adamantly opposed to losing European level positive action programmes for women (Laatikainen 2001: 99–100).

Detailed studies such as these illustrate the opportunities of working together and pursuing gender equality that these various women's organizations and women's policy agencies have. They also show the differences of opinion among them. Those closer to the decision-making power of the Commission can, for example, be complicit with its discourse of competition and flexibility whilst the women's movement can take a more critical stance. This reflects the battles over the meaning of gender equality and how best to achieve it.

Conclusion

The European Union policy-making processes provide different opportunities for advancing gender policy. Ranging from the Community method to the intergovernmental and co-ordination methods, the varying roles assigned to the EU institutions also impact on gender policy. Overall, the more accessible and democratic the policy-making process is, the easier it has been to advance gender equality. In the EU, this has usually been ensured in cases where the Parliament acts as a key partner in governance. The bureaucratic and opaque decision-making of the Council has required powerful feminist allies to push policy forward. The deregulation favoured by the co-ordination method promotes similar bureaucratic tendencies and civil society groups and democratic institutions have had difficulties in intervening.

Nevertheless, the EU has played a central role in facilitating the creation of a European women's policy network that consists of women's policy agencies in its own structures and more independent civil society organizations. Some of these were created as early as the 1980s and 1990s, including the Parliament's and the Commission's women's policy agencies and the European Women's Lobby. Others are currently being established, including the European Gender Institute or the new WES, a network for the promotion of women entrepreneurship that maps directly onto the more neoliberal economic priorities of the EU. It is evident that the creation of the European women's policy network has given the EU the opportunity to listen to the types of actors that it needs for its own policy-making. For the actors themselves this can have a negative impact on the plurality of claims as well as promoting problematic framings that are compatible with the dominant frame used by the EU (Rolandsen Agustín 2008). Nevertheless, some of these organizations, such as the European Women's Lobby, have acquired a 'feminist life of their own', seeking to increase their autonomy vis-à-vis the Commission.

Chapter 5

The EU Gender Policy: Reconciling Work and Family

This chapter discusses a key EU debate within gender policy: that around the reconciliation of work and family. The debate is interesting for a number of different reasons. First, the notion of reconciling work and family plays a key role in EU rhetoric on social policy more generally. The debate illustrates the tendency of social policy concerns that initially give priority to, for example, gender equality to be overtaken by economic issues and framed in a way that gives priority to market concerns. Second, reconciliation policies cover a wide range. In the EU, they are defined as policies that directly support the combination of professional, family and private life and cover childcare services, leave facilities, flexible working arrangements and financial allowances for working parents. This is an example of a policy field where member state variations are huge. Two broad trends comprise: first, collectivizing care by providing tax-funded care programmes, such as paid parental leave and subsidised public childcare, and second, privatizing care by encouraging family members to take on care responsibilities without compensation or supporting and regulating care given by volunteers (Haas 2003: 95). Finally, reconciliation of work and family is promoted through both hard law and soft law measures and is thus embedded in the changing modes of EU governance, making it possible to evaluate them from a gender perspective.

This chapter will analyze the EU reconciliation policies ranging from directives on pregnant workers, parental leave and part-time work to soft law regulation of childcare services. Directives provide the minimum standards for member states' policies on maternity leave, pregnant workers and parental leave. The EU policy-making context and processes had to change significantly before these directives could be enacted. However, the discussion also shows that the involvement of social partners – employers and trade unions – in the negotiations for the directive has been challenging from a gender perspective. The policy-making processes have changed in other ways too. Regulation with soft law in difficult areas such as childcare takes place through the Open Method of Co-ordination (OMC) and this chapter will explore the challenges that relate to that mode of governance from a gender perspective.

Reconciliation as an example of gender policy

The notion 'women's policy' refers to 'the area of political action and activity that particularly concerns (or targets) women or groups of women, or where issues are forced onto the agenda by women' (Hoskyns 1996: 29). The term 'feminist policy', in turn, has been used to evaluate whether policies have feminist results (Mazur 2002: 30–1). This chapter uses the more general concept 'gender policies'. In contrast, to women's policy, analyzing gender policy allows for a focus on constructions of the roles of both women and men. In contrast to feminist policy, the aim is not to measure feminist success but rather to explore how a variety of policies can be framed as contributing to gender equality. So rather than taking the meaning of gender equality as given, the aim is to analyze how the content of gender equality is constructed in the process and with what consequences (Bacchi 1999, Holli 2003, Lombardo, Meier and Verloo 2009).

Reconciliation of work and family has become a key EU gender policy debate. The language of reconciliation is, however, not new and it first emerged in EU documents in 1974 in the Community Social Action Programme where it was seen as a means to improve employment. This has indeed also been the key motivation behind the current policies. Feminist scholars and activists are, however, keen to point to other usages and alternative constructions. For example, in the UN in the 1980s, reconciliation was a concept related to gender equality. When gender equality, rather than improving labour market participation, is the goal, the emphasis of reconciliation policies would be, for example, on equal sharing of childcare responsibilities between the two parents. The EU has oscillated between the two ways of defining the issue. In the First Action Programme (1982–5), reconciliation was still about equal sharing of family responsibilities as a precondition to equal treatment in the labour market. The objective was to improve the quality of life and the sharing of all social life, including decision-making posts (Stratigaki 2004: 44). By the time the Second Programme (1986–90) was formulated the goal had shifted to combining work and family by increasing parental leave, relevant infrastructure and flexible working time for working mothers. In other words, there was a shift from a more holistic approach to a narrower 'women in the labour market' approach. In 1994, a White Paper on European Social Policy was issued and the objective of reconciliation was closely linked to the flexibility of labour (Stratigaki 2004: 44).

As a result, feminist commentators have become increasingly critical of the language of reconciliation. They suggest that it is usually based on gender-neutral language and is taken to mean the 'harmonization' of paid and unpaid work for women, rather than 'harmonization' in the sense of equal sharing between women and men at the household level (Lewis 2006: 428; see also Meier *et al.* 2007: 118). As Maria Stratigaki argues: '*Sharing* is a term associated with equality of women and men, defining a policy objective in the area of gender relations, whereas *reconciliation* derived from labour market analysis and has a more economic orientation' (2004: 31, emphasis in the original). Reconciliation policies that do not tackle existing gender inequalities can end up reproducing and consolidating women's roles and responsibilities as primary carers (Stratigaki 2004: 32).

This is a familiar trend and debate in the EU where social policy is often justified in terms of its benefits for the dominant economic growth and competition agenda. Women, in particular, become an 'untapped labour reserve' where women's labour market participation is seen as a means to increase competitiveness and the tax base of European welfare states (Lewis and Giullari 2005: 81). Within this frame of analysis, discrimination in the labour market needs to be tackled because it harmfully distorts competition. Reconciliation policies, in turn, enable the Commission to meet such growth targets as increasing women's labour market participation to 60 per cent by 2010 as outlined in the Lisbon strategy which aims for more competitive and productive European societies. Reconciliation policies also supply remedies for another worry in the EU where women as mothers are the key: declining birth rates and demography. Better reconciliation of work and family is here seen as the key to women not having to choose between a career and a family.

Legislating for equality: pregnancy, maternity and parental leave directives

Progress in EU gender policy has often been tied to the fate of EU social policy. Issues such as the length of and compensation for maternity, paternity and parental leave are the key to women's labour market participation, and fall into the field of social policy in the member states. Many member states have been reluctant to give the EU a meaningful competence in the field. It is here that some of the major challenges to feminist approaches lie.

Initially, the field developed through European Court of Justice case law and this case law was later developed into binding directives. The *Dekker* case was the first time the Court considered the rights of pregnant workers under EU law. The case was brought before the ECJ by a Dutch court in 1988. Mrs Dekker applied for a job with a Dutch company, VJV, and after an interview was found to be the most qualified candidate for the job. She was three months pregnant at the time, and while the hiring committee recommended employment, VJV management decided not to employ Dekker because its insurer would not cover the necessary maternity pay. Dekker instigated legal proceedings against VJV, claiming that she had been discriminated against on the basis of her sex. The case was referred to the ECJ for a preliminary ruling on the protection of Dekker under Article 141 and the Equal Treatment Directive (Cichowski 2003: 503). In its 1990 ruling, the Court found that discrimination in employment opportunities on the grounds of pregnancy constitutes direct sex discrimination that goes against the Equal Treatment Directive. The ruling in effect created new European rules by providing explicit protection of pregnant workers under EU law (Cichowski 2003: 503).

Later that same day, the Court made a similar ruling in a case originating from the Danish courts, the *Hertz* case, concluding that the dismissal of a pregnant employee also amounts to discrimination under EU law (Cichowski 2003: 503). However, the Court left open the possibility that protection against dismissal for pregnancy might not apply to women on fixed contracts. The Court did not address the issue that many employers do not hire young women on long-term contracts because they do not want to bear the potential economic costs of pregnancy and child-care (Hobson 2000: 95).

Developments in case law alone would not have been enough to push for directives in this field. The EU policy-making environment and decision-making structures have been changed in fundamental ways that impact on legislation in the field of reconciling work and family. Important changes include the move to co-decision-making between the Parliament and the Council, qualified majority voting, the inclusion of social partners and the subsidiarity principle. Chapter 2 showed how, in the 1980s, a number of draft directives were blocked in the Council by recalcitrant member states. Especially in the 1980s, the UK threatened to use its veto every time the Commission proposed a new binding directive on aspects of social policy like parental leave or the rights of part-time workers (van der Vleuten 2007: 9). The structures which created this situation changed towards the end of the 1980s and in the 1990s, first with the Single European Act 1987 and then with the Treaty of Maastricht (1992).

The Treaty of Maastricht introduced, first, a new legislative mechanism of *co-decision* that strengthened the Parliament's influence on legislation (Chapter 4). Second, it allowed for *qualified majority voting* in issues dealing with living and working conditions, training and equal opportunities for underprivileged groups, and health and safety protection. Third, it *involved social partners*, management and labour, in the legislative process (Heide 1999: 385). The new neo-corporatist approach called 'Social Dialogue' allowed organizations representing labour and management at the EU level to prepare draft directives for Council approval. After the Treaty, the Commission could choose to present a social policy issue either as one concerning safety at work, to be decided by qualified majority voting, or as an issue to be put before the social partners (Nousiainen 2009). Directives on parental leave, burden of proof and part-time work were re-introduced via the social partners. Finally, the Treaty of Maastricht constitutionalized the *subsidiarity principle*, according to which Community action shall be undertaken only if the same objective can be 'better achieved' by the Community than by the individual member states. In all other cases, activities should be left within the scope of the nation states (Rossilli 2000: 2). These provisions were written into the revised Chapter on Social Provisions of the Amsterdam Treaty (1997), which was signed by the UK.

The negotiations of the Maastricht Treaty politicized the general public and revealed a gender gap in support for the EU. The general decline of mass public support for the EU started in the autumn of 1991 and gender gaps in this support were clear in the popular referenda in Denmark, Sweden and Norway (Liebert 1997: 201). Even after controlling for other structural variables, for political orientations or political involvement, it was reported that men were generally more supportive of European integration than women (Nelsen and Guth 2000, Liebert 1997: 203, Gabel and Whitten 1997, Gabel and Palmer 1995). In the first Danish referendum in 1992, it was Danish women in particular who voted against the Maastricht Treaty. This gender gap can also be seen in the feminist criticisms of the EU fuelled by the stagnation in EU gender policy in the 1980s (see Chapter 2). It partly explains the perceived need to speak to 'women' and to 'women's concerns', such as reconciling work and family, at EU level.

In this new context, several important pieces of legislation were adopted. The Pregnant Workers Directive 1992 gave rights to pregnant women and those who are breast-feeding. Commissioner Papandreou did not present the directive as one of the gender equality directives, but linked it to a set of directives on heath and safety at work so that it would only require a qualified majority in the Council. Whilst the Parliament and the Commission promoted longer leave periods, the Council of Ministers – and Italy in particular – resisted (Guerrina 2005: 70). In the end, the directive only set minimum requirements, including fourteen weeks of maternity leave and the provision of pay or an allowance at least equivalent to sickness benefit. It contained a provision protecting pregnant workers against dismissal but the provision is weaker than that afforded by the 'old' gender equality directives. The directive was silent about the right of a woman to return to her job or an equivalent job at the end of her maternity leave; nor did it cover employees on short-term and temporary contracts (van der Vleuten 2007: 157; Guerrina 2005: 69–70).

Even in its watered-down form the directive required changes in all member states except Denmark. Member states were specifically forbidden to level down their national provisions to what the directive required (Beveridge, Nott and Stephen 2000: 145). Furthermore, rulings by the Court gave breadth to the directive, for example by highlighting the duties of employers regarding adjusting the workplace to the needs of pregnant workers (Cichowski 2003: 507). While the directive provided minimal protection at EU level as a result of UK insistence, women activists throughout Europe have pushed for greater pregnancy protection under EU law through litigation. The result has been an extensive case law on pregnancy and maternity rights (Cichowski 2002: 232).

The *Parental Leave Directive* 1996 under the Social Protocol (initially excluding the UK) provided for periods of time off work for mothers and fathers in certain circumstances. It was eventually agreed to by the UK in 1997. Negotiations for the directive took place under the Social Protocol and were conducted by the social partners. Despite the usefulness of reaching an agreement, the procedure reinforced the economic agenda and priorities through the roles played by the employers and employees' unions (Guerrina 2005: 77). The directive gave fathers and mothers the right to a minimum of three months' benefits on the birth or adoption of a child. It modified an earlier decision of the court in the *Hoffman* case, which did not recognize fathers' rights to parental leave. Again the directive reflected the lowest common denominator. Its main purpose was the reconciliation of parental and professional responsibilities for working parents. The duration of the leave was three months and the entitlement was valid for parents of children up to 8 years rather than up to 2 years (Stratigaki 2004: 47–8).

The new directive left such fundamental but difficult issues as pay and the right to social security benefits during leave to be decided at national level (van der Vleuten 2007: 150). In most countries, entitlement to leave was already at a standard superior to that envisioned in the directive. The directive marked considerable improvement only in three member states: Ireland, Luxembourg and Belgium. Ireland, Luxembourg and the UK had no previous entitlement to parental leave (Bruning and Plantega 1999: 196). Because the UK had opted out of the Agreement on Social Policy, it was not obliged to comply (Stratigaki 2004: 48). It finally had to comply under the Amsterdam Treaty in 1997, but it was granted a two-year compliance period. Six other member states (Austria, Germany, Greece, Italy, the Netherlands and Portugal) had to make minor changes to their existing parental leave systems (Morgan 2008). In 1998, the EC began infringement proceedings against Italy, Luxembourg and Portugal for failing to comply with the parental leave directive and by 1999, these countries had parental legislation in place (Haas 2003: 94).

The directive was adopted in a political environment of an increasing need for flexibility in the labour market. The potential for transforming gender roles, and mandating men to take on an equal share of family responsibilities, was therefore not realized (Hobson 2000: 96, Stratigaki 2004: 48). From a symbolic point of view, parental leave offered the opportunity to demonstrate that the social partners could find solutions to directives blocked by the Council (Stratigaki 2000: 42). The main purpose was thus to reconcile parental and professional responsibilities and not to promote equal treatment for women and men, indicating the lack of strong commitment among social partner organizations to gender equality. Once again genuine gender equality concerns had to give way to other priorities (cf. Skjeie 2006). The participation of women in the negotiations for the directive was very limited due to the low numbers of women in the trade unions and employers' organizations (Stratigaki 2000: 42).

There have been some ongoing changes in the field. Women's organizations, such as the European Women's Lobby, have been calling on the Commission and the Council to revise the directive on parental leave in order to establish a longer leave, better paid and shared equally between the two parents. The Social Partners (trade unions and employers) concluded their negotiations for improvements to the Parental Leave Directive in 2009 (see Nousiainen 2009). The Pregnant Workers Directive is currently also under scrutiny by the social partners and the Commission. In 2008, the Commission put forward a legislative proposal that proposes 18 weeks' continuous leave, which adds four extra weeks to the current European legislation.

TABLE 5.1   *EU directives on gender equality since 1992*

Year	Directive	
1992	Pregnant Workers Directive	92/85/EEC
1993	Working Time Directive	93/104/EC
1996	Parental Leave Directive	96/34/EC
1996	Directive on Occupational Social Security	96/97/EC
1997	Directive on the Burden of Proof	97/80/EC
1997	Part-time Workers' Directive	97/81/EC
2002	Equal Treatment in Employment Directive	2002/73/EC
2004	Goods and Services Directive	2004/113/EC
2006	Recast Directive	2006/54/EC

The Part-time Workers Directive (1997) and the Directive on the Burden of Proof (1997) in cases of discrimination based on sex are two other examples of directives negotiated by the social partners. The first guaranteed equal treatment for full-time and part-time workers with respect to pay and working conditions while leaving the matter of statutory social security to the member states. This guaranteed part-time workers, the majority of whom are women, some basic social rights at the European level without intervening significantly in national systems of social security (Bleijenbergh *et al.* 2004: 315). The second directive included a legislative definition of indirect discrimination for the first time, and provisions aiming to adjust the rules on the burden of proof in sex discrimination cases. There were some basic disagreements between the employers and workers' representatives on both directives. For example, in the case of the directive on part-time work the two sides disagreed about the definition of a part-time worker and whether to have a broad or a narrow definition (for a detailed discussion see Bleijenbergh *et al.* 2004). In the end the directive aims to guarantee part-time workers equal treatment within the labour market rather than a minimum level of social welfare (Bleijenbergh *et al.* 2004: 315).

Both directives were weak. The one on the burden of proof, for example, merely confirmed what had already been laid down by the Court's case law. Member states did not see the interests of victims of discrimination as their priority, being primarily concerned about the costs that any shift in the burden of proof in social security cases would involve. All costly elements were eliminated from the draft and the co-operation procedure left the EP powerless in the face of a unanimous Council (van der Vleuten 2007: 158–9). The case also illustrated that the decision-making procedure on social policy, in which the social partners play a key role, lacks democratic control. The Parliament only has an advisory role on texts that have already been agreed by the social partners so that the direct democratic control of the contents of policy-making are limited. There is also little indirect democratic control through the Council, the unwritten rule being that it accepts the contents of an agreement or else rejects it (Bleijenbergh *et al.* 2004: 322). This places the responsibility on the European social partners to make their procedures more transparent and accountable and, for example, to include women in their decision-making structures.

The Equal Treatment in Employment Directive 2002, by

contrast, was negotiated under the co-decision procedure between the Parliament and the Council and made some significant amendments to the 1976 Equal Treatment Directive. In this case, the strengthened role of the Parliament created more opportunities for advancing gender equality than the consultation and co-operation procedures, as member states can no longer adopt a directive against the will of the Parliament which is an actor clearly in favour of stronger gender equality legislation (van der Vleuten 2007: 161; see also Clavero and Galligan 2009: 105). In contrast to the Social Dialogue and the involvement of social partners, the Parliament's involvement lifted the directive to a level above the lowest common denominator.

In three readings, the Parliament managed to add new elements to the amended directive requiring more legislative changes in more member states (Ahtela 2005: 60). The directive contains a clear definition of the different types of discrimination. Direct discrimination occurs 'where one person is treated less favourably on grounds of sex than another is, has been or would be treated in a comparable situation'. Indirect discrimination occurs 'where an apparently neutral provision, criterion or practice would put persons of one sex at a particular disadvantage compared with persons of the other sex, unless that provision, criterion or practice is objectively justified by a legitimate aim, and the means of achieving that aim are appropriate and necessary' (for a discussion see Ahtela 2005: 63–5). The directive also strengthened the protection of women in case of pregnancy and maternity, including the right to return to the same job after maternity leave. It provides for sanctions and obliges member states to create specific bodies to ensure compliance with equality legislation, and to issue follow-up reports every four years (van der Vleuten 2007: 161).

Importantly, the directive incorporated sexual harassment into hard law for the first time and defined it as forbidden discrimination. Both sexual and gender harassment were given explicit definitions and member states were obliged to draft national legislation on criminalizing harassment (Zippel 2009: 140). The EU's definition of harassment is victim-centred in that harassment is defined as unwanted behaviour from the victim's point of view, eliminating the issue of the perpetrator's intentions and motivation (Zippel 2009: 148). For example, the employers' association UNICE wanted to leave the issue to the member states and to avoid European legislation on harassment. The gender equality advocates and the

European Parliament were, however, strongly in favour of legal action in the field (Zippel 2004 and 2006). Limitations of the directive include the exclusion of sexual harassment that takes place outside the workplace and the absence of a number of such difficult issues as prevention, implementation and enforcement on the member states (Zippel 2009: 149–51).

Some of this complex legislation was brought together and simplified with the enactment of the Recast Directive (2006). The scope of a recast exercise in the EU is in general limited and it can aim at simplifying and reshaping existing laws rather than reforming them completely (Burrows and Robinson 2007: 187). Whilst the legislation on gender equality is scattered across various directives, treaties and case law, it was somewhat surprising in comparative terms that the Commission chose to use the recast technique on sex discrimination because it has usually been used for 'harmonisation of technical regulatory measures' rather than substantive issues such as gender equality (Burrows and Robinson 2007: 188). The Recast Directive brought the Equal Pay, the Equal Treatment, the Occupational Social Security and the Burden of Proof directives together in one single text. The vast jurisprudence of the European Court of Justice was also taken into account and for example, the ECJ decision that discrimination against transsexuals is gender discrimination became a general principle of law and was included in the preamble of the new directive (Burrows and Robinson 2007: 189).

Despite the technical nature of the recast exercise the new directive signalled a move from a narrower notion of equal treatment to more substantive equality. This was evidenced, for example, by the directive incorporating the concept of positive action as a horizontal principle applying across all the provisions to which it refers (Clavero and Galligan 2009: 106). Furthermore, the European and national courts may choose to interpret the Recast Directive in an 'imaginative way' and hence give more substance to it, for example by introducing the distinction between direct and indirect discrimination into the equal pay arena (Burrows and Robinson 2007: 187).

The Recast Directive was based on Article 141 EC of the Amsterdam Treaty, which meant that it could only cover the field of employment matters. As a result, for example, the Pregnant Workers and the Parental Leave directives were both excluded from the Recast Directive because of their different legal base relating to the protection of health (Masselot 2007: 162). As these two directives were left outside the recasting exercise some important inconsistencies between the directives such as the definition of indirect discrimination were left untouched. Noreen Burrows and Muriel Robinson (2007: 195) argue that 'pregnancy and maternity provisions have been seen as an exception to the principle of equal treatment and as a matter to be dealt with by special and separate rules'. Although the ECJ has ruled that unfavourable treatment on the ground of pregnancy is gender discrimination, pregnant workers and those on maternity leave continue to be treated as workers on sick pay in the EU (Burrows and Robinson 2007: 195).

To summarize, the shift of power from the Council to the social partners had an ambivalent impact on gender equality. It permitted the unblocking of Community legal instruments, but provided little evidence to suggest that the social partners would show greater commitment to the promotion of women's rights (Stratigaki 2000: 44). The corporatist procedure has resulted in gender directives which, compared to other social policy directives, stand out because of the high number of non-binding provisions they contain (van der Vleuten 2007: 153). The legitimacy of the Social Dialogue has also been questioned in terms of the democratic representativeness of the social partners involved in the process (Nousiainen 2009). It is well known that women continue to be underrepresented in both the employers' and workers' unions' decision-making bodies, but there are also questions of size and geographic spread and power in relation to these bodies.

On the other hand, the co-decision-making procedure that enhanced the role of the Parliament had positive consequences for gender equality, as evidenced by the enactment of the Equal Treatment Directive 2002. The directive contained some progressive definitions of direct and indirect discrimination and of sexual harassment that member states have had to transpose to their own legislation. In 2008, the Commission took action against those member states who have failed to do so; for example Finland and Estonia have had to clarify the definition of sexual harassment in their national legislation. Sara Clavero and Yvonne Galligan (2009: 115) argue that 'In shifting towards a relatively more democratic, or at least a more deliberative, form of decision-making, the tendency of the Council to dilute, block and veto gender directives is more circumscribed than before.'

However crafted, these employment and social policy directives have usually led to more or less uniform rules that have been incorporated into national law, creating, at least in theory, a relatively harmonized area of law throughout the EU (see, however, Chapter 9). Overall, directives represent 'hard law' and clear-cut standards to assess transposition to national law or alternatively possible non-compliance, although the member states may have some leeway in transposing them. This makes it easier for both the Commission and women's organizations to hold member states' governments accountable and to push them forward towards progressive gender policy (Verloo and van der Vleuten 2009, van der Vleuten 2005 and 2007). The case is slightly different for the soft law that is used to regulate another aspect of reconciliation policies: childcare services.

Regulating through soft law: childcare policy

The EU competence in social and employment policy has been limited. As a result, a number of issues have been framed in terms of anti-discrimination (see Chapter 8 on poverty) or protection of health (see Chapter 7 on violence) in order to find a legal basis for EU action in the field. New soft law tools have, however, enabled an expansion of the EU role in the field of social policy, including for example childcare, which would otherwise fall outside its competence (Beveridge, Nott and Stephen 2000: 149, Büchs 2007). The soft law measures set standards, raise expectations and have considerable indirect influence on the interpretation of the main 'hard law' instruments, particularly in the context of national legislation (McCrudden 2003: 4).

Childcare is a social policy area where there is great divergence within member states making it an attractive field in which to use soft law measures. Linda Haas puts forward a four-way typology of care policy models in Europe. In the *privatized* (non-interventionist) *care model* (Greece, Italy, Portugal and Spain) care is a private responsibility undertaken primarily by mothers or extended family members. Fathers are not encouraged to make use of leave benefits (Haas 2003: 96). In the *family-centred care model* (Austria, Belgium, France, Germany and Luxembourg) policy-making is shaped by a traditional religious heritage and a strong public commitment to the preservation of the traditional family. Women's contribution to the economy is recognized but men are still responsible for family income provision (Haas 2003: 100). In the *market-oriented care model* (Ireland, the Netherlands and the UK) countries hold strong traditional values concerning the role of women and men and there is a clear lack of support for working parents.

Instead, these countries encourage employers to become more actively involved in helping employees combine work and their family role. Finally, in *the valued care model* (Denmark, Finland and Sweden) care is supported by the state and care work is valued and professionalized (Haas 2003: 104).

The central and eastern European countries which joined the EU in 2004 and 2007 went through dramatic changes in terms of social policy and welfare in the 1990s. Each of them had to balance the tension between a tradition of extensive welfare provision and income redistribution, and the residualist social policy advocated by a global neoliberal economic framework (Steinhilber 2006: 68). The reforms had significant gender implications through changes in maternity and childcare benefits and in transfers to families. For example, Poland chose a radical economic transformation strategy, while the Czech Republic combined neoliberal and social democratic elements by maintaining a high level of social solidarity (Steinhilber 2006: 68–9). Nevertheless, their shared features include a conservative family model, where social or family policy is not used to advance gender equality, and moverover, policies target nuclear families and do not take other family formations (single parents, same-sex partnerships) into account (Steinhilber 2006: 81).

Because most of these care regimes emphasize the private nature of care arrangements, it is not surprising that within Europe only a minority of countries have achieved a continuity of public responsibility for childcare. The data for childcare services tends to be scarce. While childcare services for pre-schoolers from 3 to 6 are often available, there is still a significant gap when it comes to services for children under 3. This reflects the persistence of the idea that the state has responsibility for children's education but that care remains essentially a private matter. In a number of countries, systems of reliable full day-care, including care during school holidays, are missing. The lack of sufficient childcare makes it harder for parents to balance work and care. In many cases, responsibility for care is often left to the family and overall it is women who are responsible for this care.

Publicly funded childcare is often combined with different care allowances. These further promote private care arrangements and usually result in women taking on the responsibility for care. Care leave is different from maternity, paternity or parental leave as it concerns older children and it is not supported by the employer but by the state. For example, Finland operates a dual strategy where municipal childcare is combined with a Home Care Allowance for children who do not take up the statutory right to a childcare place. Care allowances are cheaper for the state and the municipalities (welfare service providers) than public childcare and coincide with traditional ideas about women's right to choose to stay at home (Kantola 2006). Feminists have often opposed care leave as it tends to reinforce women's roles as dependant on the male breadwinner and in the home. Care leave thus does not change gendered patters of labour (Morgan and Zippel 2003).

Feminist views on childcare differ too. In the UK, women's movement activists regarded childcare as an uninteresting topic for a long time, whilst in Finland they saw it as a key to gender equality early on (Kantola 2006). This reflects and reinforces different national understandings of childcare as a public (Finland) or a private (UK) matter. Feminist discourses on childcare have, for example, emphasized its role in providing equal opportunities for women in accessing the labour market and the state's responsibility for the provision of professional and reliable public childcare places (Kantola 2006).

Despite this diversity in the member states there have been attempts at EU level to push for a childcare directive. The European Childcare Network, established by the Second Action Programme on Equal Opportunities in 1986, and the European Parliament have been calling for this since the 1990s and have sought to frame childcare as a 'citizenship right' (Bleijenbergh *et al.* 2006: 322). The Childcare Directive that they advocated would have required member states to develop publicly funded services for one- to ten-year-old children. The Commission did not support the draft and the UK was particularly opposed to it (Avdeyeva 2006: 41, Bleijenbergh *et al.* 2006: 322, Randall 2000: 349). As a result, a much weaker recommendation on childcare was adopted in 1992. In addition to not being binding, the recommendation's provisions were much weaker than the network's proposals.

In the negotiations, the principle of subsidiarity meant that childcare was seen as a policy issue where national and regional governments, local authorities and social partners should decide how and to what extent employed parents were supported (Bleijenbergh *et al.* 2006: 323). Furthermore, in contrast to child welfare, the Commission framed the recommendation in terms of economic efficiency to suit the EU goal of establishing a European market (Bleijenbergh *et al.* 2006: 323). The network itself was dismantled in 1996. Despite the watering down of the directive and the change in the framing of the issue, the recommendation represented a significant expansion of EU policies to a new field (Stratigaki 2004: 43). However, the measures failed to significantly increase childcare provision in the member states.

Since these developments, regulating for childcare has taken place through the Open Method of Co-ordination. The Lisbon Strategy for Jobs and Growth, which commenced in 2000 and was relaunched in 2005, marked a period of growth in EU social policy. Its three goals were more jobs, more competition and greater social cohesion (Daly 2007: 4). The new soft law policy-making process which it introduced was called the Open Method of Co-ordination (OMC) (see Chapters 4 and 6). In general, the OMC deals with areas of policy in which there are great differences between the member states (Trubek and Trubek 2005: 347–8). The OMC represents a new governance model that differs radically from the top-down, rule-based, centralized approaches discussed above. First, it is based on joint definitions by the member states of initial objectives, indicators, and in some cases guidelines. Second, member states draw up national reports or action plans that assess performance in light of the objectives and metrics, and propose reforms accordingly. Third, these reports are peer reviewed by other member states and include mutual criticism and exchange of good practice, backed up by recommendations in some cases. Finally, member states re-elaborate their plans and, at less frequent intervals, the broader objectives and metrics in the light of the experience gained in their implementation (Trubek and Trubek 2005: 347–8, Scharpf 2002: 625). The first and most developed example of the OMC was the European Employment Strategy (EES), initially launched in 1997.

The key target of the EES is to increase the employment rate of men to 70 per cent and that of women to 60 per cent by 2010 (see Chapter 6 for a detailed analysis). The EES promotes public provision of childcare or other supportive measures that facilitate the reconciliation of work and family. The European Council in Barcelona affirmed in 2002 that member states should remove disincentives for female labour force participation and strive, in line with national patterns of provision, to provide childcare by 2010 to at least 90 per cent of children between 3 years of age and the mandatory school age and at least 33 per cent of children under 3 years of age. In March 2006, the European Council reiterated its commitment to the attainment of the Barcelona targets in the European Pact for Gender Equality. The Commission's Roadmap for equality between women and men (2006–10) also calls for achievement of the Barcelona targets on childcare and development of other care facilities that meet the care needs of older people and of people with disabilities. The Roadmap states that the quality of care services is to be improved in member states and the qualifications of staff, mainly women, developed and better valued.

Jane Lewis (2006: 422) notes that authors come to very different conclusions about the benefits of the OMC: 'the more "internalist" the approach, focusing narrowly on the form of the OMC, the more optimistic conclusions ..., but when the OMC is put alongside other developments in economic policy and competition law, the conclusions ... tend to be more pessimistic'. The EU's childcare policy is one area where the OMC is being tested and thus provides insights into these concerns from a gender perspective.

Highlighting the positive aspects of this agenda, Claire Annesley (2007: 199) suggests that the EES represents a move towards a 'supported European adult worker model social system' where all adults (including women) are expected to work and are supported in doing so. The new soft law tools have thus enabled the EU to make policy recommendations in areas where there are big national differences, the example here being childcare. The EES and OMC have also increased the political relevance and visibility of childcare (Plantega 2004: 8). In the best cases, the OMC leads to policy learning between member states. At a minimum, countries have to provide comparable childcare data, which can help policy makers and activists to pinpoint both progress and remaining problems (Morgan 2008).

However, more critical observations can be articulated about the policy-making process. First, the non-binding nature of the policy has created some problems. The OMC and the reports and recommendations that go with it are unlikely to bring about drastic changes in childcare policies in countries that seriously lag behind in provision. The Barcelona targets are far from being met. In 2007, only five member states met the EU target of child care for 33 per cent of children aged 0–3 (Belgium, Finland, France, Sweden and Denmark), and only eight met the 90 per cent target (Belgium, Finland, France, Sweden, Denmark, Italy, Germany and Spain). At the other end of the spectrum, Greece, Ireland, Lithuania and Poland present the lowest coverage of pre-school childcare. Only in Finland, Sweden and Denmark is early childcare provision enshrined as a social or statutory guaranteed right.

In some cases, national action plans can be mere 'window dressing' or contain inflated claims of progress (Verloo and van der Vleuten 2009). This is facilitated by the fact that EU childcare policy lacks a clear vision and operates within the terrain of diverging national policies (Morgan 2008: 51). As a result, the statements of different EU institutions oscillate between egalitarian discourses of public childcare, women's employment, and men's involvement in care, and more neo-familialist policies of lengthy parental leave and part-time work for mothers that encourage women to stay at home as primary carers (Mahon 2002). This lack of clarity leaves considerable leeway for member states to interpret the targets in their own way, which, in turn, raises questions about the quality of childcare and the quality of women's employment (part-time or full-time care services; availability versus affordability of services; public or private services) (Morgan 2008, Plantega 2004). Markets can provide care that is too expensive for low-income families. When high cost childcare is combined with care leave policies a number of women may choose to stay at home. Furthermore, a focus on the quantity rather than quality of care shifts attention away from the gendered patterns of care provision that might privatize care further and force women to stay at home.

Second, the influence of civil society actors is limited in the EES and they can only influence the direction of the strategy indirectly, through the Commission or the European Parliament. National action plans and EU targets are not debated in national parliaments and there is little media attention to the issue (Morgan 2008: 47). Instead, a small number of bureaucratic actors dominate the process of drafting the national reports to the EU (Morgan 2008: 48). This renders the process bureaucratic rather than political or democratic. For example in the UK, the public visibility of the strategy has been limited and there have been few opportunities for challenging the government's interpretation of the implementation of the strategy (Richardt 2005). As a result, women's organizations and activists have not had an impact on the implementation of its priorities. In Germany, by contrast, interest groups have mobilized around the policy and have had some success in influencing its implementation (Richardt 2005: 3). Furthermore, soft law, unlike hard law, does not allow interest groups to enforce compliance by calling on a third party, such as the European Court of Justice (ECJ), on the matter (Richardt 2005). It is worth recalling that some women's policy actors, such as the British Equal Opportunities Commission (EOC) were very effective in using litigation strategy through the ECJ to advance gender equality legislation in the UK (see Chapter 9). This opportunity has been closed off by the new mode of governance through the OMC.

In this context, actors at the European level have become active in childcare policy and are perhaps better placed in terms of intervention. The European Women's Lobby (EWL) launched a 'Who Cares?' campaign in 2006 and issued a position paper on childcare. The EWL articulates care as a crucial dimension of gender equality:

> The lack of affordable, accessible and high quality care services in most European Union countries and the fact that care work is not equally shared between women and men have a direct negative impact on women's ability to participate in all aspects of social, economic, cultural and political life. (EWL 2006: 1)

The campaign and the position paper grew out of the frustration with member states not meeting the Barcelona targets of childcare. The position paper calls for a full implementation of the Barcelona targets on childcare and the Roadmap for Equality (EWL 2006). Themes of the campaign include, among others, gender stereotypes about care and the concerns of domestic migrant care workers. The socialist party group (PES) has also adopted a high profile on the issue and launched its own campaign. In addition, the Expert Group on the Situation of Women in the Labour Market, headed by Jill Rubery, played an important role in keeping gender equality on the agenda.

Conclusion

Reconciliation of work and family has become an important social policy area in the EU and the policies adopted range from directives on pregnant workers, part-time work and parental leave to targets on childcare. The language has filtered down from the EU to the member states and case studies illustrate that, for example, Spain has adopted a number of measures to improve the reconciliation of work and family as recommended by the EU (Meier *et al.* 2007: 115).

Policies on reconciling work and family can be motivated by economic, demographic and gender equality goals and arguments. In the EU, social policy, equal opportunities policy and the reconciliation of work and family have to operate within the hegemonic aims of competition, growth and efficiency. So much so that Jane Lewis argues that 'when the expansion of hard, anti-discrimination law is placed alongside the emphasis on increasing labour market participation ... the picture has the potential to resemble much more the American model, which rests in large part on the primacy accorded the market, backed up by anti-discrimination measures that permit access to the market' (Lewis 2006: 432). Maria Stratigaki too argues that the primary meaning of reconciliation has shifted from a notion promoting equality between women and men to enhancing efficiency and productivity through women's labour market participation (Stratigaki 2004: 36). A co-opted concept such as this poses particular problems for feminist activists as it is difficult to mobilize against claims that appear to be one's own (Stratigaki 2004: 36).

When reconciliation is framed in gender-neutral way and the policy lacks gender analysis, it is readily based on traditional notions of women and men and their respective gender roles. As a result, women continue to be represented as the primary care givers and reconciliation policies target women rather than men (Meier *et al.* 2007: 118). Men continue to be mentioned in some EU policy documents. For example the 1992 Council Recommendation on childcare proposed measures to promote the increased participation by men in the care of children. Increasingly, however, gender equality is defined primarily in terms of women's labour market participation with diminishing attention to promoting the equal sharing of unpaid care work between men and women and to changing the behaviour of men (Lewis 2006: 433, Stratigaki 2004: 44). Successful reconciliation does not mean equality between the genders but can mean an individual woman succeeding in combining work and family. In this context, 'jobs for women' have tended to be defined in terms of part-time work and flexible working hours. Women have entered flexible employment with little hope of job or income security (Lewis and Giullari 2005: 82).

Reconciliation policies also only target certain women and certain types of families. They remain silent about the position and the rights of same-sex families, rendering the EU reconciliation policy heteronormative. There is also a disjuncture with the debate on global care chains that would highlight new racial hierarchies that are emerging in the care sector in Europe. In global care chains, care work in rich countries is shifted from middle-class women to migrant women, who in turn often have dependant children of their own who have to be cared for by other family members or someone from a still poorer background in the home country (Hochshild 2000, Yeates 2009). Gender, race, ethnicity and class are intertwined to reproduce racial hierarchies as migrant women and women from minority ethnic groups or lower caste groups are brought in to service the care requirements of households situated higher up the racial/ethnic scale (Yeates 2009: 42). Global care chains are particularly prevalent in gender regimes where men are not encouraged to take up their care role and the state does not provide childcare support for families so that they have to make 'private choices'. In Europe, household services are a highly significant source of employment for foreigners – often non-EU, undocumented migrant labour – in Spain, France, Greece, Italy and the UK (Yeates 2009: 28).

Chapter 6

Gender Mainstreaming in EU Policy-Making

Gender mainstreaming takes the EU agenda and tools for further-ing gender equality beyond anti-discrimination, equal opportuni-ties and positive action measures. Theresa Rees defines gender mainstreaming as 'the promotion of gender equality through its systematic integration into all systems and structures, into all poli-cies, processes and procedures, into the organisation and its culture, into ways of seeing and doing' (Rees 2005: 560). Gender mainstreaming thus enables the expansion of EU gender policy from fields traditionally considered propitious for gender equality, such as family policy, to new ones including training policies (Rees 1998), employment (Rubery 2003), trade (Hoskyns 2007, True 2009), development (Debusscher and True 2008) and structural funds (Braithwaite 2000). This 'new' approach, gender main-streaming, has come to signify modernity in gender equality policy (Daly 2005: 441). Positive interpretations of the potential of gender mainstreaming have indeed stressed that it makes gender equality a horizontal concern that needs to be addressed by every-one. Gender mainstreaming has the potential to change masculine structures and policies by mainstreaming gender into all policy fields and legislation (Rees 1998: 46). It also requires the develop-ment of new policy tools and thereby 'links a revolutionary goal, e.g. the end of sexual inequality, to rational public administrative tools' (Woodward 2003: 69). These new policy tools have included gender impact assessment and gender budgeting.

Despite its radical potential, gender mainstreaming has not led to transformative change in European policy-making and legisla-tion. Rather it has been embedded in, and has added to, some problematic trends in EU policy-making more broadly and in gender equality policy in particular. First, it is becoming evident that the transformative potential of gender mainstreaming is lost in the process of implementation. This relates closely to the softness of the policy-making tools used to promote gender main-streaming (Beveridge 2008, Hafner-Burton and Pollack 2009, Woehl 2008, Woodward 2005). Like the Open Method of Co-ordination (OMC) (see Chapters 1, 4 and 5), its goals are embod-ied in an array of recommendations and policy programmes, but generally these are not binding and lack effective enforcement mechanisms.

Second, the soft gender mainstreaming tools and techniques, including gender impact assessment and gender budgeting, have consequences for gender equality policy more broadly. They have led to the increased use of indicators and statistics, where one of the effects is to reduce complex gender equality issues to simple technical measures. In practice, gender mainstreaming has been advanced in terms of various projects rather than systemic change in policy-making structures. This, in turn, has resulted in 'the projectification of gender equality' whereby resources and funding are directed towards short-term projects rather than structural change or permanent bodies (Brunila 2009). This comes close to what some scholars have termed the 'technical version of gender mainstreaming' (Walby 2005, Rees 2005), but it has implications beyond gender mainstreaming. The development shifts attention away from the way in which gender (Evelyn and Bacchi 2005) and gender equality (Lombardo, Meier and Verloo 2009, Squires 2007, Walby 2005a) are contested notions.

This chapter will, first, explore gender mainstreaming in the EU. How is gender mainstreaming advanced in the EU and with what tools? The EU development policy will be used as an example of a mainstream policy area where gender mainstreaming has had some, albeit unsystematic, impact. Second, the chapter will provide an assessment of gender mainstreaming in the EU. What kind of gover-nance tool is it? What forms does it take? Is it effective in furthering gender equality in EU policy-making? The chapter will illustrate the problems that the assessment uncovers in relation to another main-stream policy area, namely employment, as represented by the European Employment Strategy (EES). The chapter shows that gender mainstreaming is constructed in particular ways in the EU (cf. Bacchi 1999, Lombardo, Meier and Verloo 2009) and maps out the significance of the constructions for the EU and its member states.

The institutionalization of gender mainstreaming in the EU

Whilst it is often presented as a novel gender policy-making tool, the history of gender mainstreaming dates back to the 1980s. The concept has its roots in gender and development debates where it figured for the first time in 1984 (Schmidt 2005: 31). In Nordic countries too, it has a long history and was known as the 'equality permeation principle' in Finland (Holli and Kantola 2007). The UN world conference on women in Beijing in 1995 was, however, pivotal in bringing international life and leverage to the concept (True and Mintrom 2001: 33). The EU played a key role in the negotiations around the concept and the Commission lobbied for the inclusion of gender mainstreaming in the UN Beijing Platform for Action 1995. Later the Commission used this international pressure to push for gender mainstreaming in the EU (Mazey 2001: 6, Schmidt 2005: 179).

Gender mainstreaming is based on the seemingly simple idea that gender should be taken account of in all policy and law making. Yet it has been given different meanings in different contexts. In Europe, the Council of Europe definition of gender mainstreaming, dating from 1998, has proved powerful. The definition has travelled so well as a policy concept that it is used as if it were an EU definition (Verloo 2005: 354). The Council of Europe defined gender mainstreaming as: 'the (re)organisation, improvement, development and evaluation of policy processes, so that a gender equality perspective is incorporated in all policies at all levels and at all stages, by the actors normally involved in policy-making' (Council of Europe 1998: 15). Political will, a twin strategy of gender mainstreaming and women-specific policy, sex-disaggregated statistics, knowledge of gender relations, knowledge of the administration, necessary funds and human resources and participation of women in decision-making bodies were identified as necessary prerequisites for successful gender mainstreaming (Council of Europe 1998: 23).

This definition of gender mainstreaming, used in many EU reports and documents (see, for example, European Commission 2007a: 2, Sterner and Biller 2008: 7), sets the gender mainstreaming agenda in particular ways. To begin with, it emphasizes that gender mainstreaming should be undertaken by actors *normally* involved in policy-making. This was motivated by the desire to move gender policy out of specific gender policy units to the mainstream but had the effect of downplaying the importance of civil society actors (Verloo 2005: 351). The adverse impact may have been to close off more participatory forms of gender mainstreaming, ones that would have encouraged the role of women's organizations and movements as gender experts in the mainstreaming process. In other words, the meaning of gender mainstreaming was 'fixed' in this definition to 'operational terms' as it centres on policy processes and on reorganizing institutions (Daly 2005: 445). Furthermore, the report did not specify the preferred tools and techniques for gender mainstreaming, which led to an emphasis on technical tools at the expense of others, thus rendering the process technocratic (Verloo 2005: 352). This further closed off the feminist movement from the new type of policy-making.

It is notable that the EU itself lacks a clear-cut definition of gender mainstreaming. EU treaties, recommendations and policy papers all give slightly different meanings to the term (Schmidt 2005: 48). One influential definition was given in the late 1990s when a Commission Communication called for 'incorporating equal opportunities for women and men into all Community policies and activities'. This meant 'actively and openly taking into account, at a planning stage' the possible effects of general policies 'on the respective situation of men and women' (European Commission 1996: 1). Yet currently there is a tendency in the Commission to avoid using the term gender mainstreaming which creates further confusion. Because the Commission initially failed to stress that women-specific measures would continue alongside gender mainstreaming, women's organizations such as the European Women's Lobby (EWL) adopted a highly critical stance towards gender mainstreaming. As a result the Commission currently prefers to 'have a description rather than just spell out the term' in order to avoid the suspicions that it raises (Schmidt 2005: 49).

Gender mainstreaming has been advanced in the EU by means of soft law since the early 1990s in the fields of development and employment and occupation, discussed below. The contents of the initial Commission Communication (1996) were transposed to the Third Action Programme on Equal Opportunities for Women and Men in 1997. The Action Programme emphasizes that gender mainstreaming requires awareness raising and training among staff (Schmidt 2005: 67–8). The first binding EU measure on gender mainstreaming was the Regulation on gender mainstreaming activities in the area of development co-operation (1998–2003) (Nielsen 2008: 40).

The mainstreaming obligation was (as from 1 May 1999) reinforced by the Amsterdam Treaty. Under Article 3 (2) EC there is an obligation for all Community actors (legislative, judiciary, executive) to contribute to gender mainstreaming. The amendment to the Equal Treatment Directive in 2002 extended the obligation to mainstream gender in matters of employment to member states (Nielsen 2008: 40). Gender mainstreaming also informed the European Commission's Framework Strategy on gender equality (2001–5) and the Roadmap for equality between women and men for (2006–10). Gender mainstreaming is thus promoted with a mix of hard and soft law in the EU.

At organizational level, the commitment to gender equality at the highest level was expressed by the setting up of a Group of Commissioners on Equal Opportunities for women and men, back in 1995, with the aim of achieving a cross-sectoral approach to gender equality (Mazey 2001: 38, Hoskyns 2008: 113). This was relaunched in 2005 as the Fundamental Rights, Anti-discrimination and Equal Opportunities Group of Commissioners, reflecting a shift of focus to multiple inequalities and multiple discrimination (see Chapter 8). An Inter-Service Group was established in 1996 to co-ordinate equal opportunities policies across the Commission. It develops gender mainstreaming activities in all Commission services through the formulation of work programmes and the monitoring of their implementation. In addition to these, several DGs have introduced 'focal points' to provide gender expertise in their various units. Finally, the High Level Group on gender mainstreaming is an informal group of high-level representatives responsible for gender mainstreaming at national level in the member states (see also Chapter 4).

Gender mainstreaming in EU development policy

Development is a broad policy area that relates to key fields such as environment, trade, external relations, human rights and agriculture. Decades of feminist research into all these fields has demonstrated that gender relations underpin and sustain them. A commitment to gender mainstreaming in development policy means that all aspects of the policy need to incorporate a gender perspective. For example, trade liberalization promoted by the EU may have a disproportionate effect on women because of unequal gender divisions of labour, resources and power (True 2009: 123). In the EU, development is the first policy field where gender mainstreaming has been applied. It is a policy field that has been particularly 'amenable' to gender mainstreaming (Lister 2006: 25). This possibly reflects the trend in gender equality policy that it is easier to address gender equality problems elsewhere than in one's own context and structures.

Gender was first included in EU development policy in the 1980s in terms of a focus on women in education and the health sector. The 'women in development' (WID) approach dominated development policy more generally and entailed a focus on women's role in development. WID proponents stressed women's access to training, education, and health services, improving women's living conditions, and promoting their participation in the production and development processes. They pointed out that attempts to integrate women into existing societal structures based on masculine norms failed to address fundamental gender equality problems and ultimately to improve the position of women in these societies. With the recognition that there was a need to focus on gender, and men and gender relations, and bring women-specific projects from the margins to the centre of policy-making, there was a shift to the 'gender and development' (GAD) approach. The new GAD approach facilitated the mainstreaming of gender across development policy (Rai 2002).

In EU development policy, gender mainstreaming first appeared in 1995 in the Communication from the European Commission to the Council and the Parliament on 'Integrating Gender issues in Development Cooperation' (Lister 2006: 19–20). This was before the 1996 Commission Communication on gender mainstreaming in EU policy-making in general mentioned above. A first binding Regulation on Integrating Gender Issues in Development Cooperation was issued in 1998 and updated in 2004. The Programme of Action for the Mainstreaming of Gender Equality in EC Development Cooperation 2001 confirmed that gender equality was an issue that cut across all development policy (Arts 2006: 32–3). These developments were influenced by the international context and supported by the UN Millennium Development Goals.

The gender mainstreaming approach has been adopted in EU development policy – with varying success – in relation to African,

Caribbean and Pacific (ACP) countries (Arts 2006), Latin America (Angulo and Freres 2006, Debusscher 2009), Mediterranean partnership countries (Freedman 2009, Orbie 2006) and Asia (Sobritchea 2006). The policies are characterized by a twin focus on gender mainstreaming and women specific-policy, confirmed in other regulations on gender mainstreaming in development policy. For example, the Cotonou Agreement 2000 dealing with the EU development cooperation with 78 ACP states calls for the integration of 'a gender-sensitive approach and concerns at every level of development cooperation including macroeconomic policies, strategies and operations' and encourages 'the adoption of specific positive measures in favour of women' (Arts 2006: 31).

Gender mainstreaming is promoted in EU development policy both in key development policy documents (such as Country Strategy Papers since 2002) and through specific policy initiatives. Here the EU most often funds various projects that aim at promoting gender equality in the regions. For example, in Latin America, the EU funded part of a study undertaken by WIDE (Women in Development Europe) analyzing the gender impact of EU–Latin America trade agreements. In MERCOSUR countries, it funded part of a project that developed gender-disaggregated statistics and indicators on education and employment. Long term programmes include one linking Latin American and European municipalities that included a network promoting women in local decision-making bodies, and another linking universities between the regions, promoting women's empowerment in the curriculum (Angulo and Freres 2006: 51).

EU gender mainstreaming in development policy illustrates a 'phenomenal commitment' to gender mainstreaming on paper. However, it suffers from huge discrepancies between theory and practice (Arts 2006: 37). Gender mainstreaming has been applied unevenly across different policy fields. It has had most impact in areas such as education and health, but has not been incorporated into trade, economic co-operation, structural adjustment and tourism policies. The negative repercussions of trade liberalization on women and gender equality are widely recognized, but the EU continues its trade liberalization policy despite resistance from some of the states and civil society organizations, including women's movements (Arts 2006: 38; see also True 2008: 133). This signals that gender equality is not an EU development goal as such but gender mainstreaming is thought to contribute to efficiency in achieving other aims, such as poverty reduction or economic growth (Angulo and Freres 2006: 48, True 2009: 125).

The areas where a gender perspective is missing include fields that receive the bulk of EU aid, such as transport and macro-economic support (Arts 2006: 38). Gender mainstreaming initiatives have also suffered from lack of resources and declining budgets. Compared to the funds devoted to issues such as AIDS, tuberculosis and malaria, the funds for combating gender equality remain modest (Arts 2006: 39 Angulo and Freres 2006: 48 Lister 2006: 26). This has resulted in implementation problems: 'Gender mainstreaming of EU development cooperation has largely remained an exercise of expressing policy priorities and intentions, which have not been followed up by active and well-supported implementation efforts' (Arts 2006: 39). Other constraints have included the lack of gender expertise in EU policy-making institutions, in this case DG Development (Arts 2006: 39, Angulo and Freres 2006: 48). The complex and bureaucratic EU organization has closed off the representation of women and women's movements in the delegations and negotiations (Arts 2006: 39–40). In the context of development policy, specific guidelines followed by all parties on how to involve civil society would be particularly relevant, as some of the partner countries are often reluctant to engage with civil society organizations that lack organizational capacity and financial resources (True 2009: 130).

Assessing gender mainstreaming in the EU

Gender mainstreaming has become a key gender equality strategy in the EU. Its central position is evidenced by the array of recommendations and policy programmes as well as networks of policy actors that endorse gender mainstreaming. Despite progressive policy on paper, implementing gender mainstreaming has proved to be a huge challenge in the EU and its member states. The following assessment of gender mainstreaming in the EU highlights three interlocking problems: (i) the EU has adopted a technical and integrationist form of gender mainstreaming; (ii) the scope and impact of gender mainstreaming has been limited instead of resulting in radical change in gender relations; (iii) gender mainstreaming is complicit with neoliberal forms of EU governance. Taken together these problems have resulted in heightened criticism from feminist scholars and disillusionment among women's organizations and activists.

Adopting an integrationist form of gender mainstreaming

On one hand, the 'stretch factor' of the gender mainstreaming concept has been argued to be a crucial element of its success (Roggeband and Verloo 2006) and the 'vague and non-specific character of the concept has probably aided [its] rapid ascendancy: everyone understands the general idea, but no one is sure what it requires in practice' (Beveridge and Nott 2000: 1). On the other hand, this vagueness has led to gender mainstreaming being defined in ways that shift the agenda away from the feminist and transformative potential of gender mainstreaming. These feminist definitions suggest that gender mainstreaming can only adequately address inequality when it pursues a transformative agenda by focusing on the structural reproduction of gender inequality and aiming to transform the policy process such that gender bias is eliminated (Beveridge and Nott 2002: 300, Rees 2005: 557, Squires 2005: 370). In such a form, gender mainstreaming addresses the methods and principles which govern the social interaction of political actors (Beveridge and Nott 2002: 302, Shaw 2002).

The EU, by contrast, has adopted an integrationist form of gender mainstreaming that focuses on experts and the bureaucratic creation of evidence-based knowledge in policy-making. Here gender mainstreaming addresses gender issues within existing policy paradigms. Promoting gender equality is not the main policy goal but a means of delivery on or subsumed under another policy (Rees 2005). This form of gender mainstreaming does not entail a focus on the participation, presence, and empowerment of disadvantaged groups via consultation with civil society organizations, which would involve a reorientation of the agenda rather than merely integrating a gender perspective into an existing agenda (Squires 2005: 371). In other words, feminist readings of gender mainstreaming that emphasize the need to transform gendered power structures are rare (Booth and Bennett 2002: 441, Lombardo and Meier 2006: 160).

Instead, the emphasis on the integrationist form of gender mainstreaming is combined with a technical version of gender mainstreaming. This is evident in the abundance of gender mainstreaming handbooks that describe how to do gender mainstreaming with the help of gender impact assessment, awareness raising, sex-disaggregated statistics, indicators and gender budgeting, and include examples of 'best practice' (see, for example, European Commission 2004a and 2007a, Dean 2006, JämStöd

2007, Keil *et al.* 2007). In the member states too, the most frequently used methods for implementation of gender mainstreaming are gender impact assessment of proposals and bills and gender budgeting, which is a special application of gender mainstreaming in the budgetary process (Sterner and Biller 2007: 13). These technical manuals, though of some importance for practitioners, can shift the debate and agenda further away from transforming gendered structures. Many of these guidelines incorporate 'representation' or 'participation' as important facets but this rarely happens in practice. As a result, there is a tendency to acquire knowledge and information about 'women' and 'men' with the help, for example, of statistics, rather than to promote their participation in the process.

The way in which doing and evaluating gender mainstreaming has come to rely on indicators, ranking and benchmarking and policy learning from best practice is not unproblematic. While this appears in a technical and apolitical guise, evaluating success through peer reviews and best practice, pioneers and laggards is a highly political process that is based on 'relative standards of performance' (Verloo and van der Vleuten 2009: 379). Actors can strategically play to the indicators to raise their scores rather than actually advancing gender equality. The way the indicators for success in mainstreaming are chosen can close off any transparent democratic debate (Verloo and van der Vleuten 2009: 382).

In some member states, gender mainstreaming was adopted only as a result of EU pressure. This has consequences for the form that gender mainstreaming takes. It is not part of a larger vision of gender equality but is rather more of 'an end in itself' and operates 'more as an operational objective' rather than as 'an approach, or strategy, to achieve gender equality' (Braithwaite 2005: 10, Daly 2005: 436). This strengthens the tendency to opt for the integrationist form of gender mainstreaming in the member states. When providing accounts of the actions taken on gender mainstreaming, member states tend to see gender mainstreaming as a 'catch-all term' which is used to refer to varying approaches and activities (Daly 2005: 439). For example, gender mainstreaming functions as a new name to refer to 'old' policy practices such as positive action measures, transversal national plans involving different departments of the administration and even equal treatment legislation. There is also evidence that 'gender mainstreaming' can be constructed in a way that serves diverse political needs. For example, in France and Greece politicians and government officials use the term 'gender mainstreaming' to refer to a move from a focus on women to a more neutral focus on gender (which is simply understood as referring to both women and men) as the main concern of equality policy (Braithwaite 2005). Sweden has arguably been one of the few countries in the EU to have adopted a gender mainstreaming approach that combats the structural roots of gender inequality in society (Braithwaite 2005: 37).

Limited scope of gender mainstreaming

Transformative definitions of gender mainstreaming stress its potential to change both organizational structures and the contents of policies and legislation. Given the integrationist form that gender mainstreaming has taken in the EU, it is not surprising that its impact and scope have been limited both (i) in the organizational structures, for example in the Commission bureaucracy, and (ii) in mainstream policy and law making.

If, at the organizational level, the challenge for gender mainstreaming is to motivate 'the actors normally involved in policy-making' as suggested by the influential Council of Europe definition (see above), there is a long way to go in the EU to achieve this. Many actors in the Commission are not familiar with the concept of gender mainstreaming and frequently confuse it with, for example, equal opportunities or positive action for women (Woodward 2003: 68). Most civil servants interviewed in Verena Schmidt's (2005) detailed study of gender mainstreaming in the Commission named factors like long working hours, short maternity leave and no parental leave, and lack of work reorganization when workers change to part-time as reasons for the poor implementation of gender mainstreaming (Schmidt 2005: 211). Arguably this constitutes a very narrow understanding of gender mainstreaming. The problems the bureaucrats mention relate to workplace equality rather than bringing a gender perspective to policy and law making. Outright resistance was common too and some interviewees held very traditional conceptions of women and men (Schmidt 2005: 217). This is likely to make it difficult to evaluate the differentiated impact of policy on women and men as well as creating challenges to definitions of the kind of gender equality gender mainstreaming promotes. The lack of clear strategy, and of a definition of gender equality and gender mainstreaming in the EU, leaves a lot of scope for resistance at almost no cost (Gerber 2007: 2).

Evaluating the specific organizational structures established to implement and oversee gender mainstreaming (see above) also reveals weaknesses. The EU gender mainstreaming machinery falls into the category of 'soft' mainstreaming and the groups established for gender mainstreaming suffer from a weak mandate and a lack of resources that hamper their effectiveness. Their activities largely consist of co-ordination meetings, attended by low- or mid-level officials within the various DGs, voluntary training exercises, and the dissemination of policy tools such as handbooks and checklists (Hafner-Burton and Pollack 2009: 122–4).They have failed to meaningfully change the incentives or the behaviour of officials outside the core network of mainstreaming advocates (Hafner-Burton and Pollack 2009: 124). Commitment varies greatly, depending on the individual (Schmidt 2005: 231). Hence the institutionalization of gender mainstreaming has not spread beyond the relatively small group of gender experts. Gender mainstreaming only has a chance of being implemented in DGs where there is a sympathetic Commissioner (Hoskyns 2008: 114).

The same trend can be discerned at the member state level, where only ten states (Austria, Denmark, Estonia, Finland, Germany, Lithuania, Luxembourg, Netherlands, Poland and Sweden) out of 27 have set up an interministerial group for coordinating and supporting the work on gender mainstreaming at governmental level. Other states only have contact persons or committees at each ministry. Some member states use their gender unit as a co-ordinator instead of an interministerial group. Seven states appear to have no special structure at all for implementing gender mainstreaming (Belgium, Greece, Hungary, Ireland, Italy, Slovakia and Slovenia). This means that a third of all member states lack a special structure for implementing gender mainstreaming in their governmental processes (Sterner and Biller 2007: 17–18).

At the policy-making level, it is evident that gender mainstreaming has gone further in some policy areas than in others. Employment, social inclusion, economic and social cohesion policy, science and research and external relations provide some examples of good practice at EU level (Woodward 2003: 75, Mazey 2001: 44). Competition, internal market and agricultural policy have proved to be more resistant (Mazey 2001: 44, Prügl 2008, Hafner-Burton and Pollack 2009: 124). In the Commission, the gender mainstreaming mandate has been enthusiastically accepted by just a few leading DGs. A much larger number of DGs show at best modest evidence of having incorporated any gender concerns into their respective policy outputs. According to Hafner-Burton and Pollack's (2008: 11) findings, 41 per cent of all DGs listed no gender-related activities in 2007 in the Commission's work programmes for the Roadmap for Equality, and another 37 per cent listed one or two activities. In other words, nearly 80 per cent of the DGs showed only very modest signs of adopting and implementing gender mainstreaming even when explicitly asked to document their activities in the field.

At the member state level too, gender mainstreaming efforts have been highly fragmented and confined either to a particular policy domain or to a specific programme within a domain and disconnected from general governmental policy on gender (Braithwaite 2005). Adopting gender mainstreaming in an 'à la carte' manner means selectively choosing some of the components of gender mainstreaming, especially some of the tools or techniques, without an overall framework (Braithwaite 2005: 5, Daly 2005: 436). Most member states have, however, incorporated gender mainstreaming into national laws, many as a result of EU pressure. Whilst twelve states (Austria, Belgium, the Czech Republic, Denmark, Estonia, Finland, Ireland, Latvia, Slovenia, Spain, Sweden and the United Kingdom) had a more detailed and systematic description, in which they express the mandatory obligation for the state to make a gender impact analysis before introducing legislation, bills or legal acts, seven member states (Belgium, Cyprus, Italy, Malta, Poland, Slovakia and the United Kingdom) reported that they have plans neither for gender equality policy nor for gender mainstreaming (Sterner and Biller 2007: 14).

Gender mainstreaming as part of new governance

Charlotte Bretherton (2001: 73) argues that gender equality has struggled against the 'tide of neo-liberal market principles and deeply embedded understandings and practices supportive of male dominance'. Gender mainstreaming has had difficulties in turning this neoliberal tide in the EU and has instead become embedded in it, and, in some cases, provided legitimacy to it. This is evident in the language that is used to promote gender mainstreaming in the EU, in the form of governance used to implement it, and the implications for civil society actors.

Jacqui True (2009: 125) suggests that the dominant frame used by the Commission when discussing gender mainstreaming in all policies is a neoliberal one, whereby arguments for gender mainstreaming are based primarily on economic factors. Gender equality then is not a goal as such, but subordinate to other, more pressing concerns, such as efficiency, productivity, development or employment. In other words, gender equality is acceptable in EU policymaking when it does not challenge that which is defined to be in the EU's interests (Hoskyns 2008: 118). Such constructions of gender mainstreaming rely on a notion of gender equality that resonates with dominant policy frames entailing embracing marketized economic goals (Squires 2007: 137). Whilst women's organizations and women's policy agencies in the EU (see Chapter 4) seek to challenge this dominant neoliberal frame, they too have been influenced by it and sometimes seek to make the 'business case for gender equality' because of its discursive and persuasive power (True 2009: 127). This language compromises transformative and feminist definitions of gender mainstreaming that might rely on a notion of gender equality that requires redistribution, participation of civil society actors and reorienting policies (True 2003: 371).

Gender mainstreaming is promoted with the new techniques of governance in the EU that foreground different forms of deregulation. As in the case of the Open Method of Co-ordination (OMC) (see Chapters 1, 4 and 5), they entail less control from above and a move away from centralized enforcement and implementation mechanisms. The EU has used soft rather than hard regulation to implement gender mainstreaming. Emilie Hafner-Burton and Mark Pollack (2009: 122–3) suggest that 'hard' gender mainstreaming would provide binding provisions entailing precise responsibilities and commitments for Commission officials, backed by strictly enforced positive and negative sanctions for compliance and noncompliance. By contrast, current 'soft' mainstreaming in the EU can be characterized by non-binding provisions with vague or imprecise aims and little or no attempt to monitor and sanction officials for compliance and noncompliance (Hafner-Burton and Pollack 2009: 123–44). Rather than changing organizational structures and committing permanent resources to the strategy in the form of budget and staff, gender mainstreaming is promoted through short-term projects in the EU and the member states. Kristiina Brunila (2009) calls this 'projectified' equality promotion, where a continuous stream of gender equality projects establishes the impression of 'progress on the way to gender equality' (cf. Skjeie

2006). In the compulsory follow-up reports, these projects are always presented as 'success stories' with a series of measureable pseudo-activities and 'products', such as brochures, seminars and badges, to prove it. This shifts attention away from the lack of continuity in gender equality work, and the ways in which priorities are set by the funding bodies rather than civil society organizations.

Another, and closely related, characteristic of the current techniques of governance used to promote gender mainstreaming is the tendency to privilege 'gender expertise' and technical knowledge, rather than provide scope for a fundamental critique of gendered structures. In the current evidence-based policy-making, knowledge and research have become key assets in the production of policy. Where external actors are able to supply knowledge that is relevant to policy they are afforded greater authority, which in turn encourages NGOs to frame their interventions in objective knowledge-based rather than interest-based terms (Marston and Watts 2003; see Kantola and Squires 2008). Indeed, many Commission officials tend to favour NGO consultation 'in the form of a technical dossier' but, for the NGOs, the more technical their submissions become, the further they may shift away from their original aims for structural change and analysis of power relations (Cullen 2009: 146).

When gender mainstreaming relies on 'expert knowledge' for implementation, women's organizations become 'gender experts'. Stefanie Woehl argues:

> While knowledge about gender has increased in the field of gender studies at universities, this knowledge is now used as a governmental technique and as expertise in an ambivalent way: gender mainstreaming is generated from the same governmental techniques that it actually seeks to transform. (Woehl 2008: 80)

This tendency may further compromise and close off criticism. It also changes the organizational structures of feminist civil society organizations. In order to produce such expert knowledge and develop their research capacity, they inevitably require increasing levels of organizational stability and funding (see also Chapter 4). The managerialist dynamics of neoliberal governance have led to the growth of consultancy services and the demand for new expertise in fundraising and organizational management, which makes activists increasingly accountable to funding bodies rather than political constituencies. The growing use of 'gender experts' and implementation of 'analytic tools' such as gender impact assessments fit in with the logic of providing 'evidence' about the likely gendered impacts of proposed policy initiatives in order to render the policymaking process more 'effective' (Kantola and Squires 2008).

In this process, the meaning of gender and gender equality is reduced to a static definition of gender as 'women' or 'men' (Baden and Goetz 1997: 7). Whilst feminists stress the differences within the categories of women and men, indicators and statistics, which have become the key tools in gender mainstreaming, are based on a unitary category of women (Verloo and van der Vleuten 2009: 397). This masks the differences between women and how 'progress' to gender equality needs to be qualified. One example comes from labour market policy where not all women have benefited to the same extent. Linda McDowell (2008) argues that although women's labour market participation has increased across the different classes and income groups, class differences in hours and earnings remain marked and seem to be increasing. It is middle-class girls, in the main, who have benefited from the expansion of university education as participation rates for young people from working-class families in the UK have barely increased (McDowell 2008: 152). Whilst appearing as a positive development in statistical terms, this polarization opens up new class divisions between women, in which middle-class women with high(ish) salaries become more like men, working on a full-time basis and with a reasonable lifetime earning capacity (McDowell 2008: 152).

Gender mainstreaming in EU employment policy

European employment trends have become a major concern for the EU as the long-term trend in the 1990s was towards declining employment trends. There has been general concern about the European failure to create jobs compared to the US (Rubery *et al.* 1998: 13, 16). One of the sustained changes in many European societies has been the growth of women's employment. While previously, as Chapter 2 demonstrated, women were regarded as the labour reserve – 'a stable inactive part of the population which is happy to be without work' (Rubery *et al.* 1998: 14) – now the EU sets specific targets in the European Employment Strategy (EES) for increasing women's employment rates. For these reasons, EU employment policy is an area where one would assume gender analysis would occur and gender policies would be implemented.

The European Employment Strategy (EES) makes an excellent case study of the success and failure of gender mainstreaming. At first, it provided a promising picture of the success of gender main-streaming, but later gender became so mainstreamed that it disap-peared both from the EES and national reports of progress in the field. The EES was first defined by the 1997 Treaty of Amsterdam with the aim of making the European labour markets the most productive and competitive in the world. The strategy is based on the Open Method of Co-ordination (OMC) discussed in Chapter 5. In relation to the EES, the stages of the OMC include Council approval of employment guidelines; member state response to these guidelines in the form of a National Action Plan (NAP); examina-tion of NAPs in the Joint Employment Report (Commission and Council); Commission recommendations to revise Employment Guidelines; and Council country-specific recommendations (Plantega *et al.* 2008: 29, O'Connor 2005: 42). Analysis of the EES from a gender perspective provides further insights into the compat-ibility of gender equality with the key values underpinning the strat-egy, namely flexibility, competition and productivity.

Initially, gender equality was strongly present in the EES as it formed one of its four pillars which included improving employa-bility; developing entrepreneurship and job creation; encouraging adaptability of businesses and their employees; and strengthening equal opportunities for women and men. This was the result of lobbying by key officials and political actors as well as pressure and new initiatives added by different member state presidencies, includ-ing Austria, Finland, Belgium, France and Sweden (Rubery 2003: 3–4). The 'equal opportunities' pillar was based on four principles: first, adopting gender mainstreaming, second, tackling gender gaps in unemployment, job segregation, pay and employment, third, reconciling work and family, and fourth, facilitating reintegration into the labour market (Plantega *et al.* 2008: 29). In the Lisbon Council meeting in 2000, the importance of gender equality in the employment strategy was emphasized both in terms of rhetoric and by setting specific targets. The Council argued that: 'Member States should strengthen their efforts to include and make visible a gender perspective across all the pillars'. Quantitative targets included a 70 per cent target for all in employment and a 60 per cent target for women's employment, to be reached by the year 2010.

The evaluations of the consequences of the first five-year period (1997–2002) for gender equality differed but the overall tone was positive. The member states and the Commission were most optimistic about the outcomes of the peer review process and the joint evaluation exercise, and argued that the equal opportunities dimension had achieved significant outcomes (Rubery 2003: 5). Jill Rubery (2003) suggests that member states put in place some form of gender mainstreaming in either employment policy or government policy more generally. There was great national variation, however, with the process being more important for some countries than others. In Greece, for example, as discussed in Chapter 9, the first phase of the EES resulted in some important changes, including the introduction of gender mainstreaming (Zartaloudis 2008).

The European Employment Strategy (EES) changed significantly after the first five-year period and the new priorities resulted in the eventual disappearance of gender from the strategy. The first phase of reduced attention to gender equality started in 2003 when the EES was brought more in line with 'the broader economic policy guidelines and the internal market strategy' (Plantega *et al.* 2008: 30). The four pillar structure was abolished and three new objectives were drafted including full employment, quality and productivity at work, and social cohesion and inclusion. The list of guidelines was simplified from 18 to 10, with guideline 6 referring to gender equality and emphasizing combining gender mainstreaming with specific policy actions (Rubery *et al.* 2004: 47). However, in practice gender was incorporated only in the first of the three new objectives where, with regard to full employment, most member states have adopted the Lisbon strategy numerical targets for women's employment and many have set them as national targets (Rubery *et al.* 2004: 47). Otherwise gender mainstreaming was weak and patchy and many policies were introduced without regard to their gender impacts. Some new steps were taken in terms of gender equality. The re-framing of the strategy included the goal that by 2010 member states should provide childcare to at least 90 per cent of children between three years old and the mandatory school age and at least 33 per cent of children under three years of age (Plantega *et al.* 2008: 30; see Chapter 5).

An evaluation of the role and the impact of gender mainstreaming in the EES illustrates the three challenges that gender mainstreaming faces in the EU and its member states discussed above, namely (i) being adopted in an integrationist form, (ii) having a limited scope and impact, and (iii) being embedded in the broader neoliberal forms of governance.

The first challenge was the way that gender mainstreaming was adopted in an integrationist, technical and bureaucratic mode. One particular problem was that the EES did not define 'gender equality', but, in line with the norms of the OMC more generally, focused on achieving specific numerical targets on, for example, women's employment rates. This meant that employment priorities were 'imported' into gender equality policies without employment policies being gender mainstreamed (Mósesdóttir and Erlingsdóttir 2005: 516). In general, gender equality became more of a derived objective of economic growth than a question of social justice (Mósesdóttir and Erlingsdóttir 2005: 528). For example, the European Council of Ministers' recommendations to member states were underpinned by an implicit model of gender equality that involves a high use of part-time and flexible employment. The appropriateness of this model for all member states can be seriously questioned from a gender equality perspective (Rubery *et al.* 2004: 233).

The lack of focus on substantive gender equality concerns at EU level left a lot of leeway for member states to interpret what constitutes gender equality and what actions they had taken to mainstream a gender perspective in their employment policy. These interpretations reflect the differences between the member states' gender regimes discussed in Chapter 1. Some countries aimed for a dual earner model (Nordic countries), others for a one and a half earner model (the Netherlands) and still others placed emphasis on women's role as carers (Spain and the UK) (Rubery 2003). Problematically, the numerical targets were irrelevant in some member states that already had a female employment rate of over 60 per cent, and did not address the most pressing gender equality concerns including the gender-segregated labour market (Mósesdóttir and Erlingsdóttir 2005: 528). Indeed, where gender equality requires substantive change in the organization of the labour market (equal pay, working time) there was very limited evidence of change and the EES was powerless to change the behaviour of employers and trade unions (Rubery 2003). The lack of a discussion of gender equality in the strategy also makes it difficult to assess the results of the EES from a gender perspective (Rubery 2003, Mósesdóttir and Erlingsdóttir 2005: 528).

Another example of the integrationist rather than transformative and feminist form of gender mainstreaming that the EES was based on was the fact that the way that the National Action Plans were drafted in the member states closed off more participatory forms of gender mainstreaming that would have integrated civil society views into gender equal policy and decision-making. The involvement of social partners in the drafting of National Action Plans was uneven; automatic in some member states, such as Denmark, Austria and Finland, but closed in others. The process was even more closed to NGOs who were not asked to contribute to the processes (Mósesdóttir and Erlingsdóttir 2005: 516). As a result, the EES and gender mainstreaming remained a top-down bureaucratic governmental process in nearly all member states.

Second, and related, the scope and impact of gender mainstreaming was limited in the EES. As progress in achieving gender equality was defined in terms of numerical targets, the National Action Plans pay a lot of attention to achieving these quantitative figures rather than to more qualitative issues. Numbers show increases in female labour force participation, but more qualitative analysis shows that a quarter of jobs in the EU are of poor quality and held disproportionately by women, young people and immigrants. Almost a third of these poor quality jobs are 'dead-end' jobs in that they offer neither job security nor employer-provided training (O'Connor 2005: 37).

What was thus apparent was that not only was gender mainstreaming not implemented at the member state level, but member states were not addressing key gender equality problems when claiming to implement it, and certainly, the gendered patterns in the labour market did not change. Progress was highly limited and characterized by great national variation (Rubery *et al.* 2004: 232). Childcare provision remained inadequate in all member states except for the Nordic countries. Leave associated with childcare continued to be primarily taken by women and this was a particular problem in the new member states where leave arrangements encourage women to stay out of the labour market for several years. Segregation by occupation and sector and the gender pay gap were continuing and persistent, if variable, dimensions of gender inequality in all member states. Few member states had embraced the principle of individualization of taxation or benefits that would encourage women's employment, and household-based means testing was increasing in many member states. (Rubery *et al.* 2004: 232.)

Third, the role of gender mainstreaming was further weakened by the process of neoliberalization of the EES within which the policy became embedded. This was particularly evident in the new phases of the EES and feminist evaluations of it. In 2005, the European Council revised the strategy in order to respond to 'weak growth performance' and 'insufficient job creation'. The Employment Strategy was combined with broad economic policy guidelines to constitute the National Reform Programme (NRP). The integrated guidelines for the period 2005–8 were to 'provide flexibility for Member States to choose local responses that best address their reform challenges, thereby fostering national owner-ship'. There is a clear increase in deregulation and a move towards overall economic policy. Three new priorities were set: attracting and retaining more people in employment, increasing labour supply and modernizing social protection systems; improving the adapt-ability of workers and enterprises; increasing investment in human capital through better education and skills. (Plantega *et al.* 2008: 30.) Eight new employment guidelines were drawn up. Gender equality is no longer included as a specific guideline but instead is scattered across the strategy (Jenson 2008: 140, Pfister 2007: 6). Gender mainstreaming and the promotion of gender equality is included only as a general principle and the visibility of gender and the attention paid both to gender equality policies and gender main-streaming declined (Plantega *et al.* 2008: 30 Rubery 2005 and 2006).

In a new trend, flexibility gained heightened attention. 'Flexicurity' policy can be described as 'a policy strategy that attempts, synchronically and in a deliberate way, to enhance the flexibility of labour markets, the work organisation and labour rela-tions on the one hand, and to enhance security – employment secu-rity and social security – notably for weaker groups in and outside the labour market on the other hand' (Wilthagen and Tros 2004: 169). The gender mainstreaming manuals provide guidelines on how to gender mainstream flexicurity (see European Commission 2007a, Plantega *et al.* 2008: 67–9). While this may illustrate the ways in which flexicurity is gendered, it also bestows legitimacy on flexicurity (it can be gender mainstreamed, an approach that takes gender into account) and may inhibit more fundamental criticisms of the frame within which the policy operates. At best, it can show, for example, that the notion of women being the second earners in the household is part of the flexibility strategy, as mini-jobs and other forms of precarious employment, which do not allow a living wage, rely on the existence of a main income source, either a husband or the state (Plantega *et al.* 2008: 69).

According to Jane Jenson (2008) the new EES reflects a move towards a new social investment policy paradigm where children and young people are targeted and policy instruments deployed to achieve goals for the future. The re-evaluation of the EES in 2005 strengthened the language of social investment with its call for the promotion of 'a life-cycle approach to work', 'expanding and improving investment in human capital' and 'adapting training systems in response to new competence requirements' (Jenson 2008: 140). Jenson argues that the social-investment perspective effectively shifts attention to the future whilst recognizing that gender inequality has traditionally been based on comparing the differences between women and men (and women and women and men and men) in the present. She suggests that the new shift may eliminate the space for gender comparison (Jenson 2008: 147).

In conclusion, gender and gender mainstreaming were present in the EES to begin with but tended to take an integrationist form and result in limited improvements in gender equality in employment policies. As the strategy evolved and underwent restructuring, the growth of the economy, deregulation and flexicurity gained in prominence and gender was sidelined. This points to the tensions between gender equality and EU economic policy.

Conclusion

Gender mainstreaming has added a third dimension to an EU gender policy that previously relied on anti-discrimination legislation and positive action. It has the potential to address some of the shortcomings of earlier policies and tools by extending the scope of gender policy to all policy-making fields and legislation and by requiring a more structured and holistic approach to understanding the origins and consequences of gender inequalities. In practice, however, gender mainstreaming in the EU has not lived up to the high hopes that gender advocates had of it. This disappointment is largely due to the way that gender mainstreaming has been defined and implemented at EU level. Instead of promoting analyses of gendered power structures, it has largely meant incorporating the gender question into existing policy frameworks in a technical way and not questioning the power structures and gendered norms underpinning them in any fundamental way. Gender mainstreaming has been the responsibility of Commission bureaucrats with little expertise on the topic and has led to a lack of civil society participation in policy negotiations. In general, it has been furthered through soft forms of governance in the EU, which raises questions about the political commitment to it. As a result the actual impact of gender mainstreaming on changing gender relations has been limited. Rather the problems illustrate its close affinities to soft EU modes of governance and the ways in which it parallels such governance strategies as the Open Method of Co-ordination. A focus on the evolution of the European Employment Strategy further illustrates that gender can be sidelined when economic values, such as competition and flexibility in the labour markets, become priorities, and that gender mainstreaming may mean providing legitimacy to policy priorities such as 'flexicurity'. This, in turn, raises questions about scope for normative and political feminist critiques of these policies.

Chapter 7

Gender Violence in the European Union

Early feminist evaluations argued that the EU has severely neglected women's bodily rights as an important aspect of gender equality (Elman 1996, Hanmar 1996). While violence has been a core concern for feminist scholars, mainstream political science has dismissed violence as a private and personal matter that did not involve power relations and fell outside the study of politics in the 'public sphere'. Similarly, mainstream EU scholars may regard the issue of violence as falling outside EU competence and policy and as a field to be tackled within the sphere of domestic policy. This chapter focuses on two forms of gender violence, namely trafficking in women and domestic violence, to show how EU level policy-making and discourses about gender violence are proliferating. The EU is breaking new ground in moving to the seemingly 'private' issue of violence against women. The emerging policy also points to an expansion of the EU gender policy agenda beyond employment and the labour market which were discussed in previous chapters. Such transnational and international activism and policy on violence have long been deemed important in changing national policies and discourses about violence. Norms about bodily integrity as central to human rights have been particularly successful transnationally and crossculturally and gender advocates use these norms to push recalcitrant governments into action (Keck and Sikkink 1998).

Trafficking in women is a policy area where the EU has the competence to enact directives to tackle the issue. When it first emerged in the 1990s, the issue initially came under the intergovernmental method (Chapter 4). The enactment of the Amsterdam Treaty 1997 moved trafficking in women to the Community method, enabling an expansion of policy-making and of legislative tools and providing a greater role for the Commission and the Parliament. International developments, including UN norms on anti-trafficking and anti-violence, and feminist activism, have politicized the issue of trafficking in women in the EU and stimulated its institutions into action. However, EU level policy makers see trafficking in women first and foremost as a manifestation of illegal migration and transnational organized crime. EU policy and legislation reflect this understanding. International bodies, civil society actors and women's and feminist organizations, by contrast, articulate the problem of trafficking as a violation of human rights and call for a victim-centred approach. Framing trafficking in women in terms of forced prostitution divides feminist actors on the topic.

Domestic violence represents another form of gender violence that is high on women's organizations' agendas in Europe. Among policy makers too there is an EU-wide consensus that the problem of domestic violence is not a private matter to be left to individuals and families but demands a public response (Krizsán *et al.* 2007: 163). However, the EU's legal basis for action is less coherent in domestic violence than in trafficking in women. This, in turn, has resulted in particular framings of the problem, for example, as one of 'public health', so as to define the legal basis for EU level action. The EU has also used soft law to expand policy into this field. The tools have included awareness raising campaigns, action programmes, recommendations, and funding programmes. The emphasis has been on collecting harmonized data on gender violence, and developing common definitions, indicators, measures and methods. Despite the softness of the policy, it can have a substantive impact on member states' policies and on civil society actors' ways of framing the issue (see Chapter 9).

EU policy on trafficking in women: illegal migration and transnational organized crime

Trafficking in women has slowly become recognized as a major problem in Europe. Women, men and children migrate, are smuggled or trafficked to Europe through various routes and often for various purposes including domestic work or prostitution. Sometimes the line between being trafficked for domestic work and prostitution is precarious, although as policy problems the two are most often separated (Agustín 2005: 97). Both can, however, be about exploitation and abusive power relations. In this chapter, the focus is on trafficking in women for sexual exploitation, which can be defined as 'the illicit commercial exchange of ... people, and specifically women, for a sexually exploitative purpose, usually involving the movement across borders' (Askola 2007a: 17).

Figures for trafficking in women are often quoted to highlight the extent and magnitude of the issue. For example, Birgit Locher quotes the estimate from the UN and International Organization for Migration (IOM) that at the end of the 1990s about 500,000 people were trafficked to the EU every year. About 75 per cent of all victims of trafficking were women trafficked for sexual purposes (Locher 2007: 21–2). Others argue that such estimates of numbers of people being trafficked are at best 'educated guesses'. For example, the IOM estimate quoted above has come to occupy the position of an 'official truth', although due to the nature of trafficking in humans it is virtually impossible to reliably assess the number of women, men and children being trafficked (Askola 2007a: 16). Despite the difficulty of establishing the extent of the problem, a trend towards the 'foreignization of women in prostitution' can be discerned in most European countries (Askola 2007a: 52, Hubbard, Matthews and Scoular 2008: 139). Trafficking in predominantly white women from the former Soviet Union, Balkans and the central and east European countries results in 'race' as a category becoming less of a clear determinant of the experience of sex workers in Europe (Agustín 2005: 98; Goodey 2004: 28). However, ethnicity remains an issue with exoticized and ethnicized portrayals of 'women from the East' (Penttinen 2007).

As a policy problem, trafficking in women has a long history. In 1921, the League of Nations' 'Convention for the Suppression of the Traffic in Women and Children' put forward an anti-trafficking norm. This was further developed in the UN 'Convention for the Suppression of the Traffic in Persons and the Exploitation of the Prostitution of Others' in 1949. The UN, the Organization for Security and Cooperation in Europe (OSCE) and the Council of Europe have all taken an active stance on trafficking in women which is seen as a fundamental human rights violation and is strongly condemned in different conventions and protocols. The two most important international human rights instruments include the UN Protocol to Prevent, Suppress and Punish Trafficking in Persons, especially Women and Children (2000), and the Council of Europe Convention on Action against Trafficking in Human Beings (2005).

Birgit Locher (2007) argues that these international norms remained dormant in the EU until the mid-1990s when they were activated by a series of factors. The collapse of the Soviet Union and later the EU enlargement with the accession of the central and east European countries led to new flows of people to western European countries that coincided with the old patterns emanating from Africa, Latin America and Asia. In this new political context, the 'dormant' anti-trafficking norm was strengthened by the emerging women's human rights norm as evidenced by the Vienna World Conference on Human Rights 1993 and the strong anti-violence norm that emerged from the 1995 UN Beijing World Conference on Women (Locher 2002 and 2007).

In the EU, trafficking in women was tackled through the inter-governmental method until the end of the 1990s (see Chapter 4). The policy consisted mainly of high level conferences and lobbying efforts that sought to politicize the issue (for a detailed account, see Locher 2007). A change in the legal basis and subsequently in the policy-making process resulted in a spurt of EU-led activity in the field. This happened in 1997 when the Amsterdam Treaty Article 29 called for an 'Area of Freedom, Security and Justice' and named as one of the objectives the 'fight against trafficking in persons'. This formulation turned tackling trafficking in women into part of the primary law of the EU and marked a formal acknowledgement of trafficking in women as a political issue under EU competencies (Locher 2007: 265). Accordingly there has been a tendency towards trying to harmonize member state laws in relation to trafficking within the Justice and Home Affairs framework for which the EU has competence. Nevertheless, the EU competence covers only certain areas such as free movement and some aspects of external migration. Other aspects that remain under member state jurisdiction include prostitution policies and criminal justice policies (Askola 2007a: 6, 12).

Two binding legal instruments were adopted at the beginning of the 2000s: the Framework Decision on combating trafficking in human beings (2002) and the directive on the short-term residence permit for victims of trafficking (2002). The Framework Decision includes a common definition of trafficking, and sanctions for traffickers in the EU (Locher 2007: 326). It incorporated many of the provisions of the UN Protocol on Trafficking in Human Beings (2000). The situation of the victims of trafficking, however, remained unaddressed. The UN Protocol requires state parties to penalize trafficking but also to protect victims of trafficking and to grant them temporary or permanent residence in the countries of destination, but the Framework Decision left out all the optional provisions on the protection of victims of trafficking (Askola 2007: 209). The 2002 directive partly addressed the issue of protecting the victims of trafficking and granted some of them a temporary right to stay in the destination country. The directive is subordinate to the national laws of the member states which are allowed to define the length of the reflection period, the availability of psychological assistance, victims' access to legal aid and rules on working and access to education (Askola 2007: 212).

More attempts to deal with the problem have occurred in recent years. A new Commission Communication on preventing and combating trafficking in human beings was adopted in 2005. This led to the adoption in 2005 of an Action Plan for greater EU wide police co-operation on people trafficking. The Action Plan calls for the root causes of trafficking, including gender inequalities, to be addressed, but most of the document is dedicated to external migration control, investigation and prosecution (Askola 2007: 215–16). While most member states have legislation against trafficking in human beings, significant differences remain, partly because of EU legally binding instruments. For example, penalties for trafficking for sexual exploitation in aggravated circumstances vary from six months to a life sentence (Askola 2007: 211). The member states also have different concerns since most are destination countries, with others being transit countries or countries of origin (Goodey 2004: 29–30).

Critical commentators on the EU policy on trafficking in women have argued that the European Commission and Council have primarily approached trafficking in women as an issue of illegal migration and transnational organized crime. Jo Goodey (2003: 422) argues that the EU's general approach to trafficking 'focuses on the criminality of illegal immigration and related aspects of prostitution, rather than the humanitarian aspect of these "crimes"'. For example, the 2002 directive views victims with suspicion, not as 'genuine victims' and sees them as potential sources of information about crime and illegal migration (Aradau 2008: 29). Equally the directive does not address the fact that victims of trafficking have nearly always experienced repeated sexual violence (Askola 2007: 212). The focus on individual victims and perpetrators neglects structural causes behind trafficking and may make policies largely ineffective (Aradau 2008: 28). For example, the EU policies target potential migrants while ignoring the issue of demand within the

Union. The European need for migrant labour, the lack of rights for migrant workers and the structural conditions of women in the labour market fuel illegal migration and trafficking (Askola 2007: 211).

Here the EU's approach reflects its stance on third country nationals, immigration and migration more broadly. The Council meeting in Tampere in 1999 and the Tampere conclusions about improving the position of third country nationals never became the dominant approach towards third country nationals in the EU. Rather the EU and member states' stance on migration and immigration has hardened significantly, leading to a worsening situation for third country nationals. For example, the EU Hague Programme on the Area of Freedom, Security and Justice called for a more effective approach to 'cross-border problems such as illegal migration, trafficking in and smuggling of human beings, terrorism and organised crime' (Council of the European Union 2004: 3). Instead of developing immigration policies, the emphasis has been on migration control policies and a unilateralist stance towards third countries (Askola 2007a: 164).

The role of civil society organizations in combating trafficking in women in the EU

In contrast to the dominant EU policy, civil society organizations at the international, European and national levels articulate trafficking in women as a human rights violation. Feminist organizations emphasize the gendered character of trafficking. Civil society actors provide both expertise and knowledge on the topic to the EU's decision makers and act as partners in governance, assuming responsibility for helping and protecting victims (see Chapter 4). Their counter-discourses about trafficking have had some impact on EU policy and strengthened the role of NGOs in policy-making. Focusing on them also brings out the differences between EU institutions on the topic. The links drawn between trafficking in women and prostitution have, however, divided European women's organizations along national lines and diminished their influence in EU policy-making.

In contrast to the dominant EU approach where trafficking in women is seen as a symptom of transnational organized crime and illegal immigration, the human rights approach is overtly 'victim-centred'. This means that it is not so concerned with establishing what kind of criminals the trafficked women might be but rather sees them as in need of protection (Askola 2007a: 4, Goodey 2003: 422). This human rights approach was also seen in the UN Protocol mentioned above that requires states to protect victims of trafficking and grant them temporary or permanent residence in the countries of destination.

The human rights frame has been particularly influential among MEPs in the European Parliament. This is evident not just from the reports drafted on the topic by the Committee on Women's Rights, but, for example, in a 1997 parliamentary debate on trafficking where every speaker invoked the human rights frame (Locher 2007: 272). The human rights approach has also influenced the policies of the European Commission and Council. It has meant that the Commission has recognized the role of NGOs in tackling trafficking in women. NGOs are seen as representing expertise in working with sex workers and possessing in-depth knowledge of victims of trafficking. The role of the NGOs working with victims was fostered in particular through the STOP (1996–2002) and Daphne (2000–8) programmes that fund NGO activities in the field of violence against women and trafficking (see below). This has produced money for different prevention projects. Since 2003, the STOP programme has been replaced with a wider programme on the Area of Freedom, Security and Justice called AGIS that aims to bring together legal practitioners, law enforcement officials and representatives of victim assistance (Askola 2007a: 170). NGO representatives have also been appointed to the Commission's Experts Group on Trafficking in Human Beings (Aradau 2008: 97).

This kind of human rights approach is not without its contradictions (see Aradau 2008: 100–4). The victim-centred approach of the NGOs coincides with the EU Commission's agenda to identify women at risk of becoming illegal migrants and being trafficked. For the Commission, helping victims in this way is a way of preventing them from relapsing into illegal immigration or trafficking. The difficulty of tackling economic inequalities leads easily to an approach emphasizing psychological therapy for victims. This subverts the human rights approach and discourse of the NGOs (Aradau 2008: 102–3).

Despite the popularity and success of the human rights frame, gender advocates remain divided on the issue of trafficking in women in Europe. This is due to the fact that trafficking in women is currently being discussed in terms of prostitution in the EU, where prostitution and trafficking in women are collapsed into one another (Hubbard, Matthews and Scoular 2008: 139, Outshoorn 2005). This collapsing goes back to the polarized feminist debate on prostitution that oscillates between two positions. On the one hand, radical feminists such as Kathleen Barry (1995) and Sheila Jeffreys (1997) define prostitution as *sexual domination* and as the essence of women's oppression. This approach is represented at the international level by the Coalition Against Trafficking in Women (CATW) founded by Barry in the US in 1991. CATW defines prostitution as a form of sexual exploitation. Prostitution is always a manifestation of violence against women, be it directly physical or subtly inscribed in the social and economic structures of society. Trafficking in women is always seen as occurring against the will of migrant women and is seen to be caused by prostitution. Thereby the best way to fight trafficking is to abolish prostitution (Outshoorn 2005: 146).

Other feminists, however, maintain that prostitution is work that women can opt for. In the *sex work perspective*, prostitution is seen as an income-generating activity or form of labour for women and men, and prostitute women's agency is emphasized (Kempadoo 1998: 9). This perspective, represented by the Global Alliance Against Traffic in Women (GAATW) based in Thailand, objects to forced prostitution but wants to separate it from voluntary prostitution (Doezema 2001 and 2002). Women can be victims of trafficking but not all women sex workers crossing borders are victims of forced prostitution (Outshoorn 2005: 147). In this context, CATW's work has been criticized for the underlying colonial and postcolonial tendencies that underpin the analyses and for racist ideas about 'developing countries' and 'Third World women' (Kempadoo 1998: 11, Doezema 2001). Feminist scholars who work with the sex work perspective often state their commitment to creating space for the voices of 'those selling sex' and argue that 'the failure to represent their issues seriously compromises this debate' (Agustín 2005: 96). Different prostitutes' organizations, such as the International Committee for the Rights of Sex Workers, which demands social security rights and legalization across the EU, support this critique.

These two distinct perspectives function as a dichotomy. The impasse represented by them seems impossible to overcome and it seems necessary to take sides. Heli Askola, however, finds some common ground between the two extremes. Both are concerned with the well-being and security of all women in prostitution, and both regard the poor and dangerous conditions as wrong, as well as sharing a criticism of the economic and social conditions in which many women find themselves (Askola 2007a: 27). Joyce Outshoorn, in turn, suggests that both share some theoretical flaws in that they essentialize male sexuality. In the sexual domination discourse, male sexuality is connected to violence and domination and, in the sex work discourse, it is a given sexual drive (Outshoorn 2005: 146).

The EU member states' prostitution policies are similarly polarised. Prostitution is illegal in two member states, Lithuania and Malta. In Latvia, Germany, Greece and the Netherlands prostitution is either regulated or institutionalized, and in Austria prostitution is legal with restrictions. In Sweden, by contrast, buying (not selling) sexual services is criminalized. In other member states, prostitution is neither legal nor illegal (EWL 2007: 34, Askola 2007, Hubbard, Matthews and Scoular 2008, Outshoorn 2005).

The key women's organization at EU level, the European Women's Lobby's (EWL) Motion on prostitution and trafficking in 1998 reflected the perspective that both prostitution and trafficking in women are about sexual domination. The position paper states that prostitution and trafficking constitute 'a fundamental violation of women's human rights' and buying and selling of bodies should be considered illegal. Furthermore, they should not be associated with the terms 'forced' or 'free' because, according to the lobby: '"free choice" is a relative factor' and 'inequality severely restricts freedom of choice'. The EWL Motion on prostitution 2001 confirmed this approach by calling for it to be made a 'crime to buy women in prostitution'.

The EWL's position has been influenced by the Swedish model of criminalizing the buying of sex and by CATW's work on trafficking in women. The 2001 Motion comments on the Swedish model very positively and argues that it is based on a 'feminist analysis of prostitution', in that it recognises that 'women in prostitution are the victims of a crime, the crime of sexual abuse and sexual violence'. In 2008, the EWL issued a joint statement with the CATW demanding that states develop effective tools to prosecute traffickers, protect victims and address the demand for women and children for sexual exploitation. The two organizations stress that criminalizing the demand for prostitution (as in Sweden) is the most effective way to address the problem of sex trafficking (EWL and CATW 2008). It also calls for recognition of the work done by grass-roots women's organizations in helping victims and the financial difficulties that many of these organizations face.

The EU institutions are more divided on the issue. In the 1980s and 1990s, the European Parliament was influenced by a feminist lobby of activists, researchers, Green politicians and prostitutes' rights movements, and took a position that leaned towards the sex work perspective. For instance, the Parliament resolution in 1993 was informed by a distinction between forced and voluntary prostitution and did not call for measures against prostitution as such (Outshoorn 2005: 151). The resolution highlighted the need for a victim-centred approach to trafficking.

The position of the Parliament on prostitution has since then been more influenced by the Swedish model of criminalizing the buying of sex. A report by the parliamentary Committee on Women's Rights and Gender Equality (FEMM) mentions the Swedish, Finnish and Norwegian models of criminalizing the buying of sex and states that 'prostitution is integrally violent' (Committee on Women's Rights and Gender Equality 2008). The European Parliament debated prostitution and trafficking in women twice in 2006, prompted by the football world championships in Germany, and adopted a motion on 'Forced prostitution in the framework of world sports events' put forward by the Committee on Women's Rights which took an active stance on the issue. The trend in Europe is moving towards coalescing around the view that female prostitution is rarely voluntary (Hubbard, Matthews and Scoular 2008).

The European Court of Justice, by contrast, has translated the principle of free movement of people to free movement of sex workers offering sexual services. In 1982, in *Adoui and Cornuaille*, where two French women were denied residence permits in Belgium on the grounds that they were suspected to be sex workers, the ECJ ruled that if a member state allows prostitution for its own nationals (as Belgium did) it cannot deny free movement for prostitution for other member states' nationals (Askola 2007a: 53–4, Flynn 1996). In 2001, in *Jany and Others,* a case concerning six sex worker women of Polish and Czech nationality, the ECJ found that the Netherlands could not deny them entry as candidate country nationals (Aradau 2008: 149–50, Askola 2007a: 54).

The ECJ has thus taken a stance on the issue and recognized prostitution as sex work (Aradau 2008: 151, Askola 2007a: 54).

Although they have coincided with the efforts of the sex worker activists' movements, the rulings have not been without contradictions. Whilst recognizing the controversial status of prostitution in member states, the ECJ upholds the principle of negative freedom: a *laissez-faire* approach where women can choose to work in prostitution. The approach is underpinned by a traditional market understanding of sex work as work that is paid for (remunerated) unlike, for example, unpaid care work in the home, which does not merit the benefits of EC free movement law. This is done, according to some feminist commentators, without policies addressing the structural constraints faced by migrant women that channel them into prostitution (Askola 2007a: 59).

In conclusion, trafficking in women has become an important policy concern for different EU actors. The EU has enacted directives based on a perspective of trafficking in women as a form of illegal migration and transnational organized crime. Human rights approaches and feminist approaches are more likely to call for a victim-centred perspective and to emphasize the structural inequalities that cause trafficking in women. The EU policy is underpinned by a number of contradictions that make it ineffective at times. Most importantly, the dominance of illegal migration and transnational organized crime can compromise more human rights-oriented action. In this context, victim support can become a way to ensure that women are not re-trafficked. The feminist frame of seeing trafficking in women as prostitution that, in turn, is about sexual exploitation, is supported by some feminist scholars and activists and contested by others.

EU policy on domestic violence

Domestic violence emerged as a concern at the European level in the 1980s in the aftermath of the UN Nairobi World Conference on Women. The first visible sign of a newly emerging European concern about domestic violence was the Parliament's Committee on Women's Rights' comprehensive, own-initiative report on violence against women drafted by a Dutch member of the Socialist group, Hedy d'Ancona (European Parliament 1986, Hoskyns 1996: 155, Hanmer 1996: 139, Locher 2007: 146). A 'heated and lengthy' parliamentary debate followed the report and over a hundred amendments were discussed, indicating the controversies surrounding the fact that the EU was breaking new ground in its gender policy (Locher 2007: 147). The Parliament adopted a *Resolution on Violence Against Women* 1986 that called for marital rape to be criminalised; female police officers and interpreters to work with women from minority communities; and systematic data-gathering and adoption of measures to increase women's safety (Elman 2007: 89). Despite the progressive nature of the Resolution its impact was minor, and the Commission and the Council largely ignored the Parliament's proposals (Locher 2007: 149).

Towards the end of the 1990s violence continued to be a novel topic for EU level decision makers. However, international pressure was building up as the UN Fourth World Conference on Women in Beijing in 1995 had listed violence against women as one of the 12 key priority areas where countries had to take action to eradicate gender inequalities. Gender advocates at EU level started to seize the opportunities provided by this international pressure and made strong references to the UN documents (Locher 2007: 253, 256).

The EU entered the field mainly with such soft policy-making tools as parliamentary reports, awareness raising campaigns, publications and declarations, and funding programmes. Again the Parliament played an important role in politicizing the issue in the EU and pushing the agenda forward. It adopted a 'Report on the need to establish a European wide campaign for zero tolerance of violence against women' in 1997 (*Eriksson report*; see Chapter 4), which presented 'violence against women' as an issue of human rights and equality (Locher 2007: 254–5). The campaign was launched in 1999 by the European Commission, together with the European Parliament, the member states and the NGOs (European Commission 2001: 5, Theorin 2001: 17).

As the issue of domestic violence gained legitimacy, other EU level actors became active too. For example, the Presidencies of Austria, Germany, Finland, Portugal and Spain hosted conferences on the topic in the 1990s and 2000s and each of them adopted EU-wide recommendations or statements on violence. The Commission published a large cross-national survey on attitudes towards domestic violence against women, which was carried out in the context of the zero tolerance campaign (European Commission 1999). Later the commitment to combat violence against women was restated in the Framework strategy on gender equality (2001–5) and the Roadmap for equality between women and men (2006–10) where the eradication of all forms of gender-based violence is one of the six priority areas. The annex declarations of the Treaty of Lisbon (see

Chapter 10) state that 'The Conference agrees that, in its general efforts to eliminate inequalities between women and men, the Union will aim in its different policies to combat all kinds of domestic violence. The Member States should take all necessary measures to prevent and punish these criminal acts and to support and protect the victims.' This may add some leverage to EU policy in the field, and in the best case, the declaration may mean that the instruments implementing gender equality in relation to domestic violence will have a 'clear legal basis' (Koukoulis-Spiliotopoulos 2008: 22).

Overall, EU policy has suffered from the difficulty of finding a legal basis for addressing the problem of domestic violence. Domestic violence as traditionally conceptualized (crime or a social problem) lay firmly within the competence of member states. This has led to a search for a suitable legal basis as, for example, in the case of the key EU tool on combating violence against women, namely the funding programme Daphne. The Commission took Article 129 of the Treaty of Amsterdam, which deals with the improvement of public health, as the legal basis for adopting the Daphne programme on violence against women (see Chapter 4; see also Kantola 2006a, Locher 2007, Lombardo and Meier 2007, Rolandsen Agustín 2008a).

The three Daphne programmes and the funding for projects channelled through them have indeed become the key tool for EU policy on violence against women (the Daphne Initiative 1997–9, the Daphne Programme 2000–3, Daphne II 2004–8, and Daphne III 2007–13). The first call was for relatively specific and prioritized projects that set up European anti-violence networks, provided training and exchanges for personnel, conducted research and raised awareness on the issue. The latter calls have had a broader remit and increased budgets, and have included local public institutions as well as new member states (Montoya 2008: 362). Yet the increase in funds is debatable as the remit as well as the number of member states has expanded, so the funding is divided between more issues and more actors. Daphne III projects, for example, are to contribute to the protection of children and young people as well as women. All applications for Daphne funding go through a competitive review process. Proposals are evaluated on their ability to present added value at the European level, their innovation, their aims to promote best practice, and their ability to permit transnational exchanges and to target transferable results incorporating result indicators (Montoya 2008: 362).

Both the legal basis that defines domestic violence as a public health problem and the Daphne programme that promotes tackling domestic violence with short-term project funding have been evaluated from a gender perspective. On one hand, Article 152 on public health protection gave the Parliament more competences in the area, because the article is covered by the co-decision procedure that requires the Council to enact policy in co-operation with the Parliament (see Chapter 4). The Parliament and the Women's Rights Committee were, for example, successful in their attempt to widen the concept of 'health' to include a World Health Organization definition where health means 'complete physical, mental and social well-being' (Locher 2007: 278, Rolandsen Agustín 2008a: 15).

On the other hand, defining domestic violence as a public health problem has been criticized for its continuing narrowness and gender blindness. For example, in the Parliamentary debate on the Daphne programme in 1999 (European Parliament 1999), female MEPs argued that the public health discourse reduced violence against women to a health problem (Kantola 2006). It was argued that it shifted attention away from wider structural issues that had to do with gender and power in society. The framing also made it easy to eclipse gender and to target groups such as victims, human beings and individuals, which then appear 'gender neutral' (Krizsán *et al.* 2007, Rolandsen Agustín 2008a: 15). The tendency to bypass gender was exacerbated by the fact that the Daphne programme currently tends to finance projects with a focus on children. Furthermore, the public health frame leads to an emphasis on alcohol and substance abuse (Rolandsen Agustín 2008a: 17). Domestic violence then becomes a smaller part of a bigger health problem and results in a belief that that eradicating the other health and social problems will eradicate domestic violence (Kantola 2006). Finally, health can also easily be related to market concerns as a challenge to public health can endanger the EU agenda of jobs, growth and competition. For example the Daphne programme istates that violence can lead to 'high social and economic costs to society as a whole' (Rolandsen Agustín 2008a: 16).

Project funding provided by the Daphne programme can be interpreted in different ways too. Providing a positive reading, Celeste Montoya (2008: 361) points to the capacity building, resource distribution and network facilitation that the funding has ensured. She sees the programmes as 'an important new source of resources for advocacy organizations' (Montoya 2008: 364). The

EU funding and the recognition that follows it also offer respectability and political leverage to women's groups vis-à-vis their national governments (Elman 2007: 110).

More critical accounts emphasize the damaging aspects of short-term project funding. While such funding has resulted in some important new insights, networks and projects, it is questionable whether short-term initiatives like these really constitute effective prevention measures. Projects can become an excuse for not placing more emphasis on more sustained action and coherent long-term policy. They put pressure on the NGOs to act and shift responsibility away from the member states (Askola 2007a: 171). About half the projects funded by the Daphne programme were involved with raising public awareness about gender violence as well as research. However, nearly a quarter focused on providing or improving victim services, such as shelters, crisis centres and hot lines (Montoya 2008: 364). Arguably these services require permanent as opposed to precarious project funding. Women's organizations have to devote a lot of human resources to applying and competing for funding, which can divert attention away from their main activities. As pointed out in Chapter 4, some might not have the initial resources to apply for funding or might lack the 20 per cent co-financing required by EU projects. Furthermore, funding calls can effectively direct the NGO agendas, and concerns over the continuity of funding may compromise NGOs' critique of EU policies (Elman 2007: 110).

Kristina Brunila (2009) coins the term 'projectisation of gender equality work' to capture the contradictions that surround project funding. Projectization is firmly embedded in market logic: it promotes the values of productivity, competition and efficiency in gender equality work (Brunila 2009: 171). In some member states, projectization brings market logic into spheres where it did not exist before, such as non-profitable NGO work in the field of violence against women. Project funding requires 'deliverables' or 'products' as end results: preferably quantifiable results or 'best practices' that are transferrable to other countries and contexts (Brunila 2009: 171). Hence it is part of the new governance strategies discussed in relation to the Open Method of Co-ordination (Chapter 5), gender mainstreaming (Chapter 6) and soft Europeanization (Chapter 9), which may appear value-neutral but, in fact, promote a particular normative model of governance that is based on managerial values.

There are other ways of framing domestic violence and these are discussed in more detail in the next section. Most recently violence against women has come to be seen as a cultural problem in Europe (Rolandsen Agustín 2008a). This relates to a more general shift whereby governments across Europe have become more active in tackling gender inequalities within minorities (Saharso 2008a). In the shift to a focus on culturalized violence committed by 'others', migrant women are seen as a particularly vulnerable group (Rolandsen Agustín 2008a: 9, Outshoorn and Oldersma 2007). Recent EU documents and debates show a heightened emphasis on female genital mutilation (FGM), traditional cultural practices harmful to women, forced marriage and 'honour killings'. The Daphne programme created the European Networks against Harmful Traditional Practices and a study undertaken by the EWL showed that only eight member states have legislation against one or more forms of cultural or religious practice, the most common form being FGM. Prevailing harmful cultural practices that were reported included 'honour'-related violence and early marriages of Roma girls (EWL 2007: 28).

Whilst feminists had identified 'women-blaming' as a problem when confronting domestic violence (Radford and Stanko 1996), those focusing on the experiences of black women identified 'culture-blaming' as a persistent problem. This meant that state actors and institutions blamed violence on minoritized cultures: 'it's a cultural thing' (Burman, Smailes and Chantler 2004: 335, 345). A debate about gender and multiculturalism was initiated by Susan Moller Okin (1999), whose view that multiculturalism was bad for women was based on a belief in western liberal states about safeguarding the rights of minority women. Other feminists have criticized the deterministic view on culture and violence that this entails, in which certain cultures are portrayed as inherently violent and harmful to women (Rolandsen Agustín 2008a: 10). Framing domestic violence as a problem of minorities may shift attention away from the gendered structures that perpetuate violence against women in European societies as a whole.

Feminist debates and activism on domestic violence in the EU

Domestic violence as a form of 'violence against women' has become a key priority for women's organizations in the EU. For example the European Women's Lobby (EWL) defines itself as an organization for gender equality and against 'violence against women', thus singling out this one issue that is regarded as pivotal to women's position in Europe. In essence, feminist activism has sought to challenge any gender neutral or gender-blind definitions of domestic violence and other forms of violence in Europe. Although domestic violence is no longer regarded as a private family matter in most European countries, it continues to be constructed in diverse ways in Europe, ranging from 'family violence' or 'partnership violence' in Finland (Kantola 2006) to human rights, criminal justice or a public health issue in countries such as the Netherlands, Slovenia and Greece (Kriszán *et al.* 2007: 164). In general, research shows that as soon as an issue reaches the policy agenda the problem tends to be defined as gender-blind 'domestic violence' rather than in terms of 'violence against women' (Kriszán *et al.* 2007: 164). Spain is an exception and the Law on Integrated Protection Measures against Gender Violence approved in 2004 uses the notion 'gender violence' rather than the more degendered 'domestic violence' (Kriszán *et al.* 2007: 165).

Feminist discourses on domestic violence themselves have been by no means uniform in the different member states. However, the Anglo-American discourses have proved to be particularly powerful. They tend to define domestic violence as a reflection of unequal power relations both in society and in families, stress its universal character and the need for women's empowerment and women's movements' autonomy from the state (Kantola 2006). In this way, domestic violence has been regarded as a serious societal problem, the root causes of which can be tackled only by making the general position of women in society better (Dobash and Dobash 1979 and 1998, Kelly and Radford 1996: 20). State institutions have tended to be seen as both patriarchal and racist and black women's experience of domestic violence as fundamentally different from white women's experiences.

In the EU, diverse feminist discourses are represented by the European Women's Lobby (EWL), parliamentarians, the Women's Rights Committee of the European Parliament (FEMM), women's organizations such as WAVE, and international NGOs, such as Amnesty International. For example, the EWL 'Charter of principles on violence against women' adopts a feminist perspective whereby violence against women is seen as a 'structural phenomenon the cause of which is a direct result of gender inequality'. The lobby emphasizes autonomy and empowerment for women and the

central role of the NGOs in achieving this. The Charter also emphasizes the recognition of diversity and differences between women.

The EWL has established several institutional structures to
promote action and policies on violence against women, often with
EU funding from the Daphne programmes. In 1997, it developed a
European Observatory on Violence against women that has 32
countries as participants and a total of 50 experts. The observatory
has thus given a voice and role to women's NGOs and experts on
violence against women, its task being to advise the EWL on strategies to address violence against women within the EU. Most
recently, the lobby has established a European Policy Action Centre
on Violence against Women in 2008 (EPACVAW) with national
observatories in five countries (Denmark, Finland, France, Greece
and Ireland) with the aim of developing 30 others. The new structure was established mainly to make it possible to apply for funding
from the Daphne III programme and thereby raise further funding
for EWL's work on domestic violence in Europe. The key aims
include better exchange of good practice across Europe and a
campaign to ensure visibility for the issue.

Other feminist organizations include Women Against Violence
Europe (WAVE) that is a bottom-up forum for women's organizations formed in the aftermath of the Beijing 1995 World Conference
and also benefiting from the Daphne programme funding. In the
1996 founding meeting, feminist organizations from Poland, the
Netherlands, Sweden, Austria, Serbia and Ireland were present
(Krizsán and Popa 2007: 19). The aims of the network include
taking common action and promoting feminist analyses of violence
against women. In practice, it has been an information source and a
'meeting point of like-minded individuals' (Krizsán and Popa 2007:
9).

In the NGO context, the UN and its CEDAW (Convention on the
Elimination of Discrimination against Women) have been perhaps
even more important for lobbying and policy change in the new
central and eastern European member states than the EU. This
shows that the EU member states are situated in a context of multi-
level governance which reaches beyond EU level. The Beijing
Platform for Action initiated domestic violence policy in many of
these countries and the CEDAW Committee and the requirement to
report ensured its continued importance and a role for civil society
actors (Krizsán and Popa 2007: 4). The Committee monitors the
implementation of national measures to fulfil the obligations under

the Convention. In 1992, the Committee adopted general recommendation 19, which requires national reports to include statistical data on violence against women, information on the provision of services for victims, and legislative and other measures taken to protect women against violence in their everyday lives, such as harassment in the workplace, abuse in the family and sexual violence. In particular, the Committee has pushed for measures that cost money: adequate numbers of shelters, legal aid, support services and training. It has also foregrounded violence against minority women including violence against Roma women, disabled women, elderly women and women from rural areas (Krizsán and Popa 2007: 7).

The CEDAW Committee's work has become increasingly professionalized and the strengthened enforcement mechanisms have increased the capacities of the Committee (Zwingel 2005). NGOs have been systematically included in the review process, issuing shadow reports carefully studied by the Committee and being heard before the state hearings. The Optional Protocol that entered into force in 2001 established an individual complaints procedure. For example, two of the cases that the Committee has dealt with concern violence against women in Europe: these were a 2003 case on domestic violence and the inability of the Hungarian state to provide protection and support for victims, and coercive sterilization of Roma women (Krizsán and Popa 2007: 9).

Whilst articulating alternative discourses about domestic violence, gender advocates have also been embedded in the broader trends of domestic violence policy, as indicated by the discussion of the project funding and its consequences above. One of the consequences of the role of the UN Beijing Platform for Action and the national action plans that it requires has been the proliferation of the use of benchmarking and indicators in the area of domestic violence (Krizsán and Popa 2007: 9, Verloo and van der Vleuten 2009). National progress is often defined in terms of indicators; quantitative data presented as statistical information. Feminist actors, such as the European Women's Lobby, have developed these indicators to draw attention to progress or lack of progress in domestic violence policy in member states. For example, its 2001 guidebook on violence against women establishes a common set of indicators and agreed benchmarks against which progress can be measured (see EWL 2001). The challenge is to simplify qualitative information into quantitative indicators without losing a sense of the complexity of the policies and issues involved. The same challenge was identified in relation to gender mainstreaming in Chapter 6.

Conclusion

Trafficking in women and domestic violence are issues that feminists have argued are a key to gender equality but that have long been either ignored or ridiculed at EU level. In the 2000s, a spurt of EU activity has taken place in both fields. As policy debates, the two represent different policy approaches in which different discourses and policies have been adopted. The EU has enacted hard law and binding directives in the field of trafficking in women, illustrating political commitment and willingness to act on the topic. The contents of these policies have, however, been underpinned by a belief that addressing trafficking in women is one way to tackle transnational crime and illegal immigration. The EU legal basis for tackling domestic violence has been less clear. For example, for the Daphne programme it was found via the promotion of public health. The framing of domestic violence as a public health problem and addressing it through project funding have narrowed down the definition of gender violence and the ways of tackling it. Feminist actors have articulated counter-discourses by stressing the power relations and gender inequalities in society as a whole that underpin and explain both patterns of violence. The human rights frame in particular has had some impact on EU policy and has brought about a slightly more victim-centred approach and given a role to the NGOs as providers of expertise and knowledge in policy-making as well as partners in governance.

Chapter 8

'Tackling Multiple Discrimination': Gender and Intersecting Inequalities

From the beginning of the women's liberation movement in Europe, feminism has been criticized by black women and lesbians for representing only the concerns of white middle-class women. Gay and lesbian rights activists, and migrant and disability rights movements have gained in visibility in the international arena over the past decade. The intersecting hierarchies of gender, race, economic class, sexuality, religion, disability and age represent a significant challenge for contemporary equality theorists. To address the legal and political consequences of these intersecting hierarchies, Kimberly Crenshaw (1991) coined the term 'intersectionality'. In her theory, black women are located at the intersection of racism and sexism and their experiences cannot be reduced to either. Anti-discrimination law and equality policy, by contrast, relies on a single-axis framework, where claims can be made on the basis of either race or sex but not both. Crenshaw (1991: 57) argued that this deprives black women of the possibility of seeking justice as black women.

The EU has emerged as a key actor in pushing for legal and political developments in the field of multiple discrimination in Europe. The developments are underpinned by legislative change at EU level, in the form of both primary law and secondary law which EU member states have to transpose into their national legislation. These changes have made it possible for the EU to legislate not only on gender but also on race and ethnicity, religion, age, disability and sexuality. Furthermore, the changes implied that each of these grounds need to be tackled not only on its own but also in conjunction with one another, thus giving rise to debates on intersectionality, or in EU language, 'multiple discrimination'.

This chapter charts these developments. First it looks at the 'separate strands' equality policy under which gender, race and ethnicity, disability and sexual orientation have been treated mainly in isolation from one another. Whilst gender policy concentrated on the 'norm woman' (the white heterosexual working mother) and only very recently started to take diversity into account, equally gender was not a visible element in the other equality policy fields either. Second, the chapter focuses on the newly emerging horizontal approach where inequalities are understood to intersect – 'multiple discrimination' – and explores the consequences of this for equalities policy and institutions.

The power of the Amsterdam Treaty

Questions about discrimination gained heightened salience after the enactment of the Amsterdam Treaty 1997 which gave powers to the Community to combat discrimination on the grounds of gender, race and ethnicity, religion and belief, age, disability and sexual orientation. Article 13 decrees:

> Without prejudice to the other provisions of this Treaty and within the limits of the powers conferred by it upon the Community, the council, acting unanimously on a proposal from the Commission and after consulting the European Parliament, may take appropriate action to combat discrimination based on sex, racial or ethnic origin, religion or belief, disability, age or sexual orientation. (Article 13 of the Amsterdam Treaty 1999)

This addressed 'an enduring weakness' in EU anti-discrimination law in that it moved beyond discrimination on grounds of EU nationality and sex (Bell 2000: 157). The wording, which preferred 'action to combat' discrimination rather than a straight prohibition of discrimination resulted in a belief that the Article would be largely symbolic. Unlike earlier measures to combat discrimination based on nationality or gender, it has no direct effect (Holzhacker 2007: 9). Locating the new article in the first section of the Treaty also meant that it was not limited to the employment sphere and that any measure required unanimity in the Council to be approved (Mabbett 2005: 105; see also Chapter 1).

Nonetheless, a decade later it has turned out to be a powerful tool to stimulate the drafting of new anti-discrimination legislation and has been extensively researched (see Bell 2002 and 2002a, Geddes and Guiraudon 2004, Waddington 1999 and 2000, Meenan 2007).

Three directives, already mentioned in Chapter 1, have been adopted on the basis of this article: the Race Equality Directive (2000/43/ EC), the Employment Framework Directive (2000/78/EC), and the Goods and Services Directive (2004/113/EC). Enshrined in Article 13 is an approach not just to tackling each of these grounds separately (vertical approach) but rather to looking into combating discrimination horizontally – across inequalities (Bell 2002a: 385). Some commentators indeed argue that vertical approaches based separately on the different grounds for discrimination could only take European anti-discrimination law so far (Meenan 2008: 5). Article 13 has resulted in a new focus on 'multiple discrimination' in Europe with a number of consequences for equalities bodies, legislation and activists, and this may, according to some, result in more effective anti-discrimination policy.

The grounds on which discrimination is prohibited have been further extended in the EU Charter of Fundamental Rights Article 21, which prohibits discrimination on the basis of sex, race, colour, ethnic or social origin, genetic features, language, religion or belief, political or any other opinion, membership of a national minority, property, birth, disability, age or sexual orientation. In other words, Article 21 covers the six grounds of the Amsterdam Treaty Article 13 and seven additional grounds. Whilst representing a commitment to a broad anti-discrimination agenda, the Charter remains non-binding. However, it has become an important reference document for the ECJ (see Chapter 10). Nevertheless, the Charter, like human rights instruments more generally, prohibits discrimination in very general terms and allows a rather wide range of justification of differential treatment. Its power to tackle discrimination is therefore also weaker than that of the EC law.

The heightened attention to discrimination in the 2000s can be explained by two different narratives. The usual story about equality policy in the EU would emphasize the economic frame and neoliberal thinking behind the reforms. For example, Schierup *et al.* (2006: 50) argue that the EU anti-discrimination directives are part of the embedded neoliberalism of the EU social model where the mechanisms behind inequality are not really addressed. A declining labour force and an increasing need for workers from outside 'Fortress Europe' necessitate 'diversity management'. Effective competition requires any discrimination that distorts the labour market to be reduced. Neoliberal governance, and New Public Management as one of its manifestations, in turn, require efficiency in government and bureaucracy and favour joined-up government. A number of case studies on different European countries have noted that the arguments in favour of creating an integrated equalities agenda and 'single equalities bodies' do indeed centre around efficiency (Kantola and Nousiainen 2008: 7, Skjeie 2008: 301, Squires 2008b: 143–4).

Another story might emphasize the strong human rights frame that has emerged at the European level of policy-making. Of the various grounds on which discrimination may occur, sex was a well developed area of Community law and policy. Race and ethnicity, religion and belief were particularly relevant to human rights in the new member states from central and eastern Europe. Deborah Mabbett argues that the inclusion of disability, age and sexual orientation 'reflected the idea that a new generation of civil and social rights should be developed in the course of modernizing and restructuring the way that European welfare states regulate the life courses and family arrangements of their citizens' (2005: 106). Some commentators have indeed suggested that the enlargement of the EU to the East was 'the backdrop, and to some extent the raison d'être' of the measures (Ellis 2002: 291). There was a need to make quick progress before progressive policy in the field could be slowed down by the entry of new more conservative member states. A further reason, according to Mabbett, was that the rights frame was attractive as it was so ambiguous (2005: 105). The scope and application of rights in different documents was uncertain. It was also unclear to what extent they were declarations of policy intentions or restatements of established positions or provision for additional protection for individuals (Mabbett 2005: 105).

Scholars are increasingly interested in exploring the potential that these new developments entail for tackling inequalities (Kantola and Nousiainen 2009). A positive assessment might highlight the upward harmonization that considering the six strands together has meant for some types of anti-discrimination provision. For example, the Race Equality Directive provided protection against discrimination in goods and services. This was later extended to protection against discrimination on the basis of gender in goods and services (Chapter 1). Hence, an integrated approach to discrimination is thought to provide 'coherence, consistency, clarity and simplicity concerning individual rights to non-discrimination' as well as 'increased effectiveness and influence of the monitoring and enforcement authorities' (Skjeie 2008: 296). It is also advocated on the grounds that it enables intersectional or multiple discrimination to be tackled better than single-focus legislation and law enforcement bodies do (Kantola and Nousiainen 2008: 18, Skjeie 2008: 296, Squires 2009).

Nevertheless, feminist scholars are cautious about these developments, and the complexities of the integrated approach are discussed in this chapter. Feminist concerns about an integrated approach include the worry that the greater emphasis on, for example, race and disabilities will be at the expense of gender issues (Mazey 2002: 229). The integration of the relevant governmental agencies may entail the dispersal of expertise, loss of contact with specific constituencies, and a diluted approach, or alternatively it might be an opportunity for more efficient deployment of resources and a stronger approach (Walby 2005: 462). Feminists have enquired whether the equality tools needed by diverse disadvantaged groups are sufficiently similar to allow them to share institutional spaces and policies rather than each needing their own (Walby 2005: 462). Mieke Verloo (2006: 222) argues in relation to gender, race, class and sexuality that these bases for inequality are so dissimilar that the tools to tackle one form of inequality (for example gender mainstreaming) cannot simply be adapted for other forms. Furthermore, some of the grounds can be competing and in contradiction in terms of policy. The two best-known examples are gender and multiculturalism and sexuality and religion (Okin 1999, Phillips 2007). In both cases, it is argued that advancing multicultural or the religious rights of certain groups can be detrimental to women and sexual minorities within and even outside these groups.

Separate strands approaches

The new EU approach where inequalities are tackled in conjunction with one another contrasts with the traditional approach where each basis of inequality is dealt with through its own policy. This section examines EU anti-discrimination policy in relation to race and ethnicity, disability and sexual orientation and compares it to gender. The focus is on the similarities and differences between (i) the policy and tools; (ii) the current level of provision; and (iii) the major actors and their claims (see also Kantola 2009b). This provides a useful background to the chapter's discussion on an integrated equalities agenda where these grounds are considered in conjunction with one another.

Policy and tools

The chapters of this book have illustrated the expansion of EU gender policy from specific fields, such as employment and the labour market, to new areas such as violence against women (Chapter 7). The book has also discussed a wide range of tools in gender policy ranging from anti-discrimination law to positive action and gender mainstreaming (Chapters 2 and 6). Whilst gender equality policy seems to have moved beyond the narrow frame of anti-discrimination policy, for the other strands discussed here – race and ethnicity, disability, sexual orientation – the Treaty of Amsterdam's anti-discrimination framework can be interpreted as empowering.

Mark Bell (2002a: 55) differentiates four periods in EU policy on racial discrimination: (i) immigrants and the EEC (1957–84); (ii) the origins of the EU policy in combating racism (1985–90); (iii) towards the Treaty of Amsterdam (1991–9); and (iv) the Race Equality Directive 2000. In the 1980s, Council opposition hampered the Commission and Parliament's efforts to combat racial discrimination at EU level (Bell 2002a: 62). It was only in the 1990s when it was becoming evident that racism might affect the functioning of the internal market that opposition in the Council started to wither. The rise in extreme right parties and racist violence in Europe as well as emerging EU policies creating a 'Fortress Europe' galvanized a cross-border EU lobby against racism (Bell 2002a: 68, Hoskyns 1996: 175). The lobby was crucial in changing views in the Council on the enactment of Article 13 in the Treaty of Amsterdam which provided a legal basis for action in the field of racial discrimination.

The rights of disabled people have not traditionally been fought for in an anti-discrimination framework but rather with an array of social policies. The emphasis has been on providing income, care and assistance (Hendriks 2005: 189). The initiatives at EU level have been limited, leaving the social policy issue to member states. The Commission has traditionally used different soft law measures, for example in the form of action programmes to promote the social and economic rights of disabled people (Mabbett 2005: 99). The Treaty of Amsterdam represents a landmark for disability rights in Europe by providing a legal basis to tackle discrimination on the basis of disability (Hendriks 2005, Waddington 2005). The Commission has also promoted 'mainstreaming' of disability in social policy. Mainstreaming here has a slightly different meaning from gender mainstreaming. The concept was introduced in the 1993 Social Policy Green Paper and was defined as 'acceptance of people as full members of society, with opportunities for integrated education, training and employment and to lead their lives independently'. Thus it implies education in ordinary schools rather than separate special education, avoiding institutionalization where possible, and facilitating employment in an open labour market rather than employment in sheltered workshops (Mabbett 2005: 108). Later, the focus of mainstreaming was extended from social provision to the policy process, which Mabbett interprets as involving 'the procedural right to participate (or at least receive due consideration) in policy-making' (2005: 108). Again, as with gender mainstreaming, the implementation of mainstreaming has not been successful and member states have accepted it only on a rhetorical level (Mabbett 2005: 109, Waddington 1999: 143).

The Amsterdam Treaty was unique for sexual orientation too in that it is the first and only legally binding international treaty that explicitly prohibits discrimination based on sexual orientation (Kollman 2008: 9). Although the European Parliament and the Commission were receptive to lobbying efforts on sexual orientation (Kollman 2008: 9), no binding measures were put in place before the 2000s. In 1984, a Parliamentary report about sexual discrimination in the workplace included sexual orientation as a form of discrimination. In 1994, the Parliament published a report entitled *Equal Rights for Homosexuals and Lesbians in the EC* (known as the Roth Report) which condemned discrimination against lesbians and gays in a range of areas and also criticized member states for excluding same-sex couples from national marriage laws (Kollman 2008: 9).

In the member states, the most heated debate has dealt with the family rights of gay and lesbian couples. Europe has witnessed a recent rapid change from a bleak picture of 'second-class citizenship status of lesbians and gay men' in the EU (Elman 2000: 730) to the transnational diffusion of same-sex unions in western Europe (Kollman 2008). Whereas in 1990, only Denmark legally recognized same-sex partnerships, by 2007 only three western European countries, Greece, Ireland and Italy, withheld such recognition at the national level (Kollman 2008: 1). Kelly Kollman calls this the 'recognition norm' and argues that it has turned out to be a powerful catalyst of policy change in western Europe. The situation remains bleak in the new central and eastern European member states where homophobia is rife. Some binding provisions have, however, emerged at the EU level. In the Directive on the Free Movement Rights of EU Citizens and their Families (2004), the EU regulates that member states recognize the legal rights of the same-sex civil or registered partners if the host country has such a same-sex union law in place (Kollman 2008: 11).

Current level of provision

As illustrated by the chapters of this book, directives on gender equality have a scope that extends from equal pay, equal treatment in employment and self-employment to pregnancy protection, parental leave, access to and supply of goods and services, and certain social rights. The most important directive on gender discrimination, the Equal Treatment Directive (1976), was amended in 2002, and was replaced by the Recast Directive (2006/54/EC) in 2009 (Chapter 4).

The speed with which the Race Equality Directive was adopted in 2000 was remarkable. The directive forbids four forms of discrimination on grounds of racial or ethnic origin: direct, and indirect discrimination, harassment and instruction to discriminate (Bell 2002a: 75). The directive's scope is wide as it covers discrimination in employment, social protection, social advantages, education, access to and supply of goods and services. Article 5 of the directive allows for positive action. The explicit inclusion of possible recourse to hypothetical comparators marks a step forward from the Equal Treatment Directive and is particularly relevant in areas where the ethnic minority population is relatively small (Bell 2002a: 75).

According to Mark Bell (2002a: 78) one of the most innovative aspects of the directive is its focus on remedies and enforcement that build on the experience of gender equality legislation. One of the remaining problems is individual litigation: as in gender equality legislation, no right of action for trade unions or other organizations to bring discrimination cases in their own name is provided. This makes it more difficult to tackle institutional forms of discrimination, including institutional racism (Bell 2002a: 78). The Commission's report to the Council and the Parliament on the Race Equality Directive shows that the directive has been particularly effective in terms of its application beyond the fields of employment and in requiring member states to establish an equality body to promote equal treatment in relation to racial or ethnic origin (Meenan 2007: 7).

The Employment Equality Directive was adopted in November 2000 and prohibits employment-related discrimination (including that related to vocational training) on grounds of religion or belief, age, sexual orientation and disability. As it applies only to the field of employment, its scope is clearly narrower than that of the Race Equality Directive. Discrimination is defined as including direct and indirect discrimination, harassment and instruction to discriminate. In addition, employers are obliged to provide reasonable adjustment for disabled people, unless this would amount to a disproportionate burden. Certain forms of positive action for all groups are allowed for in member states but left to them to decide on (Waddington 2005: 109). The directive does not contain a definition of disability, which means that it is up to the member states to define disability in national legislation when transposing the directive (Waddington 2005: 117).

The scope of the Race Equality Directive is somewhat broader than that of the gender equality directives, especially in relation to the fields of social security and private insurance, where European law allows the use of sex but not race as a factor defining contributions and benefits (Kantola and Nousiainen 2009: 466). Discrimination on the other grounds is only prohibited in employment. In July 2008, the Commission presented a draft directive that would bring the other grounds into line with the protection in the Race Equality Directive. If the Commission's legislative move is successful, gender equality will be less well protected than the other six grounds, especially in relation to education and social welfare. In a relatively short period of time, a reversal of the hierarchy of protection has taken place: the first has become the last. The situation has created unrest among feminists involved in European politics and law (Kantola and Nousiainen 2009: 466).

Actors and claims

As illustrated in Chapter 4, EU institutions, such as the Commission, have played a key role in the construction of European civil society. Civil society actors in relation to the other inequalities were set up with Commission funding and support in a similar fashion to the European Women's Lobby. Migrants' Forum was established in 1991 to represent the interests of migrants and to act as a consultative body to the Commission (Williams 2003: 126). As a result of internal disputes and organizational difficulties, the Forum failed to emerge as a central actor in policy on racism (Bell 2002: 85). The European Network Against Racism (ENAR) was established in 1998 with the support of the EU and has taken up a role as an 'independent critic' of EU policy (Bell 2002: 86). The European Disability Forum has been very active in lobbying for a disability directive similar to the Race Equality Directive (Mabbett 2005: 104). The European branch of the International Lesbian and Gay Alliance is the LGBT network which lobbies the EU to adopt policies that enhance the legal standing of gays, lesbians and transgender people (Kollman 2008: 9). It was founded in 1997 to professionalize European lobbying and received some networking funds from the Commission.

Although these actors come together to co-operate in the European Social Platform (see Cullen 2009), the institutionalized separation between the strands is evident. Claims for gender equality and equality in relation to race, ethnicity and migration were institutionalized into largely separate and discrete organizational forms (Williams 2003: 121). While the European Women's Lobby did little, to begin with, to represent the interests of black, ethnic minority, and migrant women, the Migrant's Forum, likewise, marginalized women's interests (Chapter 4). However, after initial worries about the loss of a focus on gender in this kind of approach, the European Women's Lobby is currently seeking to develop a policy on intersectionality (Lombardo and Verloo 2009, Rolandsen-Agustín 2008).

The institutional dimension to EU policy on racism was represented by the creation in 2000 of the EU Monitoring Centre on Racism and Xenophobia, based in Vienna. The opening of the Monitoring Centre was delayed, its budget was insufficient and its role ambiguous (Bell 2002: 85). In 2007, it was replaced by the EU Fundamental Rights Agency (FRA), the task of which is to provide assistance and expertise to ensure respect of fundamental rights in policy-making. It collects 'objective and comparable information and data' to advise the EU and the member states and to promote public awareness raising. Although its mandate has been broadened to cover other bases of discrimination, it privileges the treatment of race and ethnicity (Lombardo and Verloo 2009).

The EU has arguably provided supranational opportunities for transnational networks that represent the claims and concerns of different minorities. These can, however, be hampered by the tech-nocratic nature (Geddes 2000) as well as the overall ethos of policy-making in the EU. As with gender policy, claims have to be framed in language acceptable to EU level policy-making. For example, the indigenous Saami people have benefited from the funding and lobbying opportunities provided by the EU. Yet the consequence has been that Saami claims must be framed within the framework of entrepreneurialism, the individualist and market-oriented discourse of which is in direct contrast with the community-centred values of the Saami people (Hobson, Carson and Lawrence 2008: 49–50). ILGA-Europe sought to frame their claims in terms of the internal market and barriers to competition and free movement. Yet the rights of sexual minorities continued to be hampered by the fact that they are not easily translated into the market-driven ethos of the EU (Bell 2002: 92, 97).

The EU has also provided new legal opportunities and proce-dures as illustrated in relation to gender in Chapter 2. For example, the European Roma Rights Center (ERRC) uses strategic litigation and the European Court of Justice to bring forward cases on racial discrimination against Roma (Goodwin 2008: 142). However there may be some problems associated with this strategy in relation to the topic under discussion in this chapter. It does not allow for a genuinely intersectional approach that would simultaneously address the problems both of racial discrimination and of socio-economic marginalization. The narrow way in which a legal issue must be framed in order to bring a complaint before a court neces-sarily fails to take into account the thick web of circumstances that result, for example, in a disproportionate number of Romani chil-dren being 'educated' in special schools (Goodwin 2008: 149). A litigation strategy denies the complexities of the situation and attempts to reduce it to a single issue, that of race (Goodwin 2008: 150). This exemplifies the challenges that legislation, courts and policy pose for multiple identities and tackling intersectional discrimination, discussed in more detail below.

Horizontal approaches: tackling multiple discrimination in the EU

In addition to tackling discrimination related to each of these grounds separately, the EU is promoting a move towards an 'inte-grated equalities agenda' and to tackling multiple discrimination.

The trend parallels feminist debates on intersectionality (see Crenshaw 1991, Goldberg 2009, Grabham *et al.* 2009, Hancock 2007, Schiek 2008, Verloo 2006, Weldon 2008, Yuval-Davis 2006). Decades of black feminist theorizing has highlighted how feminist studies took the white woman as the essential norm, and anti-racism policies and activism considered the black man as the norm, both ignoring the experiences of black women (hooks 1984, Hill Collins 1991, Anthias and Yuval-Davis 1992). Many feminist scholars now argue that focusing on people at intersections of groups – black women, young black men, disabled women, lesbians or gay men – is most effective in understanding marginalization and privilege (García Bedolla 2007: 233).

Black and ethnic minority women are the most common focus of intersectionality theory and research. In Europe, the concerns of black, ethnic minority and migrant women – a term that covers women in member states whose origins lie in third-world countries or in southern European migration countries –include legal residency status that is dependent on a male partner. They can be particularly vulnerable to exploitation within domestic service or as home workers within the service sector, catering and clothing industries and the sex industry, as well as to racism in the workplace (Williams 2003: 127). These issues were left without voice and representation in the EU institutions and gender policy.

To address the legal and policy consequences of the discrimination faced by black women, Kimberly Crenshaw (1991) coined the term 'intersectionality':

> Consider an analogy to traffic in an intersection, coming and going in all four directions. Discrimination, like traffic through an intersection, may flow in one direction and it may flow in another. If an accident happens at an intersection, it can be caused by cars travelling from any number of directions and, sometimes, from all of them. Similarly, if a back woman is harmed because she is in the intersection, her injury could result from sex discrimination or race discrimination. (Crenshaw 1991: 67)

The reliance of anti-discrimination law on a single-axis framework, where claims can be made on the basis of either race or sex but not both, deprives black women of the possibility of seeking justice as black women (Crenshaw 1991: 57). A focus on the interaction of different structures of inequality results in a fuller and more developed picture of the oppression and discrimination faced by different groups of people (Weldon 2008).

Intersectionality thus emphasizes that different groups – women, men, black, white, disabled, gay, lesbian – are not internally homogenous. For example, violence against disabled women is more widespread than violence against able-bodied women. Policy, by contrast, is often directed at only one aspect of an individual's identity, as the discussion above on EU policy on race and ethnicity, sexuality and disability illustrated. For example, trafficking in women can be viewed as only a gender issue although it has a strong ethnic dimension (Chapter 7). Legally, courts restrict people's lived experience of discrimination by holding that multiple discrimination should be restricted to a combination of only two grounds (Fredman 2008: 77). For example, in Norway, the single equalities body – the Ombud for Gender Equality and Anti-Discrimination – had to deal with a case of a Muslim headscarf when a woman had been dismissed from her job as a shop assistant because she refused to remove her headscarf at work (Skjeie 2008: 304). The Ombud split the case into, first, indirect gender discrimination, and second, direct religious discrimination. The employer was found to be guilty on both grounds (Skjeie 2008: 304).

The tools that the EU has had to tackle intersectionality have traditionally been either weak or non-existent (see, for example, Bell 2002: 212–13). Over the past five years, multiple discrimination has nonetheless entered the EU equality policy-making agenda. In the European Parliament, these debates have been initiated by the Committee on Women's Rights and Gender Equality. One report brings out recent cases of the sterilization of Romani women in two member states, Slovakia and the Czech Republic. Medical staff and government officials justify sterilization without consent through racialized constructions of Romani women as unable to control their own sexuality or their own fertility, and as inadequate mothers who have too many children whom they cannot look after (Center for Reproductive Rights 2006, cited in Freedman 2007: 54, Koldinská 2008 and 2009). Lívia Járóka (PPE-DE) who was the *rapporteur* for the Committee on Women's Rights and Gender Equality on the situation of Roma women in the European Union argued in the parliamentary debate (1 June 2006): 'Instead of facing the problem of reconciling family and work, the average Roma woman must fight every day to put food on the table without having a job, waiting for benefit and at the mercy of loan sharks.' Her statement illustrates how a mainstream EU gender equality policy approach – reconciling work and family (Chapter 5) – does not further gender equality for Roma women but may be irrelevant for them. Viktória Mohácsi (ALDE, Hungary) argued in the same debate that 'Member State governments are often trying to address the problem of Roma women with a paternalistic approach. They fail to ask for the opinion of the Roma women, or indeed of any women, on the fight against the discrimination.' The statement illustrates the lack of mechanisms that would ensure representation, participation and voice for the groups at the intersection of marginalization based on gender and ethnicity in the policy-making processes (Chapter 3 and 4).

The European Parliament also debated the situation of disabled women in the EU (26 April 2007). Again the debate took place on the basis of the Committee on Women's Rights and Gender Equality report, which highlights the dimensions of gender discrimination that disabled women face in their everyday lives in Europe. Ilda Figueiredo (GUE/NGL, Portugal) drew links between neoliberal policies and discrimination: 'We cannot go on prioritising the nominal convergence criteria of the Stability and Growth Pact and, in turn, cutting public investment, as has happened in Portugal, leading to the closure of maternity wards, emergency services, health services and schools. This undermines human rights, especially in the more vulnerable sections of society, as in the case of women and the disabled. It is wrong to declare that we want equal opportunities for all and to launch a propaganda campaign, only to pursue neoliberal policies that exacerbate inequality and social injustice.' Her comments juxtapose the EU's market ethos with the social rights of those who are most vulnerable.

It is evident that Romani women are discriminated against because of their gender, ethnicity, social and economic background and disabled women on the basis of their gender and disability. What legal basis is there for tackling such forms of multiple discrimination in the EU? The gender directives are single ground directives and do not mention multiple discrimination, but soft law measures, the gender equality programmes in particular, contain references to multiple discrimination (Kantola and Nousiainen 2009). For example, the Roadmap for equality between women and men 2006–10 has the declared purpose of 'combating multiple discrimination, in particular against immigrant and ethnic minority women' (Nielsen

2008: 35). The preamble of the Ethnic Equality Directive states that 'the Community should … aim to eliminate inequalities, and to promote equality between men and women, especially since *women are often the victims of multiple discrimination*' and a similar provision is found in the Employment Framework Directive (Nielsen 2008: 33, emphasis added).

The multiple discrimination agenda started to emerge with the European Commission Green paper *Equality and Non-Discrimination in an Enlarged European Union* in 2004. The Green Paper both evaluates progress since the enactment of the Amsterdam Treaty and seeks to set out the agenda for future reform. Overall there is an emphasis on and a preference for an integrated equalities agenda in the Green Paper. For example, it comments positively on the establishment of 'single equalities bodies' in some member states (European Commission 2004: 12). The Green Paper still operates with an economic and employment centred frame where EU policies of non-discrimination are seen as a measure to create economic growth through a rise in labour market participation (Rolandsen Agustín 2008: 511). The European Women's Lobby (EWL) was sceptical about the Green Paper's integrated approach to equality and argued it might result in a decrease in the allocation of funding and resources to women's organizations (Rolandsen Agustín 2008: 513). Other perceived dangers included the eclipse of gender, conflicting interests (for example between religion and gender), and institutional competition (Lombardo and Verloo 2009).

Despite these worries the EU multiple discrimination policy was further developed in a report financed by and prepared for the European Commission entitled *Tackling Multiple Discrimination*. Again the labour market is considered the sector where multiple discrimination occurs most often (European Commission 2007: 5). The report recommends extending the scope of EU anti-discrimination legislation to cover age, disability, religion/belief and sexual orientation in the fields of social protection, social advantages, education and access to goods and services. It also recommends that multiple discrimination be factored into all equality mainstreaming (European Commission 2007: 7).

It is interesting to note that in the report the EU has opted for the language of multiple discrimination as opposed to intersectionality – the preferred concept in feminist theory (Kantola and Nousiainen 2009: 468). In the report, multiple discrimination is defined as describing:

A situation where discrimination takes places on the basis of several grounds operating separately. For instance an ethnic minority woman may experience discrimination on the basis of her gender in one situation and because of her ethnic origin in an other. A different term used to describe this form of discrimination is additive discrimination. (European Commission 2007: 16)

Intersectional discrimination, by contrast, refers to a situation where several grounds operate and interact with each other at the same time in such a way that they are inseparable (European Commission 2007: 17). Overall, the report illustrates that member state ministries, national equality bodies and NGOs had little experience in dealing with multiple discrimination.

The preference for the term of multiple discrimination, as opposed to intersectionality, may be attractive to policy-makers because of its simplicity. It promises that the different axes of inequality are similar to one another, matter to the same extent and can be treated with an anti-discrimination approach (Kantola and Nousiainen 2009: 468). Each of these assumptions has been challenged in feminist debates on intersectionality. First, Mieke Verloo illustrates convincingly that the different bases of inequality are not similar and they are differently framed in terms of their relevance as policy problems (2006: 221). The categories for inequality differ, for example, on the dimension of choice (a person can choose her religion but not age), on the dimension of visibility (a person can hide sexuality but not gender), and on the dimension of change (age and disability can change but many will not change their sex). The categories are also differently situated in relation to legal institutions such a family law and various institutionalized group-based rights to self-determination (Kantola and Nousiainen 2009: 468).

Second, feminist theory on intersectionality considers which category of discrimination matters most in a given situation to be an empirical question. Ange-Marie Hancock (2007: 64) differentiates between a 'unitary approach', a 'multiple approach' and an 'intersectional approach' to the study of race, gender, class and other categories of difference in political science. Whilst the unitary approach addresses one category at the time (for example gender) as the most relevant or most explanatory, multiple and intersectional approaches address more than one (Hancock 2007: 67). For multiple approaches, categories matter equally in a predetermined relationship to each other. In intersectional approaches, on the other hand, the relationship between the categories is an open empirical question. Intersectionality conceptualizes the categories as resulting from dynamic interaction between individual and institutional factors. And whilst the unitary approach focuses on either individual or institutional levels of analysis and the multiple approach on both, the intersectional approach sees the individual as integrated with the institutional (Hancock 2007: 64).

Hancock further argues that it is the additive and multiple approaches that lead to competition rather than co-ordination between marginal groups. The unitary approach is universalizing in that it considers one category as the most salient for political explanation. It also assumes that individual memberships are permanent. This leads to 'Oppression Olympics' where groups compete for the title of being most oppressed to gain the attention and political support of dominant groups (Hancock 2007: 68). Most importantly, it leaves the overall system of structural inequality unchanged. The multiple approach that treats, for example, gender and race as parallel phenomena results in the same problem. It produces 'an additive model of politics leading to competition rather than coordination among marginal groups for fringe levels of resources rather than systemic reform that could transform the entire logic of distribution' (Hancock 2007: 70).

In the current approach multiple discrimination is tackled with a narrow anti-discrimination frame. Hence intersectionality becomes defined as anti-discrimination (Kantola and Nousiainen 2009: 469, Lombardo and Verloo 2009). Anti-discrimination's advantage can be that it costs less than redistributive measures and it shifts the blame to non-state actors, such as employers or service providers (Geddes and Guiraudon 2004: 346). However, Sandra Fredman argues that 'Intersectionality becomes more visible through positive duties to promote equality than under a complaints-led approach, since those responsible for instituting change are required to identify group inequalities and to craft solutions, rather than reacting to self-identified complaints' (Fredman 2008: 73). With positive measures – in contrast to anti-discrimination – the initiative lies with policy makers, service providers and employers. Change becomes systematic rather than random or ad hoc as the institutional and structural causes of inequality can be diagnosed and addressed collectively and institutionally. The duty to bring about change lies with those with the power and capacity to do so, not with the 'victim of discrimination' (Fredman 2008: 79–80.) However, constraints similar to those that are now present in combating intersectional discrimination can also appear to limit the use of positive measures. Authorities and employers may have a rather narrow approach to positive action, seeing it as a means to economic utility rather than to equality as such. That at least has been the experience in Finland, where a positive duty to promote gender equality has been in force for more than two decades (Holli and Kantola 2007, Nousiainen 2008). Reliance on positive duties puts much faith in the expertise and motivation of the authorities and organisations that are under such obligations.

Here the omission of class from the EU's categories becomes relevant. Class-based inequalities can hardly be tackled with an anti-discrimination agenda (Kantola and Nousiainen 2009: 469). For example, understanding poverty is fundamental to making the situation of the Roma – arguably the most marginalized people in Europe – better. As socio-economic inequalities are increasing dramatically, anti-discrimination law should be considered alongside policies tackling poverty. It certainly cannot be the only or even the main measure for distributive justice. During recent decades, social and economic inequality has increased in Europe. It may be an exaggeration to blame identity politics, and still less anti-discrimination, for the fact of rampant poverty. It seems, however, that anti-discrimination is a tool for recognition of identities (albeit victimized ones) rather than for redistribution, although it also can pave the way to distributive policies. Instead of blaming anti-discrimination for its failure to deliver, it may make sense to question why European social policies have concentrated so much on discrimination (Kantola and Nousiainen 2009: 469).

The link between intersectionality and discrimination has perhaps become central in European politics partly because of the political deficits of the EU as a polity and its limited social policy. The absence of social legislation is consistent with the principle of subsidiarity and member states are left in charge of the social justice policies that would often be so central to achieving gender equality. In these circumstances, the EU has to enhance its social legitimacy by other means, such as anti-discrimination, as more effective social policies for combating poverty are not available (Kantola and Nousiainen 2009: 469).

Towards single equality bodies?

Institutionally, this growing concern with multiple equality strands has generated equality reviews in many European countries, with significant numbers of states recently changing their institutional arrangements for promoting equality. Several countries have created 'single equality bodies' that bring law enforcement and implementation under one roof instead of having a separate body for each inequality. This is a model supported by the European Commission as a solution to tackling multiple discrimination. At the same time the EU's own institutional arrangements for promoting equality remain stratified by different identity categories (see Lombardo and Verloo 2009; see also Chapter 4). Furthermore, some key challenges in tackling multiple discrimination, such as loosening the requirement to find a suitable comparator, which is clearly a huge challenge when multiple categories are involved (see Kantola and Nousiainen 2009), are not on the agenda. A move towards single equality bodies is seen as sufficient at this stage.

Until the 2000s, European law made no demand on member states to establish equality bodies. The Race Equality Directive in 2000 was the first EU non-discrimination directive to do so in relation to race and ethnicity. A similar requirement pertaining to gender equality was added to the Equal Treatment Directive in 2002 (Bell 2008, Nousiainen, 2009). The EU requirements for equalities bodies are rather vague and set only minimal standards for the member states. The bodies are to be independent of the government and to have the competence to assist victims of discrimination. They are also to have powers to conduct surveys and studies, and to publish reports, recommendations and research. The Recast Directive (2006) adds the requirement that the national gender equality body has to have the competence to exchange information with corresponding European bodies (Nousiainen 2008a), reflecting among other things the establishment and the tasks of the new European Institute for Gender Equality (EIGE) (see Chapter 4).

Again the pressure from the EU towards the type of integrated equalities agenda represented by the single equality bodies emanates less from hard law than from soft law. For example, the equality directives do not require that equality laws be unified but the choice of legislative means used to transpose directives is left to the member states (Kantola and Nousiainen 2009: 470). However, with an increasing number of grounds recognized as potentially giving rise to discrimination, the unification of equality law and bodies has become a preferred solution. In its non-binding reports, the EU encourages a move towards 'national equality bodies that cover all protected grounds in all fields' and sees such a solution as an effective way to address multiple discrimination (European Commission 2007: 5). Arguments in favour of creating an integrated equalities agenda and single equality bodies also centre on efficiency and favour joined-up government (Kantola and Nousiainen 2009: 470).

The UK, for instance, has created an Equality and Human Rights Commission (EHRC), which is responsible for enforcing equality legislation on age, disability, gender, race, religion or belief, sexual orientation or transgender status, and encourages compliance with the Human Rights Act (Lovenduski 2007, Squires 2008b and 2009). The new member states from central and eastern Europe, which had no ombudsmen prior to entry to the EU, have followed the model of single equality bodies from the start for economic and efficiency reasons (Koldinská 2009). Two Nordic countries, Sweden and Norway, which had a strong tradition of promoting gender equality, are following the same trajectory (Bergqvist *et al.* 2007, Skjeie and Langvasbråten 2009), while another, Finland, has opted for separate equalities bodies (Kantola and Nousiainen 2009a). Whilst the EU is putting pressure on member states to tackle this issue, convergence is only limited and member states continue to opt for different solutions, as theories about Europeanization would suggest (Bell 2008; see Chapter 9).

In particular, many member states have several equality bodies dealing with different aspects of equality work: deciding or conciliating cases, positive duties and equality politics. The EU hard law requires only that equality bodies monitor discrimination and the minimum standards for equality agencies do not refer to powers needed for proactive measures (Nousiainen 2008a). For example, there is no reference to positive duties or gender mainstreaming which many national gender equality bodies engage in. This shifts attention away from proactive measures for promoting equality. Yet, positive duties to promote equality have been considered a more promising route for institutionalizing intersectionality than anti-discrimination measures, because positive actions are not hampered by the problems connected to the scope of protection or finding a comparator (Fredman 2005).

The current EU approach reflects a human rights based model of equality bodies (see Nousiainen 2008a). The Nordic tradition, by contrast, is based on the ombudsman type of bodies that have to be able to take proactive measures. Human rights bodies are responsible for presenting opinions, recommendations and reports, disseminate information and do research. Their independence is underlined to ensure neutrality and objectivity. Kevät Nousiainen (2008a) argues that the prevalence of these human rights norms for equality bodies in the EU downplays the features that are typical for equality bodies entrusted with social policy aims and proactive promotion of equality. Independence from government may be important for monitoring purposes, but less useful when pushing for positive action or gender mainstreaming (Nousiainen 2008a). The EU is thus promoting a specific model of women's policy agencies, which is proving to be particularly influential in the new member states from central and eastern Europe that did not have a pre-existing bodies but are establishing them according to EU standards (Koldinská 2009).

Conclusion

The ways in which different inequalities based on, for example, gender, race and ethnicity, disability or sexual orientation, intersect and result in particular forms of discrimination is gaining heightened attention in the EU. Under the powers provided by the Amsterdam Treaty (Article 13 EC), the EU has started to develop its anti-discrimination policy both in relation to each of the six strands mentioned and to the ways in which they intersect. This has enhanced the understanding of multiple discrimination in Europe. In theory, intersecting inequalities could be tackled both within specific equality policy fields (the vertical approach) or within an integrated equalities agenda (the horizontal approach). In the first approach, this would mean that gender equality policy would need to account for the concerns of, for example, ethnic minority women, young black men, disabled women and lesbians. Similarly, policies on racial and ethnic discrimination would have to be based on an understanding of the gendered hierarchies that these policies may perpetuate or reproduce. In the second approach, the integrated equalities agenda, intersecting inequalities are seemingly easier to grasp but similarly here also there is a need to develop ways of 'tackling multiple discrimination' or taking intersectionality into account. Whilst the language of multiple discrimination is currently on the EU agenda, the tools and practices to address it are far less developed.

Chapter 9

Gendering Europeanization in the Enlarged Union

Research on Europeanization has become a central aspect of studying the EU over the past decade. The increased focus on Europeanization reflects the different stages in the European integration theory. Whilst previous approaches were dominated by bottom-up theorizing and explored the flow of ideas and policies from member state level to EU level (see Chapter 2), currently the changes in the European polity, its growing powers and impact on the member states shift the focus to Europeanization. The shift has been facilitated by institutional developments in the EU where ECJ judgements and qualified majority voting may run counter to member state interests (Caporaso 2008: 25).

Europeanization concerns an increasing number of countries as a consequence of the various rounds of enlargement. The 1970s saw an enlargement to the west when Denmark, Ireland and the UK (all in 1973) joined the EU, the 1980s to the south with Greece (1981), Portugal and Spain (1986) becoming members, the 1990s to the north with Austria, Finland and Sweden joining (1995). In the 2000s, Cyprus, the Czech Republic, Estonia, Hungary, Latvia, Lithuania, Malta, Poland, Slovakia and Slovenia (2004) and Bulgaria and Romania (2007) constituted the eastern enlargement. Croatia and Turkey are current candidate countries and Iceland is likely to apply for membership too. Europeanization is also having an effect beyond membership and candidacy as the cases of, for example, Norway and the Balkan countries illustrate.

Conceptualizations of Europeanization have evolved considerably over the years. In its simplest form, the term Europeanization highlights the role of European politics and institutions in domestic politics and refers to the processes by which domestic structures adapt to European integration (Caporaso 2008: 27). Rather than being a theory, Europeanization is regarded as a phenomenon that needs to be explained (Vink and Graziano 2008: 12) and its

189

gendered and gendering patterns understood. This process is shot through with power and involves identity constructions and representations illustrated by the way in which the different enlargement rounds are represented. The 1990s northern round was represented in terms of its positive impact on enhancing the status of gender equality in the Union. The 2000s eastern enlargement was discussed in terms of mass migration of labour, prejudices based on ethnicity and gender, the Roma and trafficking in women or prostitution (Einhorn 2006: 2). Hierarchies have also emerged between Europeanization in the old and new member states. The rights of the citizens of the new member states which joined the EU in 2004 and 2007 were not as extensive as those from the old member states in terms of full freedom of movement (Liebert 2008: 24). Nira Yuval-Davis (1997) refers to 'multilayered citizenship' to describe the kinds of hierarchies that entail more rights for some and less for others.

This chapter focuses on the Europeanization of gender policy. The first part of the chapter discusses the well-established research on Europeanization through hard law both in the old and the new member states. The second part analyzes the new trends in Europeanization research: foregrounding of the role of soft law, actors and discourses in the processes of Europeanization. The chapter discusses the latest enlargement round in terms of Europeanization. However, in the light of the power structures, it is important to take into account the specific features of the relationship between the EU and the former socialist states. For example, whilst Europeanization is today discussed as both a top-down and a bottom-up process, the asymmetrical power relationship between the two meant that the accession countries were mainly 'downloading policy, with few opportunities for uploading' (Grabbe 2005: 4). The accession process was faster and more thorough than the adaptation of the former EU-15 member states and there was very little scope for negotiating transitional periods (Grabbe 2001: 1014).

Theorizing gender and Europeanization

As a phenomenon or a process to be explained, Europeanization focuses essentially on questions of change and continuity. Some broad key questions in relation to gender include: What happens to local, national and European gender regimes when they interact with one another? How does such a powerful transnational actor and polity as the EU shape national gender policies, institutions and norms? How much diversity is preserved in Europe in relation to gender equality? How do national and local actors use the EU both at member state and transnational levels and how does this in turn shape EU policies and opportunities for action?

In Europeanization theory, the notions of 'fit' and 'misfit' have been central when theorizing the pressure for domestic change. The concepts are based on an understanding that it is possible to discern both national and European models in relation to particular policy fields and compare and contrast these in order to discern their differences and similarities. According to the theory, in cases of 'good fit' between the domestic level and the EU, there is little pressure for change and, in cases of misfit, the opposite is the case (Caporaso 2008: 29). In gender policy, for example, the Equal Pay Directive analyzed in terms of 'goodness of fit' in the UK and France showed greater pressures towards Europeanization in the UK than in France (Caporaso and Jupille 2001). However, misfit can also lead to resistance and result in no change, symbolic change without substantive content, and active attempts to subvert the European policy (Börzel and Risse 2003: 58, Caporaso 2008: 29). Even in cases of little or no apparent change, the interaction with the EU level of policy-making can lead to subtle changes and effects on member state policies (Radaelli and Pasquier 2008: 37).

The domestic level is seen as crucial in explaining Europeanization. The so-called bottom-up approaches to Europeanization take the domestic level as their starting point and argue that EU policies are neither a necessary nor a sufficient condition for Europeanization (Radaelli and Pasquier 2008: 41). Rather 'domestic mediating factors' that include 'nearly every domestic structural condition that affects the impact of European integration' shape the outcomes (Caporaso 2008: 30). These factors can range from cultural, institutional, discursive, formal and informal institutions, to norms, state and civil society structures, and traditions of litigation (Liebert 2003).

For example, *Gendering Europeanization* edited by Ulrike Liebert (2003) measures the impact of public opinion, elite learning, and domestic factors on Europeanization and evaluates it by looking at the equality directives from the 1970s up to 2000, as well as the timing of their implementation and whether this is below or above average. This research emphasizes the importance of the meanings that European norms acquire and of varying reactions that Europeanization provokes across different domestic contexts

(Liebert 2003b: 256). The key factors that shape Europeanization of gender policy include member states' gender regimes, court activity, public pressure, dominant frames, and policy advocacy coalitions (Liebert 2003b: 260).

This diversity poses challenges to anyone trying to argue that Europeanization of, for example, gender policy would result in the emergence of a European (EU) model in member states. A number of scholars now argue that convergence is 'neither theoretically predicted nor empirically likely' and rather that there is a 'continual arbitrage between national differences, different adaptational pressures, different mediating institutions and outcomes' (Caporaso 2008: 31). This is also true in relation to the domestic gender regimes in Europe first discussed in Chapter 1. Domestic actors have autonomy and can choose to use the European policy in different ways, sometimes embracing it and sometimes resisting it, which results in a differentiated impact of Europeanization in member states and beyond (Liebert 2003b: 263).

Europeanization through hard law

The impact of European hard law – treaties, directives and ECJ rulings – has provided scholars with ample material to study the processes of Europeanization. Despite the presumption of hard, clear-cut standards on the basis of which to measure 'compliance', member states vary greatly in their transposition and implementation of EU legal norms. This section explores, first, what mechanisms for Europeanization are provided for the EU and domestic actors by hard law. Second, it focuses on the change that these processes result in.

Europeanization that takes place through hard law is based on the supremacy of EU law, its direct and indirect effect in member states, and the responsibility for transposition of treaty provisions and directives that the member states have (Liebert 2003: 20). The backbone of these 'legal compliance mechanisms' is Article 226 ECT which grants the Commission the right to monitor member state compliance and sanction noncompliance through the ECJ. In its monitoring work, the Commission relies heavily on monitoring by external actors including citizens, firms and public interest groups and the European Parliament (Börzel 2006: 133). Here the supremacy and the direct effect of EU law provides these citizens and groups with the opportunity to litigate to get their EU rights enforced against the resistance of their governments (Börzel 2006: 147). The ECJ has organized a transnational legal community by actively seeking co-operation with national courts (van der Vleuten 2005: 469).

Anna van der Vleuten (2005) has coined the term 'pincers' to further explore the conditions for compliance. Pincers describe the pressure from above and below on the member state. 'Pressure from above' refers to the supranational power of the EU, namely the Commission mechanisms of monitoring, infringement, the ECJ mechanisms of direct effect, binding judgements, and penalty payments. For example, between 1980 and 1990 the Commission sent 19 letters of formal notice concerning the three gender equality directives. 11 cases were settled by correspondence between the Commission and the member state. Eight cases were referred to the Court (van der Vleuten 2005: 477). National courts were active too. Between 1980 and 1990 they referred 28 cases that concerned equal pay and equal treatment to the ECJ, and from 1990 to 2000, 102 cases. German courts referred 33 cases, Dutch courts 21, and French courts 5 (van der Vleuten 2005: 477).

This pressure from above needs to be combined with the pressure from below provided by national actors and their resources. This pressure is often exercised in co-operation with transnational actors who supply expertise and information. Supranational actors can also influence implementation at national level by mobilizing domestic actors including courts and movement actors (van der Vleuten 2005: 468). Countries can be very differently positioned in relation to these mechanisms. For example, in terms of litigation, some countries have been very successful, whilst others lack a tradition of litigation. In other words, the EU enforcement system in fact empowers those actors that already actively participate in domestic and European politics. Noncompliance is the highest in member states where soci-etal actors are the weakest, and vice versa; a process that Tanja Börzel calls the 'empowerment of the already powerful' (Börzel 2006: 130). Again the empowering effect offered by the EU compli-ance system is filtered through domestic structures that provide indi-viduals and groups with differing degrees of court access and resources to use it (Börzel 2006: 135). The dilemma then becomes that the tools are least effective where they are most needed (Börzel 2006: 149).

In gender studies, a frequently cited example of an effective liti-gation strategy is the British women's movement and groups that

have effectively used this strategy against their recalcitrant government (Alter and Vargas 2000, Sifft 2003: 150). Overall British
courts have asked for more preliminary rulings in gender matters by
the ECJ than every other country except Germany (Sifft 2003: 149).
Women's rights in relation to the labour market and care leave
arrangements have been furthered in this way although the UK did
not go beyond minimum standards, for example in relation to
maternity leave and pay (Sifft 2003: 154, 157). The existence of a
strong women's movement willing to use litigation on, for example,
equal pay has also been shown to be a crucial factor facilitating
Europeanization in hard law (Tesoka 1999).

Such strategies have been less common in other big member
states such as France, where collective action suits have not in
general been important political tools in the struggle for women's
rights and ECJ court cases have been less numerous than in other
countries (Reuter and Mazur 2003: 53, Caporaso and Jupille 2001:
42). Domestic institutional structures can indeed hamper the use of
this strategy. For example, the corporatist nature of the German
polity disadvantages groups promoting women's rights, as gender
issues have to be channelled through organizations that might be
resistant towards them (Tesoka 1999: 13)

Hence, whilst court activity and litigation are important avenues
for Europeanization of hard law, they are not necessarily enough.
The German case shows high court activity where a lot of cases have
been referred to the ECJ by German courts on gender issues. Yet,
governments have remained recalcitrant in implementing legal
gender norms. This suggests that the link between court activity and
advancing Europeanization in relation to hard law in member states
is not straightforward (Liebert 2003b: 264). In fact what becomes
important are political actions (see below for more detail). For a
long time, German feminists showed little interest in using the
European institutions to push for gender equality in their own country (Macrae 2006: 538; see also Miethe 2008: 120). For some this
was a function of a basic distrust of legislative avenues. Others who
were more interested in using existing political institutions considered the national level to be more important than the EU level
(Macrae 2006: 538).

It is evident that even hard law mechanisms have a differentiated
impact on member states' gender regimes. A key question that has
intrigued scholars is the kind of change that Europeanization of
gender policy has produced in old member states. Ulrike Liebert's

(2002) study on the transposition of equal opportunity directives 1975–2000 in six member states used two dimensions to measure change: the speed and extent of transposition. Her findings show that Sweden transposed all directives in due time and adequately, followed by Spain, the UK and France in the middle, and Italy and Germany behind (Liebert 2002: 245). As Sweden and Spain have traditionally been based on different gender regimes, the one a Nordic egalitarian model and the other a more traditional southern one (see Chapter 1), the findings illustrate that good compliance practices are not related to the characteristics of the gender regime as such or simple notions of 'fit' or 'misfit' between the national and the European regimes. Liebert suggests in fact that key factors include the publicly perceived legitimacy of the EU and domestic agency in using the EU (Liebert 2002: 249).

Spain's good record in transposing directives reflects a commitment to both Europe and equality under socialist governments (Lombardo 2004, Threlfall 1997, Valiente 2003). Whilst some norms, such as requirements on sexual harassment, were implemented before binding directives, others such as the Pregnant Workers Directive 1992 had a more mixed record (Lombardo 2004: 123). In general, conservative governments were more resistant to transposing gender equality directives than socialist ones. The EU, however, continued to provide important back-up, support and continuity for gender equality bodies and gender equality under conservative governments, and this facilitated domestic pressure for Europeanization of gender policy (Lombardo 2004: 130).

Germany represents a particularly strong clash – or 'misfit' – between the European gender regime as represented by the Equal Pay and Equal Treatment Directives and the German gender regime based on a strong male breadwinner and female caregiver model (Kodré and Müller 2003: 84, Liebert 2003c: 482). Instead of putting heightened pressure on Germany and pushing the country towards common European standards, the implementation of EU gender directives has been limited in Germany (Tesoka 1999: 7, von Wahl 2005: 82). Between 1970 and 2000 a quarter of the ECJ requests for rulings on gender equality were presented by German courts and related to conflicts on equal pay and equal treatment. The Commission also initiated several infringement procedures against the country (Kodré and Müller 2003: 84). Despite the active resistance of German governments, pressure from the EC has forced the country to adapt to the EU standards. The controversies surrounding the *Kalanke* case (see Chapter 2) functioned as an important turn-ing-point that raised awareness about EU level gender policy-making, and politicized the issue, paving the way for a partial move away from the male breadwinner model (Kodré and Müller 2003: 113, Liebert 2003c: 484). For instance, in 1994, German legislation was changed to permit women to work night shifts in industry under certain circumstances. In 2000, the German army was opened to women after a ruling by the ECJ that German law contradicted the EC legal norm of equal treatment between women and men when it barred women from the army (Liebert 2003c: 485). As a result Germany has come to represent a 'hybrid regime' combining elements of both German and EU gender regimes (Macrae 2006: 523).

It is commonly stated that the three Nordic countries that are EU members – Denmark, Finland and Sweden – have contributed more to EU gender policy than they have gained from it and that the EU was seen as a threat to women's rights in these countries (see, for example, Lister *et al.* 2007: 5, Roth 2008: 4). Sweden in particular, and some feminist activists in the country, have sought to export the Swedish model of gender equality to the EU and via the EU to member states (Hellgren and Hobson 2008: 219, Towns 2002: 158). One example already discussed in this book is prostitution (see Chapter 6) and others include childcare, individualized taxation and social security (Hellgren and Hobson 2008: 220).

However, the EU hard law on equal treatment and non-discrimi-nation has had a significant impact on these countries too. The Nordic gender equality model has been based on positive action measures and promotion of gender equality through co-operation with the social partners rather than on strong anti-discrimination legislation. The so-called Tham professors' case in Sweden illus-trates the clash of these two models. The Tham professors, created in 1995, were 20 professorships earmarked for women and one of the most celebrated cases of positive action. These quotas in acade-mia were then taken to the ECJ which found in 1998 that they conflicted with EC equal treatment law.

Overall, the EU directives have moved the countries towards stronger provision against discrimination. The Commission has in the past found the Danish transposition of the equal pay directive inadequate and the infringement procedure resulted in Denmark appearing before the Court. There was a clash between the Nordic model of ensuring equal pay through collective agreements and the

EU anti-discrimination model, on which the Court found that the Nordic model did not adequately ensure pay equity (Martinsen 2007: 552). The EU law also expanded the meaning of equal treatment and extended the rights of Danish pregnant workers against dismissal and indirect discrimination (Martinsen 2007: 552). Similar changes took place in Finland and Sweden, with the countries' membership in the 1990s resulting in changes in their equality legislation (Holli and Kantola 2007, Nousiainen 2005, Olsson Blandy 2005). Although Norway is not an EU member state its gender policy has nevertheless been closely influenced by EU's anti-discrimination policy (Skjeie and Langvasbråten 2009).

In the 2000s, the EU anti-discrimination model has been further strengthened by the Amsterdam Treaty and the anti-discrimination directives enacted on the basis of it (see Chapter 8). Despite an initially sluggish approach to transposing the Racial Equality Directive 2000 and the Employment Equality Directive 2000, drafted on the basis of the new powers conferred by the Treaty, by the end of 2006 all member states had adopted new legislative measures in response to the directives (Bell 2008: 36). A focus on these most recent changes illustrates some of the challenges relating to Europeanization through hard law.

First, whilst the EU requires member states to make extensive changes in this field, substantial gaps remain between the standards set by the directives and by national law (Bell 2008: 36, Guiraudon 2008: 297). Focusing on two issues, the list of grounds on which discrimination is forbidden and the establishment of equality directives, Mark Bell (2008) shows considerable divergence in the member states despite EU directives on these issues. For example, several states contested the use of 'race' in their anti-discrimination law. Austria uses the term 'ethnic affiliation', Sweden 'ethnic belonging', and France 'real or presumed' race (Bell 2008: 37).

These considerations surrounding the transposition of the anti-discrimination directives result in challenges to the notion of compliance. In addition to prohibiting discrimination on certain grounds, the Racial Equality Directive requires the establishment of equality bodies in relation to discrimination based on racial or ethnic origin. A similar requirement is made in the 2002 Equal Treatment Directive on gender equality. However, numerous different adaptations of this exist in member states due to the high degree of flexibility for states in the form and structure of such bodies (see Chapter 8). One can therefore question the usefulness of 'compliance' as it masks great differences in, for example, the equalities bodies that must be set up according to the directives. Compliance can also mean different things for different member states. According to Virginie Guiraudon (2008: 304), implementation of the recent anti-discrimination directives was one of the fields in which the Commission insisted strongly on compliance before candidate states were held to have satisfied the conditions for accession to the EU. Consequently the Commission may appear to have used the accession criteria to be particularly strict with the new member states even if it can be argued that the old member states fared little better (Guiraudon 2008: 304). This shows that the Commission addresses perceived laggards much more strongly than member states which were perceived to be policy leaders (Guiraudon 2008: 304; see also Verloo and van der Vleuten 2009).

Second, the anti-discrimination model promoted by this Europeanization through hard law is based on the UK and the Dutch models which have, in turn, been strongly influenced by the US model. So we need to qualify the notion "Europeanization": 'anti-discrimination as a policy frame being largely a US import to Europe when it comes to race/ethnicity and handicap [sic]' (Guiraudon 2008: 297). Key elements of the model include the centrality of the notion of (direct and indirect) discrimination in employment and provision of goods and services, civil suits, an independent body to examine complaints, and ethnic monitoring (Guiraudon 2008: 303). These do not necessarily address the most pertinent discrimination issues in the member states. Bell argues that for a number of member states that lack an immigration history comparable to that of, for example, the UK or France, a thorough exploration in the EU of issues around 'ethnic origin' would have been crucial. For example, the question of outlawing discrimination against the Roma in a number of European countries as well as against Russian or stateless minorities in the Baltic states would have benefited from such a debate (Bell 2008: 38). The EU anti-discrimination model is based on an individual rights model but it is doubtful whether individual litigation is a sufficient response to the inequalities faced by the Roma community at the intersection of ethnic and gender discrimination and poverty (Bell 2008: 38, Goodwin 2008).

In conclusion, Europeanization of hard law is often studied in terms of compliance and the change that this produces in member states. A number of examples illustrate progressive change towards European norms, as for example in Germany. However, the EU and national level interactions can result in diverging patterns and trends in gender policy and little convergence on gender regimes. One can also enquire whether directives respond to all national needs when based on certain models.

Hard law in the new member states: conditionality

As argued above, the 'eastern enlargements' of 2004 and 2007 can be studied in terms of Europeanization but they also draw attention to specific features of the process, for example by highlighting the importance of accession and conditionality in Europeanization. The accession process resulted in the promotion and spread of EU institutions, policies and norms into the candidate countries before full membership of the Union. This has been widely regarded as a top-down bureaucratic process based on hierarchical power relations: 'High volume and intrusiveness of the rules attached to membership, have allowed the EU an unprecedented influence on the restructuring of domestic institutions and the entire range of public policies in the CEECs' (Schimmelfennig and Sedelmeier 2008: 88).

Enlargement, like Europeanization in general, is a process that can be studied in terms of its impact on the political culture of the countries, on specific policy fields (including gender equality) or on state structures and institutions (Schimmelfennig and Sedelmeier 2008: 89). In terms of state structures and institutions, for example, it has been argued that the accession process strengthened technocratic and top-down policy-making in the accession countries as the Commission negotiated mainly with teams consisting of ministerial bureaucrats from the accession countries (Grabbe 2001).

Conditionality has become the key concept when studying the enlargement process. A policy of conditionality can be defined as international organizations promising 'rewards (such as financial assistance or membership) to target states on the condition that the states fulfil one or more conditions (such as policy adjustments or institutional change) set by the international organizations' (Schimmelfennig and Sedelmeier 2008: 88–9). In the EU accession process, political conditionality was established by the Copenhagen European Council in 1993 (known as the Copenhagen criteria) which included: (i) the stability of institutions guaranteeing the rule of democracy; (ii) the rule of law; and (iii) human rights and respect for and protection of minorities. These criteria formed a precondition for accession negotiations (Schimmelfennig and Sedelmeier 2008:

89). Once the negotiations opened the focus shifted towards specific EU rules (*acquis communautaire*) that candidate countries were expected to transpose into domestic law. The Agenda 2000 formulated in 1997 outlined a clear accession process, provided a timetable and called for annual evaluations, known as Regular Reports, of each country's progress towards meeting the membership standards (Seppanen Anderson 2006: 106).

Before the EU imposed conditionality, CEEC governments adapted EU rules sporadically. Once a given issue area became subject to the EU's conditionality, rule adoption increased dramatically. However, the salience that the EU attached to particular areas is a key factor in rendering conditionality credible; social policy, for example, was seen as less important than other areas (Schimmelfennig and Sedelmeier 2008: 93). After accession normal hard and soft law Europeanization mechanisms come into play. However, some differences between the old and new member states may remain. In some cases, the communist legacy meant that there were no old institutions and practices to overcome in the CEECs and hence less institutional resistance when compared to the old member states (Grabbe 2001: 1014–15).

Interpretations of the position of gender equality in the accession negotiations and its impact on the new member states differ. Of the 31 chapters under negotiation, Chapter 13 on Employment and Social Policy contained EU legislation on gender equality. Most commentators agree that prior to the EU accession process, gender was marginal in the CEECs and the EU brought the issue onto the political agenda (Einhorn 2006: 17). Yet in practice, compliance or non-compliance with EU gender norms did not assist or impede the accession of the CEECs, which illustrates that the position of gender equality was not as central in the accession process as many would have hoped (Steinhilber 2002).

Positive changes as a result of the accession process included legal change in relation to equal opportunities in the form of both the revision or supplementation of old laws and the drafting of new ones (for an overview see Sloat 2005). Provisions on equal pay, equal treatment in statutory social security schemes and maternity leave existed under state socialism. As a result, norm adoption in this field has been more effective as citizens are more aware of these rights than of the new ones introduced by EU requirements, such as the burden of proof in discrimination cases, part-time work regulations and equal treatment for the self-employed and their spouses

(Sloat 2005: 54–5). However, policy agencies and monitoring bodies were established to oversee the implementation and enforcement of these laws (Koldinská 2009, Kriszán and Zentai 2006).

The enlargement clearly brought with it hopes for gender equality, and women's organizations were active in using the tools and the frames provided by the EU. Yet many argue that despite the EU's formal commitment to gender equality, in practice EU accession meant 'a process of economic alignment and integration. In this process, concerns not only for gender equality, but also for citizenship and social justice are marginalized' (Einhorn 2006: 23).

When critiquing the enlargement process from a gender perspective, terms such as 'missed opportunities' (Bretherton 2001), 'window dressing' (Hašková 2005: 1088), and mere 'technical reforms' (Koldinská 2009) are often employed, suggesting no profound change. According to critics, insufficient attention was paid to gender equality in the accession negotiations and documents either by the EU or the accession countries. For example, in the Polish application for membership gender was 'marginalized from the beginning' and women, gender or gender equality were not mentioned (Regulska and Grabowska 2008: 142).

Candidate countries showed large variations in transposing and implementing EU requirements. The Commission's regular reports on each of the candidate countries shed some light on the issue. In the final monitoring evaluations Romania, Bulgaria and Estonia were identified as having significant progress to make, while Latvia, Slovakia and Poland represented good, if incomplete progress, in transposing EU gender equality measures. The Czech Republic, Hungary, Lithuania and Slovenia were seen as making considerable efforts to transpose and create effective structures for implementing gender norms (Clavero and Galligan 2009: 111).

Leah Seppanen Anderson (2006: 103) explains the differences in transposing gender norms in the Czech Republic and Poland by the extent of organized opposition to EU gender laws and the commitments of the political party in government. For example, feminist mobilization was greater in Poland prior to and during the accession process because of the politicized abortion issue, and therefore the variation between the two countries cannot be explained by the presence and strength of a feminist social movement. Rather, the opposition represented by the Catholic Church played a major role in Poland and resulted in poor transposition of EU gender norms in the country (Seppanen Anderson 2006: 114).

Even in the countries that had made considerable progress, a number of problems remained. In their Regular Reports the Commission criticized countries such as theCzech Republic for failing to introduce adequate gender legislation. Problems included the lack of enforcement of gender equality legislation, and failures in the introduction of positive action measures and the implementation of gender mainstreaming. Furthermore, gender equality bodies suffered from limited responsibilities and personnel who lacked expertise on gender equality, and from infrequent interactions between the state and the NGOs (Hašková and Křižková 2008: 160, Křižková 2007: 4).

In general, the reforms associated with the accession process were often undertaken in a technocratic manner without a substantive discussion about the gender equality problems in the country (Křižková 2007: 5). For example, the Czech Republic adopted a strategy of mechanically introducing required aspects of equality law that constituted preconditions for EU membership. The specific problems that needed tackling in the country were not considered (Hašková and Křižková 2008: 160). In Hungary, gender equality was treated with a high level of generality, omitting detailed policies or specific tools for implementing policy objectives, which was a symptom of the lack of political will and commitment to the issue. Such an approach did little to address the needs and concerns of Hungarian women (Kakucs and Pető 2008: 179). Not surprisingly then, policy debates and changes on gender equality did not result in a comprehensive gender equality strategy in Hungary. After having passed the Act for Equal Treatment and Promotion of Equal Opportunity in December 2003, Hungary fares quite well in the *de jure* fulfilment of all the formal legal requirements relevant to gender equality imposed on her by the EU. This successful legal harmonization, however, has been accompanied by persistent and pervasive obstacles to the practical realization of the newly formulated standards (Kriszán and Zentai 2006).

Despite these challenges, conditionality continues to be important and relevant in cases such as Turkey, a controversial candidate country. The European Commission has included gender conditionality within the category of political criteria, which also spans across the stability of institutions guaranteeing democracy, the rule of law, rights, and the respect for the protection of minorities in Turkey (Aldıkaçtı-Marshall 2008: 200). This has resulted in significant changes in Turkish law and strengthened women's rights in the country. In particular, the revisions of the civil code, the penal code and labour law in the 2000s have changed the legal status of women in the country. The revision of civil law raised the legal age of marriage for girls from fifteen to eighteen and put them on a par with boys. It turned the husband and wife into equal spouses in marriage and strengthened women's divorce rights. The reforms in the penal code strengthened women's individual rights, in that violence against women is now conceptualized as a crime against the individual rather than society or family, indicating that women can no longer be regarded as someone's property. Sexual harassment in the workplace and rape in marriage were criminalized. The issue of so-called 'honour killings' is also covered but with some loopholes which have been strongly criticized by feminist activists in the country. Sixteen weeks of paid maternity leave and a reversal of the burden of proof in cases of discrimination were included in the new labour law (Aldıkaçtı-Marshall 2008: 200–1). Criticisms of the Turkish reforms remain, however, and the country's women's movements and activists continue to push for reforms.

Europeanization through soft law

The Europeanization through hard law described above is currently being complemented by Europeanization through soft law, which produces different kinds of pressures on member states. Soft law draws attention to the different mechanisms and paths through which Europeanization may work. For example, the Open Method of Co-ordination (OMC) (see Chapters 5 and 6) results in 'more subtle impacts of socialisation processes, ideational convergence, learning, and interpretations of policy paradigms and ideas' (Radaelli and Pasquier 2008: 38). It gives a role to different actors and highlights the role of the diffusion of common frames and discourses.

More specifically, this kind of Europeanization through soft law works through (i) defining what problems domestic policy-makers should tackle vis-à-vis specific policy domains, such as employment or competitiveness; (ii) reinforcing the idea that a policy line is good, bad or necessary; (iii) restricting and limiting the policy options and courses of action for domestic actors; and (iv) providing potential courses of action, learning, and good practice (López-Santana 2006: 482). In other words, Europeanization through this form of governance can result in common framings of policy problems across member states leading to shared practices in terms of responses to the problems (Bruno, Jacquot and Mandin 2006: 533).

Some argue that soft law can have more impact in the member states than hard law. For example, Virginie Guiraudon (2008: 305) suggests that in the case of anti-discrimination, the EU soft norms or instruments such as monitoring and benchmarking have had more impact in certain countries than the required transposition of directives. Whilst the transposition of directives is a long term process, other more managerial norms and tactics result in reports, the setting up of monitoring bodies and co-operation with civil society groups in a much shorter time-span (Guiraudon 2008: 305). The impact of soft law can be further enhanced by the financial incentives attached to it, for example through structural, research and developmental programmes that have facilitated the implementation of gender mainstreaming in countries such as Greece, Ireland, Portugal and Spain where the overwhelming share of spending is concentrated (Liebert 2003c: 488).

The European Employment Strategy (EES) is an advanced area of soft law, as discussed in Chapter 6. Despite its general failure to achieve progress in many gender equality measures (O'Connor 2008: 88), it has been argued that it implies comprehensive and structural transformations and a pressure for change in the member states with conservative and Southern European social policy traditions based on strong male breadwinner/female carer model (Aybars 2008: 63). In other words, the EES has had a bigger impact in some of these member states than in others. In some cases, it has even been argued to have been more effective than hard gender equality law. To illustrate this argument a study of Greek employment policy suggests that the EU hard legislation and directives of the 1980s and 1990s resulted in qualitative rather than quantitative reforms (Zartaloudis 2008). This means that hard law did not change some of the gendered problems of the Greek labour market, such as the low participation rate of women. Rather it was the use of the EES and the OMC as examples of soft law that resulted in both qualitative and quantitative change in the 2000s. Active labour market measures were strongly gender-mainstreamed, resulting in a reconciliation policy, a number of new institutions and measures and funds for them, as well as the engagement of social partners in promoting gender equality (Zartaloudis 2008: 20). The case also illustrates that as soon as the EU priorities in the area were reshaped away from an active approach of promoting gender equality (see

Chapter 6), the emphasis on gender equality decreased in Greece. Hence one can conclude that the challenge in this case is not so much the softness of the EES but rather the loss of commitment and visibility on the issue of gender equality by the EU (Zartaloudis 2008: 21, 30).

In contrast to these positive assessments, critiques of soft law Europeanization have also been put forward. Measures such as 'mutual learning', 'peer review', 'exchange of good practice' are often represented as neutral governance techniques. They do, however, represent a specific normative model of governance that is Europeanized to member states, one that relies on foregrounding competition and managerial values (Bruno, Jacquot and Mandin 2006: 521–2). In this 'government by numbers' and 'governance by standardization of knowledge', indicators, scoreboards, and quantitative data have a tendency to reduce political issues into simple figures that are then represented as facts. This could be interpreted as signaling a move 'from integration by law to Europeanization by figures' (Bruno, Jacquot and Mandin 2006: 528–30).

Gender mainstreaming is a specific example of Europeanization that takes place mainly through the impact of soft law. This can exacerbate some of the problems identified in Chapter 6 in relation to the effectiveness and implementation of gender mainstreaming. The soft mechanisms provided by soft law have in general resulted in poor implementation in a number of European countries, for example in Italy, and the focus on gender equality has been only incidental in the National Action Plans (NAPs) of the European Employment Strategy (EES) (Velluti 2008). The softness of the measures also enable processes of 'window dressing' – varying interpretations of what counts as implementation of gender mainstreaming (Verloo and van der Vleuten 2009). The problems have become even bigger after gender lost its position as one of the four pillars of the EES. Gender mainstreaming can also be Europeanized with a very particular meaning. In talking about its 'twisted usage' scholars have suggested that gender mainstreaming has been Europeanized not as a tool to reduce gender inequalities but as a means to promote more labour force participation and labour market flexibility (Bruno, Jacquot and Mandin 2006: 531). This twisted usage is based on an impression that gender equality can be simplified in this way. Arguably soft law leaves more room for such interpretations than the standards set by hard law.

These challenges are also illustrated by the position of gender mainstreaming in the accession process of the CEECs to the EU. Despite the EU commitment to gender mainstreaming in the Amsterdam Treaty, gender equality was addressed narrowly in terms of the equal opportunities directives in the context of Chapter 13 in the accession process. This sidelined the potential role that gender mainstreaming could have played in other policy fields. In other words, gender equality was understood as 'a particular policy field rather than a guiding principle for all policy areas' as implied by gender mainstreaming (Locher and Prügl 2009). The consequences of this lack of priority and endorsement of gender mainstreaming have been studied, for example, in Hungary. The country did not adopt any strategic policy document that would introduce gender mainstreaming but instead there were 'only erratic signs showing gender mainstreaming awareness of the policymakers' (Kriszán and Zentai 2006: 138). Where gender mainstreaming was referred to as a policy approach, its form, contents or implementation were not developed. For example the key European Employment Strategy (EES) documents, the Hungarian National Action Plan for Social Inclusion 2004–2006 and the National Employment Action Plan 2004 contained references to gender and gender mainstreaming, but remained on a general level (Kriszán and Zentai 2006: 145).

A focus on the CEECs also illustrates that what counts as 'best practice' in gender equality to be copied in member states is highly dependant on the context. For example, long maternity and parental leaves can be considered as valuable for women in countries where unemployment is low. However, in countries where unemployment rates are high such supposedly women-friendly policies can be used to push women out of the labour market at a rate faster than men (Fuszara 2008: 104–5). Here women's movement activists in the old member states and in the CEECs may have differing constructions of gender equality, the former pushing strongly for longer leave policies, a view shared by the European Women's Lobby (EWL), and the latter adopting a more sceptical point of view. Kristina Koldinská (2008a: 124) suggests that the OMC has been structured and implemented in a way that does not take into account the new member states, which makes it harder for these countries to adopt the best practices promoted by the method.

To sum up, Europeanization through soft law works through a different logic to Europeanization through hard law. Some interpretations stress its positive impact in achieving more far-reaching change in member states than Europeanization through hard law.

Others draw attention to the ways in which soft law governance as evidenced in the Open Method of Co-ordination (OMC), the European Employment Strategy (EES) and gender mainstreaming are underpinned by norms of competition and managerial values resulting policy problems being reduced to sheer numbers, indicators and figures. In addition, soft law measures are often poorly implemented in both member states and the EU institutions, as shown by gender mainstreaming. This poor implementation gives rise to questions about the effectiveness of soft law in achieving desired change.

Europeanization and the role of actors and discourses

Whilst the role of domestic and transnational actors has been self-evident when studying Europeanization of gender policy, sociological and constructivist perspectives on Europeanization have drawn attention to the neglect and underestimation of the role of actors and discourses in much of the mainstream debate (Jacquot and Woll 2003: 4, Schmidt and Radaelli 2004). Here, it is argued, the interaction between the actors, discourses and institutions at the European and national levels – 'soft pressures of European integration' (Della Porta and Caiani 2006: 78) – is crucial for the processes of Europeanization. In studies on gender and Europeanization, actors include elites, norm entrepreneurs, epistemic communities or policy advocacy coalitions, women's and feminist movements (Liebert 2003: 27). Their role as policy or norm entrepreneurs is considered to be crucial in that they facilitate the transfer of the European policies and frames, without which Europeanization would be limited to a minimal, legal implementation with little impact on actual gender inequalities (Liebert 2003: 25–7, Macrae 2006: 539).

On one hand, mechanisms of Europeanization that use information and persuasion as their tools can change 'beliefs, opinions, attitudes, values on the part of domestic actors' (Liebert 2003: 23). On the other hand, a focus on the role of actors has shifted interest to 'the usage of Europeanization' by different actors in member states. Actors need to seize the opportunities provided by the EU in the member states in order for them to be transformed into political practices, and this usage is argued to be necessary for any impact of the European integration process on national political systems (Jacquot and Woll 2003: 4–6). The notion of political, strategic, usage of Europeanization can be defined as 'the mediation done by an actor to transform a material or immaterial resource provided by the European institution into a political action' (Jacquot and Woll 2003: 6). Creative usage may mean that domestic actors use the EU in different ways, reappropriating EU norms and paradigms to implement their own policies or claiming EU pressure even when there is none (Radaelli and Pasquier 2008: 38).

In feminist theory, this is known as the 'boomerang effect' where national and local actors bypass the sometimes recalcitrant state level of policy-making and take their claims to the international level. After successful formulation of new international norms on, for example, violence against women, national actors are able to get back to their own governments and require the implementation of these norms (Keck and Sikkink 1998). For example, the former Swedish Equal Opportunities Ombudsman (*Jämo*) seized the window of opportunity provided by the EU to advance equal pay in Sweden (Olsson Blandy 2005). The Swedish model is traditionally characterized by corporatist tripartite negotiations on pay, where gender equality tools include positive action and collective rights. The EU model, by contrast, relies on strong laws, litigation and the individual's legal rights. The EU provided the Swedish Ombudsman with an opportunity to enforce a new model based on individual rights and anti-discrimination policy in the regulation of wages (Olsson Blandy 2005: 220). Hence it promoted new frames and discourses in Sweden that were based on framing equal pay as a human rights issue and a discrimination issue that also required a new set of actors – including courts – to take a more active role (Olsson Blandy 2005: 220). The opportunities that the EU has provided for women's movements have also been explored in Spain (Lombardo 2004) and Italy (Donà 2004 and 2006).

Alongside the focus on the role of the actors in Europeanization, the transfer of ideas, discourses and frames as central in shaping the process has become a focus of research (see Kantola 2006, Verloo 2007, Lombardo, Meier and Verloo 2009, Rolandsen Agustín 2008a, Zippel 2006). How does the EU discursively construct or frame particular policy problems and how do these interact with national constructions? Under what conditions does a particular 'frame' or 'discourse' become dominant, how is it adopted and articulated in the member states? As discourses are historically variable ways of specifying knowledge and truth that are shot through with power, institutionalized as practices and form the identities of subjects and objects (Foucault 1980, Howarth and Stavrakakis

2000: 3–4), they are as deeply rooted in societal contexts as political institutions. This makes it a challenge to study the way that they 'travel' between the different levels of multi-level governance. Analyzing policy frames in European politics has illustrated the multiple constructions of policy problems, solutions and the variation in the voices that define these in particular contexts (Verloo 2007, Lombardo, Meier and Verloo 2009). Some frames are easily adopted in member states, others resisted by different actors. For example, feminists in the CEECs have resisted western models and constructions of gender equality (Einhorn 2006: 11).

Discourses and frames are articulated and drawn upon by a range of political actors in the Europeanization processes. Mediation by political actors takes place in relation to both hard and soft law although the two foreground a different set of actors, as discussed in Chapter 1. In general, the presence of civil society actors in public debates in the member states varies according to the field of EU competences, with less presence in fields such as monetary policy and European integration where the EU competence is high (Della Porta and Caiani 2006: 89). This illustrates that some debates remain highly elitist and difficult for actors such as NGOs to participate in. Europeanization of public discourse can, then, reduce the chance for civil society actors to participate in the debate, although this may change over time and through learning processes (Della Porta and Caiani 2006: 89).

Soft law measures, like the OMC, provide actors with a general, yet sufficiently vague framework, which they can interpret to increase their political discretion (Jacquot and Woll 2003: 6). Soft law makes it necessary to consider the ways in which discourse and frames at EU level open up or close off political opportunities at the national level: 'EU frames that are easily fitted in the national legal and institutional context are the most difficult to challenge, as they require groups with power resources and strong brokering partners to contest both their own governments and EU legitimacy' (Hellgren and Hobson 2008: 212). A focus on the actors that actually take part in the OMC process illustrates that the strategy 'reproduces' power relations rather than challenging them (Pascual 2008: 182).

In the CEECs, the accession process profoundly shaped the context in which the women's movements as actors in Europeanization operate (see also Chapter 4). A positive reading emphasizes that the accession process empowered women's NGOs in the new member states, for example in Poland, the Czech

Republic and candidate countries such as Turkey (Aldıkaçtı-Marshall 2008: 196, Fuszara 2008: 104, Regulska and Grabowska 2008: 148). The EU's approach to NGOs was markedly different from that of the former communist states in that it stressed the need for government consultation with civil society in policy-making processes. This made it possible for women's organizations to put pressure on their national governments to adopt equal treatment and non-discrimination legislation. The governments in the CEECs had to both consult women's NGOs and institutionalize this consultation, leading to the establishment of new consultative bodies (Regulska and Grabowska 2008: 148). Furthermore, women's movement organizations chose to interpret EU directives in stricter ways than their governments in order to pressurize for more progressive reforms (Hašková 2005: 1088).

In Turkey too, the positive effect of Europeanization on women's organizations has been particularly pronounced. Feminist organizations have effectively used the opportunities provided by the EU conditionality and successfully placed such issues as 'honour killings' and virginity tests on the public agenda with the help of EU pressure and the national secular media (Aldıkaçtı-Marshall 2008: 197). One of the important tasks was to argue that the recent legislative changes which, for example, make the legal position of women better are not just a result of exogenous EU pressure but also of national demand and lobbying by women's organizations. This has been used to counter arguments that the EU reforms are alien to Turkish society (Aldıkaçtı-Marshall 2008: 204–5). Women's organizations also remain critical of the recent changes and push for more, for example in terms of virginity tests, 'honour killings', abortion and discrimination on the basis of sexual orientation (Aldıkaçtı-Marshall 2008: 205).

More critical interpretations of the Europeanization of women's movement organizations in the new member states stress that the accession process was a bureaucratic rather than a parliamentary and a political process. In the technocratic approach adopted by the EU and accession countries, national governments, rather than parliaments, played a central role in the accession process and delegated the task to officials rather than to politicians (Grabbe 2001: 1017). In the long run, this may have had the impact of increasing perceptions of a democratic deficit, and of a lack of legitimacy of the EU in these countries. Women in particular were underrepresented at the accession negotiation tables, among both the representatives of the EU and the delegations from the candidate countries (Steinhilber 2002: 4). There were no women in powerful positions within the EU to apply pressure to advance gender equality in the process (Locher and Prügl 2009). Short deadlines resulted in the exclusion of broader civil society (Kakucs and Pető 2008: 180). Co-operation between the EU women's organizations, such as the EWL, and women's organizations from the CEECs started so late that it did not 'significantly contribute to the capacity of CEE women's NGOs to participate in civic dialogue, advocacy and lobbying at the EU level before accession', according to Kinga Lohmann (2005: 1114), the chair of the Karat Coalition.

Overall, the success of NGOs in gaining access to their national governments in the CEECs varied greatly despite EU emphasis on involving civil society. For example, in the Czech Republic NGOs were sidelined in the EU accession process (Einhorn 2006: 39). In Poland, in order to ensure a yes vote for EU membership in the referendum, the Polish government made a highly controversial deal with the powerful Catholic Church in the country. In return for support for EU membership, the government silenced the proponents of change in the country's strict anti-abortion law (Regulska and Grabowska 2008: 149). This effectively illustrated that the government's willingness to co-operate with women's NGOs and to further gender equality was limited. The women's organizations also felt abused by the new structures. They had to provide expertise in gender questions to government officials without being paid for their work and the issues that were addressed were dictated by the EU gender equality agenda rather than by country-specific equality problems (Hašková 2005: 1090).

Indeed in some cases the EU seems to have provided tools for lobbying at the national rather than supranational level of policy-making. For example, the women's movements in the Czech Republic intensified their efforts to influence government policy through the newly established gender equality bodies, whilst the European level of policy-making was perceived as remaining distant (Hašková 2005: 1090). This was exacerbated by the fact that the European Commission was reluctant to take direct feedback from the women's movements which drafted a 'shadow report' on the government's gender equality priorities. Whilst the organizations had hoped to attract EU attention to the remaining problems, the Commission were unwelcoming to such attempts and called for the problems to be solved 'at home' (Hašková 2005: 1093).

The new avenues for project funding for NGOs that the accession process provided posed some serious challenges for women's organizations in these countries. Many of them were highly reliant on foreign money, and with EU accession this was cut as international donors assumed that these funds were no longer necessary (Fuchs and Payer 2007: 166, Hašková and Křižková 2008: 164, Roth 2007: 473, Sloat 2005: 441). For example, the ASTRA federation, which seeks to prevent a backlash against reproductive rights in the conservative new member states, had its funding cut after EU accession and faced severe financial difficulties. The financial problems were further exacerbated by the NGOs not having the experience, knowledge or human resources to apply for EU funds. Here the EU's accounting rules, late payment schedules, bureaucracy and inaccessibility seriously undermine local NGOs' access to EU funding (Fuchs and Payer 2007: 168). Alternatively they did not meet the requirements of EU donors, for example to have sufficient matching funds, called 'co-funding' (Roth 2007: 473). EU funds are difficult to acquire for staff costs, administration or capacity building but are instead available for networking, media, technology and communications work, and leadership development (Fuchs and Payer 2007: 168). This can result in the 'projectisation of gender equality' work (Brunila 2009; see also Chapter 7) and the redirection of policy priorities and constructions of women's concerns towards those preferred by the funding bodies (Forest 2006: 178). Scarce funding has led women's NGOs to compete for resources and sometimes hindered the formation of alliances between them in these countries (Hašková and Křižková 2008: 164, Sloat 2005: 444).

It has also resulted in many re-labelling their activities away from women's or feminist issues in order to qualify for EU funding programmes on development or human rights (Fuchs and Payer 2007: 166). Feminism has been a pejorative term in most central and eastern European countries, associated either with foreign western ideologies or the official communist equality ideology. Furthermore, many of these countries have experienced a conservative backlash with a new central role for the Catholic Church and patriarchal family structures (Fuszara 2005). The EU principle of subsidiarity has shifted the financial aid agendas to national governments who then allocate money to NGOs. This poses problems for feminist organizations who are forced to look to national governments for funding whilst being critical of their policies (Fuchs and Payer 2007: 167). It empowers national governments to give resources to those actors favourable to their agenda. In some countries, for example in Latvia, this has also revealed a backlash against feminist organizations. The fact that EU funding, such as the structural funds, is mediated through government ministries has enabled some conservative governments to withold funds from organizations critical of their policies.

Conclusion

Europeanization is an increasingly complex phenomenon that can be studied in terms of hard law and soft law, as well as ideas, discourses, norms and frames, and different political actors. Its impact on member states and candidate countries is by no means uniform; instead a great deal of diversity in national gender regimes has been preserved in member states. It is also a hierarchical process shot through with power relations, in that Europeanization processes mean different things for different member states. This challenges some of the key concepts in Europeanization theory, such as compliance, and points to the usefulness of new concepts such as 'political usage by actors'. However, the lack of uniform uni-directional change in member states towards a European gender regime does not diminish the importance of understanding some broad trends. One of these is the tendency towards deregulation and soft governance implied by soft Europeanization. Whilst appearing to be value-neutral, such forms of Europeanization promote a particular managerialist form of governance that has the potential to change national gender equality policies and the context where gender advocates operate in subtle and often hidden ways.

Chapter 10

Conclusion

Feminist studies of the European Union seek to make sense of a field that has become enormously complex. Gender equality has been an issue in the EU since the inclusion of Article 119 on equal pay in the Treaty of Rome 1957 but has since widened to the recognition of equality between women and men as a fundamental principle of democracy for the whole of the EU. Gender equality is present not only in gender-specific policies, such as women's participation in the labour market, reconciliation of work and family, and political representation of women in parliaments, but it also informs the basic principles and functioning of the EU institutions wherever gender mainstreaming is implemented. Whilst a few decades ago it made sense to study which member state or EU institution initiated particular policy initiatives, such as the equal pay or equal treatment directives, the range of actors involved in gender policy-making has now widened, making this task ever more difficult. 27 member states also convey multiple meanings and understandings of women, men, gender and gender equality (see Verloo 2007).

This concluding chapter will, first, analyze the Lisbon Treaty from a gender perspective and discuss its significance for the EU gender regime. Second, the chapter will evaluate the EU in terms of its *gender policy*, gendered *institutions and processes*, *actors* and *discourses*, and the multi-faceted interaction between the EU and the member states, namely *Europeanization*.

Looking ahead: The Lisbon Treaty

The EU decision-making structures and processes will undergo some significant changes under the Reform Treaty signed in Lisbon in December 2007. The Lisbon Treaty provides that the Union shall have a single legal personality, and be founded on the two amended treaties, which shall have the same legal value, the three pillars being merged. In order to come into force the Lisbon Treaty had to be ratified by all member states, which delayed the process (Koukoulis-Spiliotopoulos 2008: 16).

It is, therefore, pertinent to ask what the negotiations for the treaty and its entry into force mean for gender equality in the EU. In the first place, a focus on the place of gender in the negotiations that preceded the treaty sheds doubt on the central democratic questions of participation, consultation, and openness in the EU. For example, in 2003, only 18 out of 105 members of the Convention on the Future of Europe were women (17 per cent), and a similar pattern can be discerned among the observers. The negotiations were also marked by a hierarchy of positions with fewer women at the top (Lombardo 2007a: 146, Mateo Diaz 2004: 214, Millns 2007: 221–2). The concerns of NGOs were marginalized too and the 'emphasis on the civil society was a rhetorical device to gain legitimacy rather than a genuine move towards a more pluralistic EU democracy' (Lombardo 2007a: 154). Civil society organizations, including NGOs and trade unions, regarded 'Social Europe' and social policy as the most important fields, whereas the final outcome prioritized the neoliberal and market-oriented tendencies of the Union (Lombardo 2007a: 155). The concerns of the organizations also included the environment, equality and non-discrimination, the role of civil society, democracy, citizenship, human rights and poverty, all issues that were largely sidelined in the treaty and the process leading up to it (Lombardo 2007: 164). This reflects the trend discussed in Chapter 4 that the EU prefers to listen to certain centralized voices that share its views. Furthermore, Chapter 8 illustrated how civil society groups representing different inequality strands were differently positioned in relation to making the market-based claims that have most value in the EU. Some concerns such as those of sexual orientation do not translate easily to this language but rely instead on human rights and justice norms.

In terms of the contents of the treaty, there are, however, some things to celebrate from a gender perspective (see, for example, EWL 2004). Gender equality is listed among the fundamental values of the Union (Article 2). Its inclusion was achieved through persistent lobbying by activists and academics in a difficult environment (Bell 2004, Lombardo 2007: 142, Millns 2007: 229). The position of gender equality means that it should be one of the yardsticks for determining whether a member state is in breach of these values and therefore liable to sanctions, as well as determining whether a state can be a candidate for accession (Koukoulis-Spiliotopoulos 2008: 18).

Furthermore, the treaty makes explicit reference to women and sexual exploitation in two of the articles on combating trafficking. Declaration 19 annexed to the Final Act of the 2007 Intergovernmental Conference confirms that domestic violence is a gender equality issue and that it is the Union's and member states' obligation to combat it in all areas (see Chapter 7). The power of this formulation remains to be seen. At best, the declaration may mean that the instruments implementing gender equality in relation to domestic violence will have a 'clear legal basis' (Koukoulis-Spiliotopoulos 2008: 22).

Gender was not, however, successfully mainstreamed into all parts of the treaty itself. Whilst gender is mentioned in relation to combating trafficking, it is absent from areas such as health, culture and education where combating cultural gender stereotypes would be pertinent, as well as finance and foreign and security policy that both have a significant gendered impact (Lombardo 2007: 145). The treaty is thus an example of the way in which the EU fails to implement gender mainstreaming in its own legislation and policies, as discussed in Chapter 6.

A lot of the debate centres around the Charter of Fundamental Rights of the European Union to which the Lisbon Treaty refers. On the one hand, a number of commentators point out that the Lisbon Treaty would strengthen a human rights approach to gender equality through references to the Charter (Beveridge 2008: 14). As a fundamental right, equality is no longer restricted to the internal market, but must be guaranteed in all areas of the Community and within all pillars (Masselot 2007: 155–6). Hence the Charter further 'enhances the visibility and the clarity of gender equality as human rights' (Masselot 2007: 157). Whilst discrimination on the grounds of nationality is still often addressed with the aim of making the internal market more effective, equality and discrimination on other grounds are now treated mainly in the fundamental rights context (Nielsen 2008: 38).

On the other hand, others, such as the European Network of Legal Experts in the field of Gender Equality and a number of academics have voiced critiques and concerns about the some of the formulations in the Charter (Koukoulis-Spiliotopoulos 2008: 16, Lombardo 2007, Millns 2007: 231). First, there are some discrepancies between the norms pertaining to gender equality in treaties (*acquis communautaire*) and secondary law (directives) on the one hand, and the Charter and the Lisbon Treaty on the other hand. The divergence and different provisions are in danger of creating confusion that may make it harder to enforce these rights. For example, the Network feels that the fundamental rights already guaranteed by EU law are stronger in a number of places than those in the Charter and the Lisbon Treaty (Koukoulis-Spiliotopoulos 2008: 16).

This confusion is created by the fact that some of the existing provisions are weakened in the new treaty. For example, the Charter's Article 23 states that 'Equality between women and men must be ensured in all areas, including employment, work and pay.' The formulation is welcome in that it covers all areas, not just traditional EC fields of competences such as employment and equal pay (Millns 2007: 231). However, it also has some weaknesses in that it does not match Article 141 of the EC Treaty guaranteeing equal pay for equal work or work of equal value. Furthermore, the Charter does not create a right for individuals to invoke it and is presented as a more general statement of intent (Millns 2007: 231). This means that the direct effect of the principles discussed in Chapter 2 is weakened (Koukoulis-Spiliotopoulos 2008: 18). The possibility of positive action is also expressed in a 'watered-down version' of the Lisbon Treaty's Article 141-4-EC counterpart and formulated as: 'The principle of equality shall not prevent the maintenance or adoption of measures providing for specific advantages in favour of the under-represented sex.' This, according to commentators, 'admits only a derogation from the equality principle and does not match the Article 141-4's acknowledgement that positive measures are means or tools to promote substantive gender equality' (Millns 2007: 231). Susan Millns suggests that 'where the content of the Charter does not match the *acquis* the very advantage of visibility and showcasing of the Charter rights becomes a disadvantage' (Millns 2007: 231).

In conclusion, neither the legal basis of gender policy nor gender mainstreaming was significantly strengthened in the long process of treaty-making. Again, 'the goal of gender equality had to give way to other priorities' such as reforming the institutions of the Union, its competencies and principles such as subsidiarity (Lombardo 2007: 151). Nevertheless, these reforms are likely to have gendered implications, as illustrated by the earlier discussions in this book and this concluding chapter on the gendered consequences of EU institutions and processes. The Treaty will also create some new high-powered jobs, which will politicize issues surrounding gender balanced representation.

Assessing gender and the European Union

Taking stock of EU gender policy as expressed by equal opportunities directives, by gender policies such as those on family and violence, or by general policies such as trade and agriculture is rather challenging because of the ever-expanding scope of this policy. The chapters in this book have discussed three fields in more detail: reconciling work, family and care, employment, and violence. The first, reconciling work and family, represents a key field of gender policy from the perspective of the European Union, and is a field prioritized in policy documents such as the Roadmap for Equality. The second, employment, was discussed as an example of a mainstream policy area where gender mainstreaming has been used to integrate a gender perspective. Finally, violence was explored as an issue that has become a top priority for feminist activists and gender equality advocates at EU level.

EU gender policy has traditionally focused on providing equal access for women to the labour market and removing discriminatory practices in the member states. The policy field of reconciling work and family continues this trend. It is a field where the EU has been able to enact binding directives on, for example, pregnant workers and parental leave. These have often only set minimum standards, not going beyond existing member state provisions, but have sometimes resulted in important changes in member states' legislation. The EU has been particularly powerful in developing an anti-discrimination policy in the field, which has also signified progressive definitions of such concepts as direct and indirect discrimination. These have extended to issues such as sexual harassment not previously defined as discrimination. Policies in the field of reconciling work and family have been shaped by institutional constraints and policy-making processes, such as the prominent role given to the social partners in drafting framework directives and the principle of subsidiarity which has curtailed centralized EU action. Care policies, by contrast, have been promoted in terms of soft law and soft regulation and their impact on member states remains more variable than that of the binding hard law.

This book's assessment of the success of gender mainstreaming in bringing a gender perspective to the field of employment was slightly more critical. Whilst gender mainstreaming has been an important tool in extending the gender perspective to fields such as development and employment policy, the dominance of economic concerns like market flexibility continues to hamper the efforts. This has resulted in the promotion of women's labour market participation in a way that means that quantitative increases are seen as a success, with a lesser focus on what kind of jobs women enter. Such structural and substantive gender equality concerns are not easily addressed when gender mainstreaming is implemented in an integrated and technical way in a policy field such as employment. Rather the policy field and gender mainstreaming interact in a way that ensures that the gender perspective does not challenge EU priorities although these may not be ideal for achieving gender equality.

Gender violence is an example of an issue that has been and is a top feminist priority that has been taken up by the EU too. This could be considered as a feminist success. Whilst trafficking in women is a field where the EU has been willing to use hard law, its policies on domestic violence have relied on soft governance and have, for example, been developed through funding programmes. Our focus on different ways of constructing and framing the two issues illustrates that constructing the policy problem emphasizing trafficking as an aspect of transnational crime or domestic violence as a public health problem can seriously narrow down the positive impact of these policies on gender equality.

EU equality policy has expanded not only to new fields but also, since the end of the 1990s, to cover multiple equality strands that include race and ethnicity, religion and belief, age, disability and sexual orientation. Whilst most member states had existing family policies promoting certain patterns of reconciling work and family, well-established employment policies, and some policies on gender violence, the issue of multiple discrimination that EU action in this field is higlighting is a new area for most member states. The term multiple discrimination requires gender to be considered in conjunction with other bases of inequality. In the EU, it also means promoting new institutional solutions to tackling inequality, for example by favouring single equality bodies in its soft law documents. In addition to merging equality bodies, some member states have drafted single pieces of legislation covering the different grounds of inequality. In the future, this trend is likely to have policy consequences and lead to debates about 'diversity mainstreaming' (see, for example, Beveridge and Nott 2002, Shaw 2004, Squires 2005 and 2007, Verloo 2006) that will enable consideration of different policy fields in terms of their impact on diverse inequalities. The challenge will be to take into account the different structural bases that these inequalities have and to address normative questions in situations where the inequalities compete; where, for example, religion and gender might point to opposite solutions.

Studying the EU institutions, actors, processes, and discourses brings to the foreground their gendered patterns. Chapter 3 illustrated both moves towards gender-balanced decision-making in the key EU political institutions and also the persistent power imbalances. Chapter 4, in turn, discussed the gender policy network that consists of European level women's organizations and women's policy agencies. The European Women's Lobby has come to occupy a central position in defining what constitutes women's concerns in today's Europe, although its power in relation to the Commission may be rather limited.

The Council, the Commission, the Parliament and the Court have all both advanced and hampered gender equality. The Council often appears as a problematic actor in gender equality policy. It has blocked reforms in the past and still does, and it has been insulated from civil society influence including the voices of gender advocates. When addressing issues relevant to gender equality, its constructions of the policy problems have emphasized aspects seen as vital to 'national interests'. One example discussed in Chapter 7 was the framing of trafficking in women in terms of transnational crime and illegal immigration. However, the rotating Council Presidencies have enabled individual member states holding the presidency to put forward gender equality as one of their priority areas. For example, the presidencies of Austria, Finland, Belgium, France and Sweden increased the pressure for gender equality to become one of the four pillars in the original European Employment Strategy. Domestic violence has also been kept on the EU political agenda by different presidencies of the Council.

The role of Commission has often been crucial in terms of gender equality in the EU. It has, for example, played a key role in the construction of women's organizations and policy agencies at EU level. It has also been relatively open to lobbying by these organizations and has integrated some of the expert information provided by NGOs into its policy-making. The Commission lobbied for the introduction of gender mainstreaming into the UN Beijing Platform for Action in the 1990s and then used this international pressure to push for gender mainstreaming in the EU.

Its powers to further gender equality have also been limited.

Chapter 3 illustrated that its hands were tied in relation to promoting gender-balanced decision-making in many of its preparatory bodies as the member states were responsible for nominations. Of course, some of these issues could be tackled by, for example, making the member states nominate both a female and a male candidate from whom the Commission could then choose a gender-balanced body. However, the Commission has also demonstrated that its political commitment to gender equality can be limited and overtaken by other concerns that appear more important or more pressing. This has been aptly illustrated by the fate of gender mainstreaming in EU policy and in the Commission.

Similarly the European Court of Justice (ECJ) has both deepened the meaning of EU legislation, for example on the rights of pregnant workers, and provided restrictive rulings as in the case of positive action. The European Parliament, by contrast, is most often discussed with reference to its positive role in promoting gender equality. A focus on the gendered patterns of representation in its Committees in Chapter 3 showed, however, that top positions continue to be male dominated and that Committee work is also segregated by gender. However, many of the Committees and MEPs have well-developed contacts with civil society organizations which provide access for gender advocates' concerns and framings of policy problems.

The chapters in the book have also provided examples of the impact of policy-making principles such as subsidiarity and processes such as the enhanced role of social partners in drafting legislation on gender equality. Both subsidiarity and the Social Dialogue are examples of the trend towards deregulation and decentralized decision-making in the EU. In relation to the position of women's organizations in the member states, Chapter 9 illustrated some of the detrimental consequences of the principle of subsidiarity: it has shifted the financial aid agenda to national governments who then allocate money to NGOs. This poses problems for feminist organizations which are forced to look to national governments for funding whilst being critical of their policies. In some policy fields, such as childcare, subsidiarity has meant that childcare is seen as a policy issue where national and regional governments, local authorities, and social partners should decide how and to what extent employed parents are supported. As a result, little progress has been made in childcare policy. Chapter 5, in turn, provided examples of the impact of the role of social partners in legislation relevant to reconciling work and family. For example, in the negotiations for the Parental Leave Directive 1996 the procedure reinforced the economic agenda and priorities through the roles played by the employers' and employees' unions (Guerrina 2005: 77). Furthermore, in terms of access and voice, and the reduced role of the European Parliament, the procedure continues to be a challenge from a gender perspective.

When studying gender and the EU from the perspective of Europeanization, the focus shifts to the complex interaction of policies, institutions, processes, actors and discourses between the subnational, national and supranational levels. On the one hand, some examples cited in the book have illustrated that the EU does put pressure on member states to move towards common policies, standards and norms. In the past, the Equal Treatment Directive 1976 contained novel provisions on direct and indirect discrimination. Currently, the issue of multiple discrimination has been placed by the EU on many member states' agendas. The EU impact can also be more subtle and indirect and it can shape member state gender equality norms with softer methods that set priorities and goals rather than definitive hard law that needs to be transposed. On the other hand, studying Europeanization shifts the focus to the actual implementation of the EU gender norms in the member states and qualifies the success of this policy. Rather than converge, member states may prove resistant and diverge in their gender policies. This pattern is further strengthened by the soft modes of governance, such as the Open Method of Co-ordination (OMC). A new trend in research, not discussed in this book, would be to extend consideration of the impact of the EU gender norms and policies beyond their impact on member states and candidate countries. Gender analyses of EU foreign and security policy (Valenius 2007) and neighbourhood policy are starting to emerge (Freedman 2009, van der Vleuten 2008). They provide further insights into the discrepancies between, for example, the Commission actions within the EU and the norms that it sets for outside countries. However, they also illustrate the growing relevance and the enhanced need to understand the EU gender policy.

Appendix: Women's Policy Agencies in the EU

Parliament

1. Committee on Women's Rights and Equal Opportunities

Background

Set up as a permanent committee in 1984, known as the Committee on Women's Rights; since 15 April 1999 has had a new name and new powers.

Responsibilities

–   Define, develop and implement women's rights in the Union and promote women's rights in non-member states.
–   Achieve and pursue gender mainstreaming.
–   Put in place and evaluate all policies and programmes concerning women.
–   Monitor and implement international agreements and conventions concerned with women's rights.
–   Information policy and research on women.
–   Equal opportunities policy (Art. 141 ECT).
–   Ongoing monitoring of budget implementation in the area of its responsibilities, on the basis of reports provided periodically by the Commission.

Activities

–   Meets every month, draws up numerous reports and opinions leading to resolutions adopted in Parliament and organizes hearings on various topics.
–   In 1999 the Committee organized a campaign against violence against women.
–   Played a part in launching the DAPHNE programme and initiative on measures to support, measures to combat violence against children, young people and women.

2. Committee on Equal Opportunities for men and women (COPEC)

Background

Parliament's COPEC is part of DG V (Directorate-General for Personnel).

Responsibilities

–   Establish a work atmosphere where everyone's dignity is respected.
–   Rearrange working hours to make it possible to combine work and family.
–   Promote part-time work.

- Make arrangements for CCP (leave on personal grounds), parental leave and family leave.
- Improve child care.
- Ensure equal opportunities in recruitment, career management, vocational training and access to decision-making positions.
- Ensure greater participation by women in internal committees and bodies.

Activities

- Draws up equal opportunities action programmes 1997–2000.
- COPEC delegates from the Council, the Parliament, the Court of Justice, the Economic and Social Committee and the Commission, and an observer from the Committee of the Regions, meet in the Intercopec (joint equal opportunities inter-committees). This makes proposals on reforms to the Staff Regulations and monitors problems concerning women and men in all areas of work.

Commission

1. Advisory Committee on Equal Opportunities for Women and Men

Background

1981: 2 representatives from each member state and from the two sides of industry at European level. Observers include the EWL, the Council of Europe, the ILO, and the EEA countries.

Responsibilities

- Assist the Commission in drawing up and implementing its policy on the promotion of women's interests, women's employment and equal opportunities.
- Maintain an ongoing exchange of information on developments and action in these areas throughout the EU.

Activities

- Exchanges information with the Commission and issues opinions or draft reports for the Commission.
- Once a year the Committee is invited by the Group of Commissioners on equal opportunities for men and women and women's rights to a joint meeting with delegations from the European Parliament, the Committee of the Regions, the ESC and the EWL.

2. Unit of Equal Opportunities between Women and Men: Strategy and Programme

Background

1976: Directorate-General Employment and Social Affairs.

Responsibilities

- Ensure compliance with EU directives on equal opportunities.
- Devise and implement action programmes to promote gender equality.
- Encourage the integration of women into the labour market and improve the status of women in society.
- Include the gender element in EU policies and activities.

Activities

- Monitors the application of equal opportunities legislation.
- Submits new legislative proposals .
- Supports transnational projects to promote equality between men and women in the areas of employment, combining work with family life, the media, decision-making and mainstreaming.
- Assists the group of European experts on equality between women and men.

3. Unit of Equal Opportunities between Women and Men: Legal Questions

Background

1983 (2005)

Responsibilities

- Ensure the effective transposition and implementation of Community legislation and initiates new legislative proposals if necessary.

4. The Group of Commissioners on Fundamental Rights, Anti-discrimination and Equal Opportunities

Background

Formerly High Level Group of Commissioners on Equality Between Men and Women (1996). Established under new mandate in 2005.

Responsibilities

- Develop policy and ensure the coherence of action taken by the Commission.
- Ensure that the gender equality dimension is taken into account in the framework of all relevant Community policies and actions, in accordance with article 3(2) of the Treaty of Amsterdam.

Activities

- Commissioners responsible for these issues meet three to four times a year.

5. High Level Group on Gender Mainstreaming

Background

An informal forum for discussion and exchange of information on gender mainstreaming set up by the Commission in 2002.

Responsibilities

– Support presidencies in identifying relevant policy areas during a European Council.
– Plan the strategic follow-up of the Beijing Platform for action.
– Assist the Commission in the preparation of the Report on Equality between Women and Men to the European Council.

Activities

– Meets twice a year, one representative from the women's policy agencies in each member state and four officials from DG Employment.

6. Higher Level Group on Gender Mainstreaming in the Structural Funds

Background

An informal group set up in 2004, high level representatives responsible for Structural Funds at national level in the Member States, chaired by the Commission.

Responsibilities

– Give input on gender mainstreaming to the authorities managing Structural Funds implementation.
– Forum to exchange best practice and experience of implementing gender mainstreaming in the structural funds at national level.

Activities

– At least one meeting per year.

7. Gender and Law Expert Group

Background

Set up under the Fourth equal opportunities Action Programme (1996–2000).

Responsibilities

– Monitor legal developments in the member states in the area of equal opportunities.

8. Gender and Employment Expert Group

Background

Set up under the Fourth equal opportunities Action Programme (1996–2000).

Responsibilities

– Analyze the obstacles, problems and challenges to women in the area of employment at European level.

9. Expert Group on Gender, Social Inclusion and Employment (EGGSIE)

Background

Set up in 1998.

Responsibilities

– Evaluate national action plans under the European Employment Strategy (EES) from a gender perspective.
– Develop gender-specific indicators.

10. Advisory Committee Women and Rural Areas

Background

Set up in 1998, made up of representatives of socio-economic organizations (agricultural producers, trade,consumers, the European Women's Lobby and workers).

Responsibilities

Provide for exchange of views and advice between Commission and the European socio-economic sector on rural development policy and specifically on its gender aspects.

Activities

Commission convenes meetings once or twice per year.

11. Family and Work European Network

Background

Set up in 1994 as part of the International Year of the Family.

Responsibilities

– Study, disseminate and exchange innovative practices in the area of combining work and family life.

12. European Monitoring Centre on National Family Policies

Background

Set up by the Commission in 1989; multidisciplinary network of independent experts coordinated by the Austrian Institute for Family Studies.

Responsibilities

Study trends in different forms of family structure, demographic change and the impact of various policies on the family.

13. Women's Information Division

Responsibilities

– Disseminate information about EU measures in favour of women.
– Maintain a permanent dialogue between the Commission and women throughout the EU.

Activities

– Monthly newsletter, 'Women of Europe' (in 11 languages; 25,000 copies distributed to women's associations, relay networks, libraries and individuals).
– Organize, every two years, a 'Prix Niki' awarded to European TV producers who portray women and men in non-traditional ways in TV programmes.
– In 1999, played a role in the European Campaign to raise awareness of violence against women.

14. Women and Development Unit

Background

Established in 1990 in the DG External Relations.

Responsibilities

– Ensure that women's needs and priorities are fully taken into account in Commission-funded development co-operation.

Activities

– Responsible for its own budget line since 1992 .
– Funds are intended to finance strategies for incorporating the needs of women into large-scale programmes rather than funding small-scale action projects for women, which would have a more limited impact.

15. Inter-service Group on Gender Equality

Background

Established in 1996, chaired by DG Employment, Social Affairs and Equal Opportunities.

Responsibilities

- Bring together representatives of all Commission services.
- Develop gender mainstreaming activities, contribute to and co-ordinate activities in the annual work programmes on Gender Equality, monitor their implementation and exchange experience and good practice.

16. Expert Group on Trafficking in Human Beings

Background

Set up in 2003, consists of 20 people appointed as independent experts.

Responsibilities

- Commission consults the expert group on any matter relating to trafficking in human beings.
- Issue opinions or reports to the Commission at the latter's request or on its own initiative, taking into consideration the recommendations set out in Brussels Declaration.

17. Group of Experts on Gender Equality in Development Co-operation

Background

Informal group, set up in 1999, formed by member states' gender experts.

Responsibilities

Discuss policy developments in relation to gender and development in the context of EU and international major events.

Activities

Chaired by the Commission, which convenes meetings annually.

18. Cooperation Helsinki Group on Women and Science

Background

1999, national representatives from all the EU member states.

Responsibilities

- Promote the participation and equality of women in the sciences on a Europe-wide basis.
- Provide a forum for dialogue about national policies.
- Help the Commission build a picture of the situation on the ground at the national level.

Activities

Has appointed national statistical correspondents to help the Commission gather and compile sex-disaggregated statistics and build gender-sensitive indicators.

19. The European Network to Promote Women's Entrepreneurship (WES)

Background

Created in 2000, composed of representatives from the national governments and institutions responsible for the promotion of female entrepreneurship in 27 countries from the EU, EEA and candidate countries.

Responsibilities

- Exchange information and good practice in the promotion of female entrepreneurship.

Activities

Commission convenes meetings twice a year.

20. Network of Gender Focal Points

Background

Informal.
Formed by representatives of Directorates-General of the Commission dealing with external relations and development co-operation as well as representatives of EC delegations.

21. Network of Focal Points on Equal Opportunities

Background

Set up in 2004.
Formed by representatives of all Directorates-General of the Commission in charge of human resources.

Responsibilities

– Ensure proper implementation of the Fourth Action Programme for Equal Opportunities for Women and Men at the European Commission.
– Contribute to the respect of gender equality in the human resources policy of the Commission.

Sources: European Parliament, Directorate-General for Research (1999) Working paper 'Institutions and bodies responsible for equality between women and men', Women's Rights Series, FEMM 10; European Commission (2006c).

Bibliography

Agustín, Laura (2005). 'Migrants and Mistress's House: Other Voice in the "Trafficking" Debate.' *Social Politics: International Studies in Gender, State & Society* 12 (1): 96–117.

Ahrens, Petra (2008). 'More actors butter no parsnips: Gaining insights into gender equality programs of the European Union', a paper presented in the ECPR Fourth Pan-European Conference on EU Politics, 22–27 September 2008, Riga, Latvia.

Ahtela, Karoliina (2005). 'The Revised Provisions on Sex Discrimination in European Law: A Critical Assessment.' *European Law Journal* 11 (1) 57–78.

Aldıkaçtı-Marshall, Gül (2008). 'Preparing for EU membership: Gender Policies in Turkey.' In Silke Roth (ed.), *Gender Politics in the Expanding European Union: Mobilization, Inclusion, Exclusion*. New York and Oxford: Berghahn Books.

Aliaga, Christel (2005). *Gender gaps in the reconciliation between work and family life. Statistics in focus*. 4/2005 Luxembourg: Eurostat.

Alter, Karen J. and Jeanette Vargas (2000). 'Explaining Variation in the Use of European Litigation Strategies: European Community Law and British Gender Equality Policy.' *Comparative Political Studies* 33 (4): 452–82.

Anderson, Leah Seppanen (2006). 'European Union Gender Regulations in the East: The Czech and Polish Accession Process.' *East European Politics and Society* 20 (1): 101–25.

Angulo, Gloria and Christian Freres (2006). 'Gender Equality and EU Development Policy towards Latin America.' In Marjorie Lister and Maurizio Carbone (eds), *New pathways in development: gender and civil society in EU policy*. Aldershot: Ashgate.

Annesley, Claire (2007). 'Lisbon and social Europe: towards a European "adult worker model" welfare system.' *Journal of European Social Policy* 17 (3): 195–205.

Anthias, Floya and Nira Yuval-Davis (1992). *Racialized Boundaries: Race, Nation, Gender, Colour and Class and the Anti-racist Struggle*. London: Routledge.

Aradau, Claudia (2008). *Rethinking Trafficking in Women. Politics Out of Security*. Basingstoke: Palgrave Macmillan.

Armstrong, Kenneth A. (2001). 'Civil Society and the White Paper - Bridging or Jumping the Gaps?' Jean Monnet Working Paper No.6/01, Symposium: Mountain or Molehill? A Critical Appraisal of the Commission White Paper on Governance.

Arts, Karin (2006). 'Gender and ACP-EU Relations: The Cotonous Agreement.' In Marjorie Lister and Maurizio Carbone (eds), *New pathways in development: gender and civil society in EU policy*. Aldershot: Ashgate.

Askola, Heli (2007). 'Violence against Women, Trafficking, and Migration in the European Union.' *European Law Journal* 13 (2): 204–17.

Askola, Heli (2007a). *Legal Responses to Trafficking in Women for Sexual Exploitation in the European Union*. Oxford: Hart Publishing.

232

Avdeyeva, Olga (2006). 'In support of mothers' employment: limits to policy convergence in the EU?' *International Journal of Social Welfare* 15 (1): 37–49.

Aybars, Ayse Idil (2008). 'The European Employment Strategy and the Europeanization of Gender Equality in Employment.' In Fiona Beveridge and Samantha Velluti (eds), *Gender and the Open Method of Coordination: Perspectives on Law, Governance and Equality in the EU*. Aldershot: Ashgate.

Bacchi, Carol Lee (1999). *Women, Policy and Politics. The Construction of Policy Problems*. London: Sage.

Bacchi, Carol (2009). 'The issue of intentionality in frame theory: the need for reflexive framing.' In Emanuela Lombardo, Petra Meier and Mieke Verloo (eds), *The Discursive Politics of Gender Equality: Stretching, Bending and Policymaking*. London: Routledge.

Baden, S. and Anne-Marie Goetz (1997). 'Who needs [sex] when you can have [gender]? Conflicting discourses on gender at Beijing.' *Feminist Review* 56 Summer, 3–25.

Banaszak, Lee-Ann, Karen Beckwith and Dieter Rucht (2003). 'When Power Relocates: Interactive Changes in Women's Movements and States.' In Lee-Ann Banaszak, Karen Beckwith and Dieter Rucht (eds), *Women's Movements Facing the Reconfigured State*. Cambridge: Cambridge University Press.

Barry, Kathleen (1995). *The Prostitution of Sexuality: The Global Exploitation of Women*. New York: New York University Press.

Barth, Erling, Marianne Røed and Hege Torp (2002). *Towards a Closing of the Gender Pay Gap: A comparative study of three occupations in six European countries*. Oslo: Institute for Social Research.

Bell, Mark (2000). 'Equality and diversity: Anti-discrimination law after Amsterdam.' In Jo Shaw (ed.), *Social Law and Policy in an Evolving European Union*. Oxford-Portland: Hart Publishing.

Bell, Mark (2002). *Anti-Discrimination Law and the European Union*. Oxford: Oxford University Press.

Bell, Mark (2002a). 'Beyond European Labour Law? Reflections on the EU Racial Equality Directive.' *European Law Journal* 8 (3): 384–99.

Bell, Mark (2004). 'Equality and the European Union Constitution.' *The Industrial Law Journal* 33 (3): 242–60.

Bell, Mark (2008). 'The Implementation of European Anti-Discrimination Directives: Converging Towards a Common Model?' *Political Quarterly* 79 (1): 36–44.

Bergqvist, Christina , Anette Borchorst, Ann-Dorte Christensen, Viveca Ramstedt-Silen, Nina C. Raaum and Audur Styrkasdóttir (eds.) (1999). *Equal Democracies: Gender and Politics in the Nordic Countries*. Oslo: Scandinavian University Press.

Berman, Jacqueline (2003). '(Un)Popular Strangers and Crises (Un)Bounded: Discourses of Sex-Trafficking, the European Political Community and the Panicked State of the Modern State.' *European Journal of International Relations* 9 (1) :37–86.

Beveridge, Fiona (2007). 'Building Against the Past: The Impact of Mainstreaming on EU Gender Law and Policy.' *European Law Review* 32: 193–212.

Beveridge, Fiona (2008). 'Implementing Gender Equality and Mainstreaming in an Enlarged European Union: Prospects and Challenges.' In Fiona Beveridge and Samantha Velluti (eds), *Gender and the Open Method of Coordination: Perspectives on Law, Governance and Equality in the EU*. Aldershot: Ashgate.

Beveridge, Fiona and Sue Nott (2002). 'Mainstreaming: A Case for Optimism and Cynicism.' *Feminist Legal Studies* 10: 299–311.

Beveridge, Fiona, Sue Nott and Kylie Stephen (2000). 'Mainstreaming and the Engendering of Policy-Making: a Means to an End?' *Journal of European Public Policy* 7 (3): 385–405.

Beveridge, Fiona, Sue Nott and Kylie Stephen (2002). 'Addressing Gender in National and Community Law and Policy-Making.' In Jo Shaw (ed.), *Social Law and Policy in an Evolving European Union*. Oxford-Portland: Hart Publishing.

Beveridge, Fiona and Jo Shaw (2002). 'Introduction: Mainstreaming Gender in European Public Policy.' *Feminist Legal Studies* 10: 209–12.

Beveridge, Fiona and Samantha Velluti (eds) (2008). *Gender and the Open Method of Coordination: Perspectives on Law, Governance and Equality in the EU*. Aldershot: Ashgate.

Beveridge, Fiona and Samantha Velluti (2008a). 'Gender and the OMC: Conclusions and Prospects.' In Fiona Beveridge and Samantha Velluti (eds), *Gender and the Open Method of Coordination: Perspectives on Law, Governance and Equality in the EU*. Aldershot: Ashgate.

Black, J. H. (2000). 'Entering the Political Elite in Canada: The Case of Minority Women As Parliamentary Candidates and MPs.' *Canadian Review of Sociology and Anthropology* 37 (2): 143–66.

Bleijenbergh, Inge, Jeanne de Bruijn and Jet Bussemaker (2004). 'European Social Citizenship and Gender: The Part-time Work Directive.' *European Journal of Industrial Relations* 10 (3): 309–28.

Bleijenbergh, Inge, Jet Bussemaker and Jeanne de Bruijn (2006). 'Trading Well-Being for Economic Efficiency: The 1990 Shift in EU Childcare Politics.' *Marriage and Family Review* 39 (3/4): 315–36.

Börzel, Tanja A. (2005). 'Mind the gap! European integration between level and scope.' *Journal of European Public Policy* 12 (2): 217–36.

Börzel, Tanja A. (2006). 'Participation Through Law Enforcement: The Case of the European Union.' *Comparative Political Studies* 39 (1): 128–52.

Börzel, Tanja A. and Thomas Risse (2003). 'Conceptualizing the Domestic Impact of Europe.' In Kevin Featherstone and Claudio Radaelli (eds), *The Politics of Europeanization*. Oxford: Oxford University Press.

Braithwaite, Mary (2000). 'Mainstreaming Gender in the European Structural Funds.' Paper prepared for the Mainstreaming Gender in European Public Policy Workshop, University of Wisconsin-Madison. 14–15 October 2000.

Braithwaite, Mary (2005). *Gender sensitive and women-friendly public policies: A comparative analysis of their progress and impact*. EQUAPOL. A 5th Framework research project funded by the European Union. Final report.

Bretherton, Charlotte (2001). 'Gender Mainstreaming and EU Enlargement: Swimming Against the Tide?' *Journal of European Public Policy* 8 (1): 60–81.

Brunila, Kristiina (2009). *Parasta ennen. Tasa-arvotyön projektitapaistuminen*. Kasvatuksen laitoksen tutkimuksia 222, Helsinki 2009.

Bruning, Gwennaële and Janneke Plantega (1999). 'Parental leave and equal opportunities: Experiences in eight European countries.' *Journal of European Social Policy* 9 (3): 195–209.

Bruno, Isabelle, Sophie Jacquot and Lou Mandin (2006). 'Europeanization through its instrumentation: benchmarking, mainstreaming and the open method of co-ordination ... toolbox or Pandora's box?' *Journal of European Public Policy* 13 (4): 519–36.

Büchs, Milena (2007). *New Governance in European Social Policy: The Open Method of Coordination.* Basingstoke: Palgrave Macmillan.

Bull, Anna, Hanna Diamond and Rosalind Marsh (2000) . 'Introduction.' In Anna Bull, Hanna Diamond and Rosalind Marsh (eds), *Feminisms and Women's Movements in Contemporary Europe.* Basingstoke: Palgrave Macmillan.

Burman, Erica, Sophie L. Smailes and Khatidja Chantler (2004). '"Culture" as a barrier to service provision and delivery: domestic violence services for minoritized women.' *Critical Social Policy* 24 (3):332–57.

Burrows, Noreen and Muriel Robison (2006). 'Positive actions for women in Employment: Time to Align with Europe?' *Journal of Law and Society* 33 (1): 24–41.

Burrows, Noreen and Muriel Robison (2007). 'An Assessment of the Recast of Community Equality Laws.' *European Law Journal* 13 (2): 186–203.

Bussemaker, Jet and Kees van Kersbergen (1999). 'Contemporary Social-Capitalist Welfare States and Gender Inequality.' In Diane Sainsbury (ed.), *Gender and Welfare State Regimes.*Oxford: Oxford University Press.

Bustelo, María (2009). 'Spain: Intersectionality Faces a Strong Gender Norm.' *International Feminist Journal of Politics* 11 (4).

Bustelo, María and Candice Ortbals (2007). 'The Evolution of Spanish State Feminism: a Fragmented landscape.' In Joyce Outshoorn and Johanna Kantola (eds), *Changing State Feminism.* Basingstoke: Palgrave Macmillan.

Butler, Judith (1990). *Gender Trouble.* London: Routledge.

Caporaso, James (2008). 'The Three Worlds of Regional Integration Theory.' In Paolo Graziano and Maarten P. Vink (eds), *Europeanization. New Research Agendas.* Basingstoke: Palgrave Macmillan.

Caporaso, James and Joseph Jupille (2001). 'The Europeanization of Gender Equality Policy and Domestic Structural Change.' In Maria Green Cowles, James Caporaso and Thomas Risse (eds), *Transforming Europe: Europeanization and Domestic Change.* Ithaca and London: Cornell University Press.

Caracciolo di Torelia, Eugenia (2005). 'The Goods and Services Directive: Limitations and Opportunities.' *Feminist Legal Studies* 13: 337–46.

Caul Kittilson, Miki (2006). *Challenging Parties, Changing Parliaments: Women and Elected Office in Contemporary Western Europe.* Columbus: The Ohio State University Press.

Celis, Karen, Sarah Childs, Johanna Kantola and Mona-Lena Krook (2008). 'Rethinking Women's Substantive Representation.' *Representation: The Journal of Representative Democracy,* 44 (2): 99–110.

Center for Reproductive Rights (2006). *Body and Soul: Forced Sterilization and Other Assaults on Roma Reproductive Freedom.* New York: Center for Reproductive Rights.

Chaney, Paul and R. Fevre (2002). 'Is there a Demand for Descriptive Representation? Evidence from the UK's Devolution Programme.' *Political Studies* 50 (5): 897–915.

Chappell, Louise (2003). *Gendering Government: Feminist Engagement with the State in Australia and Canada.* Vancouver: University of British Columbia Press.

Childs, Sarah (2006). *New Labour's Women MPs: Women Representing Women.* London: Routledge.

Childs, Sarah (2008). *Women and British Party Politics.* London: Routledge.

Chiva, Cristina (2005). 'Women in Post-communist Politics: Explaining Under-representation in the Hungarian and Romanian Parliaments.' *Europe-Asia Studies* 57 (7): 969–994.

Cichowski, Rachel A. (2002). '" No Discrimination Whatsoever" Women's Transnational Activism and the Evolution of EU Sex Equality Policy.' In Nancy A. Naples and Manisha Desai (eds), *Women's Activism and Globalization: Linking Local Struggles and Transnational Politics.* London: Routledge.

Cichowski, Rachel A. (2004). 'Women's Rights, the European Court, and Supranational Constitutionalism.' *Law & Society Review* 38 (3): 489–512.

Cichowski, Rachel A. (2006). 'Courts, Rights and Democratic Participation.' *Comparative Political Studies* 39 (1): 50–75.

Cichowski, Rachel A. (2007). *The European Court and Civil Society: Litigation, Mobilization and Governance.* Cambridge: Cambridge University Press.

Clavero, Sara and Yvonne Galligan (2005). '"A job in politics is not for women": Analysing barriers to women's political representation in CEE.' *Czech Sociological Review* 41 (6): 801–23.

Clavero, Sara and Yvonne Galligan (2009). 'Constituting and Reconstituting the Gender Order in Europe.' *Perspectives on European Politics and Society* 10 (1): 101–17.

Cockburn, Cynthia (1995). 'Women's Access to European Industrial Relations.' *European Journal of Industrial Relations* 1 (2): 171–89.

Cockburn, Cynthia (1996). 'Strategies for gender democracy: strengthening the representation of trade union women in the European social dialogue.' *European Journal of Women's Studies* 3 (1): 7–26.

Commission of the European Communities (2001). *European Governance: A White Paper.* Brussels, 25.7.2001, COM(2001) 428 final.

Commission of the European Communities (2005). Report from the Commission to the Council, the European Parliament, the European Economic and Social Committee and the Committee of the Regions on on equality between women and men, 2005. Brussels, 14.2.2005, COM(2005) 44 final.

Commission of the European Communities (2006). *A Roadmap for equality between women and men 2006–2010.* Communication from the Commission to the Council, the European Parliament, the European Economic and Social Committee and the Committee of the Regions. SEC(2006) 275.

Committee on Women's Rights and Gender Equality (2008). *Draft Report on prsoti-tuiton and its health consequences on women in member states.* Rapporteur Maria Carlshamre. European Parliament 2007/2263(INI).

Conaghan, Joanne (2005). 'Extending the Reach of Human Rights to Encompass Victims of Rape: *M.C. v. Bulgaria.*' *Feminist Legal Studies* 13(1) :145–57.

Conaghan, Joanne and Susan Milln (2005). Special Issue: Gender, Sexuality and Human Rights. *Feminist Legal Studies* 13 (1): 1–14.

Connell, Robert W. (1987). *Gender and Power.* Cambridge: Polity Press.

Council of the European Union (1999). Review of the implementation by the Member States and the European Institutions of the Beijing Platform for Action. 11829/99 SOC 340.

Council Resolution of 27 March 1995 on balanced participation of women and men in decision-making. OJ C 168, 4.7.1995.

Council Recommendation 96/694 of 2nd December 1996 on the balanced participation of women and men in the decision-making process OJ L 319 10.12.96 p.11.

Council of the European Union (2004). *The Hague Programme: Strengthening Freedom, Security and Justice in the European Union.*

Crenshaw, Kimberly (1991). 'Demarginalizing the intersection of race and sex: A Black feminist critique of antidiscrimination doctrine, feminist theory and antiracist politics.' In Katherine Bartlett and Rose Kennedy (eds), *Feminist Legal Theory: Readings in Law and Gender*. San Francisco: Westview Press.

Cullen, Paulina (1999). 'Coalitions working for social justice: Transnational non-governmental organizations and international governance.' *Contemporary Justice Review* 2 (2): 159–77.

Cullen, Paulina (2009). 'Pan-European NGOs and social rights: Participatory democracy and civil dialogue.' In Jutta Joachim and Birgit Locher (eds), *Transnational Activism in the UN and the EU: A comparative study*. London: Routledge.

Dahlerup, Drude (2006). 'Introduction.' In Drude Dahlerup (ed.), *Women, Quotas and Politics*. London: Routledge.

Daly, Mary (2005). 'Gender Mainstreaming in Theory and Practice.' *Social Politics: International Studies in Gender, State and Society* 12 (3): 433–40.

Daly, Mary (2007). 'Whither EU Social Policy? An Account and Assessment of Developments in the Lisbon Social Inclusion Process.' *Journal of Social Policy* 37 (1): 1–9.

Davis, Rebecca Howard (1997). *Women and Power in Parliamentary Democracies: Cabinet Appointments in Western Europe, 1968–1992*. Lincoln and London: University of Nebraska Press.

Dean, Homa (2006). 'Methods and good practices for gender mainstreaming.' *European Trade Union Institute for Research, Education and Health and Safety (ETUI-REHS)*. ETUI-REHS, Brussels.

Debusscher, Petra and Jacqui True (2008). 'Lobbying the EU for gender-equal development.' In J. Orbie and L. Tortell (eds), *The European Union and the social dimension of globalisation: How the EU influences the world*. London: Routledge.

De Groote, Jacqueline (1992). 'The European Women's Lobby.' *Women's International Studies Forum* 51 (l): 49–50.

Della Porta, Donatella and Manuela Caiani (2006). 'The Europeanization of Public Discourse in Italy: A Top-Down Process?' *European Union Politics* 7 (1): 77–112.

Della Porta, Donatella and Mario Diani (2006). *Social Movements: An Introduction*. Second Edition. Blackwell Publishing.

Denza, Eileen (2002). *The Intergovernmental Pillars of the European Union*. Oxford: Oxford University Press.

Deshormes, Fausta (1992). 'Women of Europe.' *Women's Studies International Forum* 15 (1): 51–2.

Dobash, R. Emerson and Russell P. Dobash (1979). *Violence Against Wives: A Case Against the Patriarchy*. New York: Free Press.

Dobash, R. Emerson and Russell P. Dobash (1998). *Women, Violence and Social Change*. London and New York: Routledge.

Doezema, Jo (2001). 'Ouch! Western Feminists "Wounded Attachment" to the "Third World Prostitute".' *Feminist Review* 67 (Spring) 16–38.

Doezema, Jo (2002). 'Who gets to choose? Coercion, Consent and Trafficking in the UN Trafficking Protocol.' *Gender and Development* 10 (1): 20–7.

Donà, Alessia (2004). 'Italy as negotiator in the EU equal opportunities policy.' *Modern Italy* 9(2): 173–87.

Donà, Alessia (2006). *Le pari opportunità. Condizione femminile in Italia e integrazione europea.* Rome/Bari: Laterza.

Dovi, Suzanne (2007). 'Theorizing Women's Representation in the United States.' *Politics & Gender* 3 :297–319.

Egan, Michelle, Neill Nugent and William Paterson (eds) (2010). *Research Agendas in EU Studies: Stalking the Elephant.* Basingstoke: Palgrave Macmillan.

Einhorn, Barbara (2000). 'Gender and citizenship in the context of democratisation and economic transformation in East Central Europe.' In Shirin Rai (ed.), *International Perspectives on Gender and Democracy.* London: Macmillan.

Einhorn, Barbara. (2005). 'Citizenship in an Enlarging Europe: Contested Strategies.' *Czech Sociological Review* 41 (6): 1023–39.

Einhorn, Barbara (2006). *Citizenship in an Enlarging Union: From Dream to Awakening.* Basingstoke: Palgrave Macmillan.

Einhorn, Barbara and Charlotte Sever (2003). 'Gender and Civil Society in Central and Eastern Europe.' *International Feminist Journal of Politics* 5 (2): 163–90.

Ellina, Chrystalla A. (2003). *Promoting Women's Rights: The Politics of Gender in the European Union.* New York & London: Routledge.

Ellis, Evelyn (1998). 'Recent Developments in European Community Sex Equality Law.' *Common Market Law Review* 35 (2): 379–408.

Ellis, Evelyn (2002). 'The principle of non-discrimination in the Post-Nice era.' In A. Arnull and Daniel Wincott (eds), *Accountability and Legitimacy in the European Union.* Oxford: Oxford University Press.

Elman, R. Amy (ed.) (1996). *Sexual   Politics and the European Union: The New Feminist Challenge.* Providence and Oxford: Berghahn Books.

Elman, R. Amy (2000). 'The Limits of Citizenship: Migration, Sex Discrimination and Same-Sex Partners in EU Law.' *Journal of Common Market Studies* 38 (5): 729–49.

Elman, R. Amy (2007). *Sexual Equality in an Integrated Europe: Virtual Equality.*Basingstoke: Palgrave Macmillan.

Engeli, Isabelle (2009). 'The Challenges of Abortion and Assisted Reproductive Technologies Policies in Europe.' *Comparative European Politics* 7 (1): 56–74.

Esping-Andersen, Gøsta (1990). *The Three Worlds of Welfare Capitalism.* Princeton: Princeton University Press.

Essed, Philomena (1995). 'Gender, migration and cross-ethnic coalition building.' In Helma Lutz, Ann Phoenix and Nira Yuval-Davis (eds), *Crossfires: Nationalism, Racism and Gender in Europe.* London: Pluto Press.

European Commission (1990). *Equal Opportunities for Men and Women – the Third Medium Term Action Programme* (1991–1995) (COM (90) 449).

European Commission (1995). *Fourth Medium-Term Community Action Programme on Equal Opportunities for Women and Men* (1996–2000) (COM (95) 381).

European Commission (1996). Commission Communication from the Commission of 21 February 1996: Incorporating Equal Opportunities for Women and Men into all Community Policies and Activities. COM(1996)67. Brussels.

European Commission (1998). *Sexual harassment in the workplace in the European Union.* Directorate-General for Employment, Industrial Relations and Social Affairs, Unit V/D.5

European Commission (1999). *Europeans and Their Views on Domestic Violence Against Women.* Eurobarometer 51.0.

European Commission (2000). *Beijing 5+: An Overview of the European Union Follow-Up and Preparations.*

European Commission (2000a) Commission report on the implementation of Council Recommendation 96/694 of 2nd December 1996 on the balanced participation of women and men in the decision-making process ((COM(2000) 120 – C5-0210/2000).

European Commission (2000b). Commission Decision relating to Gender Balance within the Committees and Expert Groups established by it Official Journal L 154, 27/06/2000.

European Commission (2001). *The Daphne Initiative (1997–1999): Overview and External Evaluator's Report of the 1998 Initiative.*

European Commission (2002). *Daphne: External Evaluator's Report on the Daphne Programme (year 2000).*

European Commission (2004). *Equality and non-discrimination in an enlarged European Union. Green Paper.* DG for Employment and Social Affairs. Unit D.3

European Commission (2004a). *EQUAL Guide on Gender Mainstreaming.* Brussels: European Commission.

European Commission (2005a). *Women and men in decision-making - A question of balance.* Publications Office.

European Commission (2005b). Report from the Commission to the Council, the European Parliament, the European Economic and Social Committee and the Committee of the Regions on on equality between women and men, 2005. Brussels, 14.2.2005, COM(2005) 44 final. 2005.

European Commission (2006). *European handbook on equality data.* Directorate-General for Employment, Social Affairs and Equal Opportunities. Unit G. 4

European Commission (2006a). *Migration and public perception.* Bureau of European Policy Advisers 4/10/2006.

European Commission (2006c). *A Roadmap for equality between women and men 2006–2010.* Directorate-General for Employment, Social Affairs and Equal Opportunities. Unit G.1

European Commission (2007). *Tackling Multiple Discrimination: Practices, policies and laws.* DG for Employment, Social Affairs and Equal Opportunities.

European Commission (2007a). *Manual for gender mainstreaming of employment policies.* Employment, Social Affairs and Equal Opportunities DG. July 2007.

European Parliament (1986). *Report drawn up on behalf of the Committee on Women's Rights on Violence Against Women (d'Ancona Report).* Document A2-44/86, Strasbourg.

European Parliament (1997). Debate on Violence Against Women. Sitting of Tuesday, 16 September 1997.

European Parliament (1999). Debate on Violence Against Women – Daphne programme. Sitting of Monday, 8 March 1999.

European Parliament, Directorate-General for Research (1999a). Working paper. The work of the Committee on women's rights 1994-1999.

European Parliament (2000). Report on the Commission report on the implementation of Council Recommendation 96/694 of 2nd December 1996 on the balanced participation of women and men in the decision-making process (COM(2000) 120 – C5-0210/2000 – 2000/2117(COS)).

European Parliament, Committee on Women's Rights and Gender Equality (2006). Background note: Showing the red card to forced prostitution. Available at

http://www.europarl.europa.eu/comparl/femm/womensday/2006/default_en.
htm Accessed 10.6. 2008).

European Women's Lobby (1998). *Position on employability and childcare*. May 1998, Brussels.

European Women's Lobby (1998a). *EWL motion on Prostitution and Trafficking*.

European Women's Lobby (1999). *Unveiling the hidden data on domestic violence in the EU*. Brussels: European Women's Lobby.

European Women's Lobby (2001). Towards a common European framework to monitor progress in combating violence against women. (EWL Policy Action Centre on Violence Against Women).

European Women's Lobby (2002). Report from the European Women's Lobby to the UN Special Rapporteur on Violence Against Women. December 2002.

European Women's Lobby (2002a). *Towards a Common European Framework to Monitor Progress in Combating Violence Against Women*.

European Women's Lobby (2003). Contribution to the 47th Session of the Commission on the Status of Women (CSW) (4–15 March) from the European Women's Lobby in relation to Violence Against Women. 2 June 2003.

European Women's Lobby (2003a). 'Women's Rights are Human Rights'. EWL's contribution to the Public hearing: Human Rights in the EU. 24 April 2003.

European Women's Lobby (2004). The European Constitution and Equality between Women and Men. 22 November 2004.

European Women's Lobby (2006). *Position paper on childcare*. 31 May 2006.

European Women's Lobby (2007). *Reality Check: When Women's NGOs Map Policies and Legislation on Violence against Women in Europe*. EWL Policy Action Centre on Violence against Women.

European Women's Lobby and Coalition Against Trafficking in Women (2008). 'Equality Now', a joint statement in the Vienna Forum on Trafficking in Human Beings 13-15 February 2008.

Eurostat (2006). News release: A statistical view of the life of women and men in the EU25. 29/2006. Eurostat Press Office, Luxembourg.

Eveline, Joan and Carol Bacchi (2005). 'What are we mainstreaming when we mainstream gender?' *International Feminist Journal of Politics* 7 (4): 496–512.

Fagan, Colette, Peter Urwin and Kathryn Melling (2006). *Gender inequalities in the risks of poverty and social exclusion for disadvantaged groups in thirty European Countries*. European Commission, Directorate-General for Employment, Social Affairs and Equal Opportunities Unit G.1.

Featherstone, Kevin and Claudio M. Radaelli (eds) (2003). *The Politics of Europeanization*. Oxford: Oxford University Press.

Ferrari Occhionero, Marisa and Mariella Nocenzi (2009). 'Gender inequalities: The integrated approach to the gender dimension in Europe.' *International Review of Sociology* 19 (1): 155–69.

Flynn, L. (1996). 'The Body Politic(s) of EC Law.' In T. Hervey and D. O'Keeffe (eds), *Sex Equality Law in the European Union*. Chichester: John Wiley & Sons.

Fodor, Eva (2006). 'Gender mainstreaming and its consequences in the European Union.' in *The Analyst* 7 (1): 1–16.

Footitt, Hilary (2002) .*Women, Europe and the Language of Politics*. London and New York: Continuum.

Forest, Maxime (2006). 'Emerging Gender interest Groups in the New Member states: The Case of the Czech Republic.' *Perspective on European Politics and Society* 7 (2): 170–85.

Fraser, Nancy (2000). 'Rethinking Recognition.' *New Left Review* 3: 107–20.

Fredman, Sandra (2008). 'Positive rights and positive duties: Addressing intersectionality.' In Dagmar Schiek and Victoria Chege (eds), *European Union Non-discrimination Law. Comparative Perspectives on Multidimensional Equality Law*. London: Routledge.

Freedman, Jane (2002). 'Women in the European Parliament.' *Parliamentary Affairs* 55: 179–88.

Freedman, Jane (2007). *Gendering the International Asylum and Refugee Debate*. Basingstoke: Palgrave Macmillan.

Freedman, Jane (2007a). 'Women, Islam and rights in Europe: Beyond a universalist/culturalist dichotomy.' *Review of International Studies* 33: 29–44.

Freedman, Jane (2009). 'Gender in the Euromed Relations.' Paper presented at the First European Conference on Politics and Gender, Queen's University Belfast, 21–23 January 2009.

Fuchs, Gesine and Silvia Payer (2007). 'Women's NGOs in EU Governance. Problems of Finance and Access.' In Heiko Pleines (ed.), *The Capacity of Central and East European interest groups to participate in EU governance*. Research Centre for East European Studies, Bremen.

Fuszara, Mařgorzata (2005). 'Between Feminism and the Catholic Church: The Women's Movement in Poland.' *Czech Sociological Review* 41 (6): 1057–75.

Fuszara, Mařgorzata (2008). 'The OMC, Gender Policy and the Experience of Poland as a New Member State.' In Fiona Beveridge and Samantha Velluti (eds), *Gender and the Open Method of Coordination: Perspectives on Law, Governance and Equality in the EU*. Aldershot: Ashgate.

Gabel, Matthew and Harvey D. Palmer (1995). 'Understanding variation in public support for European integration.' *European Journal of Political Research* 27:3–19.

Gabel, Matthew and Guy D. Whitten (1997). 'Economic conditions, economic perceptions, and public support for European integration.' *Political Behavior* 19 (1): 81–96.

Galligan, Yvonne and Sara Clavero (2008). 'Researching Gender Democracy in the European Union: Challenges and Prospects.' *RECON Online Working Paper* 2008/5.

Galligan, Yvonne, Sara Clavero and Maria Calloni (2007). *Gender Politics and Democracy in post-socialist Europe*. Leverkusen Opladen: Barbara Budrich Publishers.

García Bedolla, Lisa (2007). 'Intersections of inequality: Understanding marginalization and privilege in the post-civil rights era.' *Politics & Gender* 3 (2): 232–47.

Geddes, Andrew (2000). 'Lobbying for migrant inclusion in the European Union: New opportunities for transnational advocacy?' *Journal of European Public Policy* 20 (4); 632–49.

Geddes, Andrew and Virginie Guiraudon (2004). 'Britain, France, and EU Anti-Discrimination Policy: The Emergence of an EU Policy Paradigm.' *West European Politics* 27 (2): 334–53.

Gerber, Alexandra (2007). 'Gender mainstreaming and becoming European: At the intersection of Polish and EU gender discourses.' Paper presented at the 10th Biennial EUSA Meeting, Montreal, Canada, 17 May 2007.

Gerhards, Jürgen, Sylvia Kämpfer and Mike S. Schäfer (2008). 'The European Union's idea of gender equality and its support among citizens of the 27 European countries.' *Berliner Studien zur Soziologie Europas*, Nr. 10.

Goldberg, S. (2009). 'Intersectionality in theory and practice.' In E. Grabham, D. Cooper, J. Krishnadas and D. Herman (eds), *Intersectionality and Beyond: Law, power and the politics of location.* Abingdon: Routledge-Cavendish.

Goodey, Jo (2003). 'Migration, crime and victimhood. Responses to sex trafficking in the EU.' *Punishment & Society* 5 (4) 415–31.

Goodey, Jo (2004). 'Sex trafficking in women from Central and East European countries: Promoting a "victim-centred" and "woman-centred" approach to criminal justice intervention.' *Feminist Review* 76: 26–45.

Goodwin, Morag (2008). 'Multidimensional exclusion: Viewing Romani marginalisation through the nexus of race and poverty.' In Dagmar Schiek and Victoria Chege (eds), *European Union Non-discrimination Law. Comparative Perspectives on Multidimensional Equality Law.* London: Routledge.

Gould, Arthur (2001). 'The Criminalisation of Buying Sex: the Politics of Prostitution in Sweden.' *Journal of Social Policy* 30 (3): 437–56.

Grabbe, Heather (2001). 'How does Europeanization affect CEE governance? Conditionality, diffusion and diversity.' *Journal of European Public Policy* 8 (6): 1013–31.

Grabbe, Heather (2005). *The EU's Transformative Power: Europeanization through Conditionality in Central and Eastern Europe.* Basingstoke: Palgrave Macmillan.

Grabham, E. with D. Herman, D. Cooper and J. Krishnadas (2009). 'Introduction.' In E. Grabham, D. Cooper, J. Krishnadas and D. Herman (eds), *Intersectionality and Beyond: Law, power and the politics of location.* Abingdon: Routledge-Cavendish.

Graziano, Paolo and Maarten P. Vink (eds) (2008). *Europeanization. New Research Agendas.* Basingstoke: Palgrave Macmillan.

Gréboval, Cécile (2004). 'Introducing Parity Democracy: The Role of the International Community and the European Women's Lobby.'Paper presented at the IDEA/CEE Network for Gender Issues Conference, 22–23 October, Budapest.

Greenwood, J. (1997). *Representing Interests in the European Union.* Basingstoke: Macmillan.

Greenwood, J. (2004). 'The search for input legitimacy through organized civil society in the EU.' *Transnational Associations* 2: 145–155.

Griffiths, Sue and Jalna Hanmer (2005). 'Feminist quantitative methodology: evaluating policing of domestic violence.' In Tina Skinner, Marianne Hester and Ellen Malos (eds), *Researching Gender Violence: Feminist Methodology in Action.* Devon: Willan Publishing.

Guadagnini, Marila and Alessia Donà (2007). 'Women's Policy Machinery in Italy between European Pressure and Domestic Constraints.' In Joyce Outshoorn and Johanna Kantola (eds), *Changing State Feminism.* Basingstoke: Palgrave Macmillan.

Guerrina, Roberta (2005). *Mothering the Union: Gender Politics in the EU.* Manchester: Manchester University Press.

Guiraudon, Virginie (2008). 'Anti-Discrimination Policy.' In Paolo Graziano and Maarten P. Vink (eds), *Europeanization. New Research Agendas.* Basingstoke: Palgrave Macmillan.

Haas, Linda (2003). 'Parental Leave and Gender Equality: Lessons from the European Union.' *Review of Policy Research* 20 (1): 89–114.

Hafner-Burton, Emilie M. and Mark Pollack (2002). 'Mainstreaming Gender in Global Governance.' *European Journal of International Relations* 8 (3): 339–73.

Hafner-Burton, Emilie M. and Mark Pollack (2008). 'Mainstreaming Gender in the European Union: Getting the Incentives Right.'Paper presented at the Annual Meeting of the American Political Science Association, August 28–31, 2008.

Hafner-Burton, Emilie and Mark Pollack (2009). 'Mainstreaming Gender in the European Union: Getting the Incentives Right.' *Comparative European Politics* 7 (1): 114–38.

Hagemann-White, Carole (2000). 'Male violence and control: constructing a comparative European perspective.' In Simon Duncan and Birgit Pfau-Effinger (eds), *Gender, Economy and Culture in the European Union.* London and New York: Routledge.

Hancock, Ange-Marie (2007). 'When Multiplication Doesn't Equal Quick Addition: Examining Intersectionality as a Research Paradigm.' *Perspectives on Politics* 5 (1): 63–79.

Hancock, Ange-Marie (2007a). 'Intersectionality as a Normative and Empirical Paradigm.' *Politics & Gender* 3 (2): 248–54.

Hankivsky, Olena (2005). ' Gender vs. Diversity Mainstreaming: A Preliminary Examination of the Role and Transformative Potential of Feminist Theory.' *Canadian Journal of Political Science* 38(4): 977–1001.

Hanmer, Jalna (1996). 'The Common Market of Violence.' In R. Amy Elman (ed.), *Sexual Politics and the European Union: The New Feminist Challenge.* Providence and Oxford: Berghahn Books.

Hantrais, Linda (ed.) (2000). *Gendered Policies in Europe.* London: Macmillan.

Hantrais, Linda and Marie-Thérèse Letablier (1996). *Families and family policies in Europe.* London: Longman.

Hašková, Hana (2005). 'Czech women's civil organising under the state socialist regime, socio-economic transformation and the EU accession period.' *Czech Sociological Review* 41 (6): 1077–110.

Hašková, Hana and Alena Křižková (2008). 'The Impact of EU Accession on the Promotion of Women and Gender Equality in the Czech Republic.' In Silke Roth (ed.), *Gender Politics in the Expanding European Union: Mobilization, Inclusion, Exclusion.* New York and Oxford: Berghahn Books.

Haussman, Melissa and Birgit Sauer (2007). *Gendering the State in the Age of Globalization: Women's Movements and State Feminism in Postindustrial Democracies.*Lanham: Rowman & Littlefield Publishers.

Hautala, Heidi (1999). 'Open Platform; A New Chapter in the Equality Story' *Equal Opportunities Magazine* 7 March, 23.

Hayes-Renshaw, Fiona (2006). 'The Council of Ministers.' In John Peterson and Michael Shackleton (eds), *The Institutions of the European Union.* Second Edition. Oxford: Oxford University Press.

Heide, Ingeborg (1999). 'Supranational action against sex discrimination: Equal pay and equal treatment in the European Union.' *International Labour Review* 138 (4): 381–40.

Helfferich, Barbara and Felix Kolb (2001). 'Multilevel Action Coordination in European Contentious Politics. The Case of the European Women's Lobby.' In Doug Imig and Sidney Tarrow (eds), *Contentious Europeans: Protest Politics in an Emerging Polity.* Lanham: Rownham & Littlefield.

Hellgren, Zenia and Barbara Hobson (2008). 'Gender and Ethnic Minority Claims in Swedish and EU Frames: Sites of Multilevel Political Opportunities and Boundary Making.' In Silke Roth (ed.), *Gender Politics in the Expanding European Union: Mobilization, Inclusion, Exclusion.* New York and Oxford: Berghahn Books.

Héritier, Adrienne (2001). 'The White Paper on European Governance: A Response to Shifting Weights in Inter-institutional Decision-Making.' Jean Monnet Working Paper No.6/01. Symposium: Mountain or Molehill? A Critical Appraisal of the Commission White Paper on Governance.

Hill Collins, Patricia (1991). *Black Feminist Thought: Knowledge, Consciousness and the Politics of Empowerment* .New York: Routledge.

Hix, Simon (2005). *The Political System of the European Union.* Second Edition. Basingstoke: Palgrave Macmillan.

Hobson, Barbara (2000). 'Economic Citizenship: Reflections thought the European Union Policy Mirror.' In Barbara Hobson (ed.), *Gender and Citizenship in Transition.* Macmillan.

Hobson, Barbara, Marcus Carson and Rebecca Lawrence (2008). 'Recognition Struggles in Trans-national Arenas: Negotiating Identities and Framing Citizenship.' In Birte Siim and Judith Squires (ed.), *Contesting Citizenship.* London: Routledge.

Hochschild, Arlie Russell (2000). 'Global care chains and emotional surplus values.' In Will Hutton and Anthony Giddens (eds) , *On the Edge. Living with Global Capitalism.* London: Jonathan Cape.

Holli, Anne Maria (2003). *Discourse and Politics for Gender Equality in Late Twentieth Century Finland.* Acta Politica 23. Department of Political Science, University of Helsinki.

Holli, Anne Maria (2008). 'Feminist triangles: Conceptual analysis.' *Representation* 44 (2): 169–85.

Holli, Anne Maria and Johanna Kantola (2007). 'State Feminism Finnish Style: Strong Policies clash with Implementation Problems.' In Joyce Outshoorn and Johanna Kantola (eds), *Changing State Feminism.* Basingstoke: Palgrave Macmillan.

Holzhacker, Ronald (2007). 'The Europeanization and Transnationalization of Civil Society Organizations Striving for Equality: Goals and Strategies of Gay and Lesbian Groups in Italy and the Netherlands.' EUI Working Papers. RSCAS 2007/36.

Hooghe, Liesbet and Gary Marks (2001). *Multi-Level Governance and European Integration.* Lanham: Rowman & Littlefield.

hooks, bell (1984). *Feminist Theory: From Margin to Center.* Boston: South End Press.

Hoskyns, Catherine (1996). *Integrating Gender: Women, Law and Politics in the European Union.* London and New York: Verso.

Hoskyns, Catherine (1996a). 'The European Union and the women within: An overview of the women's rights policy.' In R. Amy Elman (ed.), *Sexual Politics and the European Union: The New Feminist Challenge.* Providence and Oxford: Berghahn Books.

Hoskyns, Catherine (1999). 'Gender and Transnational Democracy: The Case of the European Union.' In Mary K. Meyer and Elisabeth Prügl (eds), *Gender Politics in Global Governance* Lanham: Rownam & Littlefield.

Hoskyns, Catherine (2000). 'A Study of Four Action Programmes on Equal Opportunities.' In Mariagrazia Rossilli (ed.), *Gender Policies in the European Union.* Oxford: Lang.

Hoskyns, Catherine (2001). 'Gender Politics in the Union: The Context for Job Training.' In Amy G. Mazur (ed.) ,*State feminism, women's movements, and job* *training: Making democracies work in the global economy.*New York and London: Routledge.

Hoskyns, Catherine (2004). 'Gender Perspectives.' In Antje Wiener and Thomas Dietz (eds), *European Integration Theory.* Oxford: Oxford University Press.

Hoskyns, Catherine (2007). 'Linking gender and International Trade Policy: Is Interaction Possible?' CSGR Working Paper 217/07.

Hoskyns, Catherine (2008). 'Governing the EU: Gender and Macroeconomics.' In Rai, Shirin and Georgina Waylen (eds), *Global Governance: Feminist Perspectives.* Basingstoke: Palgrave Macmillan.

Hoskyns, Catherine and Shirin Rai (1998). 'Gender, class and representation: India and the European Union.' *European Journal of Women's Studies* 5 (3): 345–65.

Hubbard, Phil, Roger Matthews and Jane Scoular (2008). 'Regulating sex work in the EU: Prostitute women and the new spaces of exclusion.' *Gender, Place and Culture* 15 (2): 137–552.

Hubert, Agnès (2001). 'From Equal Pay to Parity Democracy: The Rocky Ride of Women's Policy in the European Union.' In Jytte Klausen and Charles S. Maier (eds), *Has Liberalism Failed Women? Assuring Equal Representation in Europe and the United States.* Basingstoke: Palgrave Macmillan.

Hubert, Agnès (2004). 'Moving beyond quotas in the EU: An emerging stage of democracy.' Paper presented at the International Institute for Democracy and Electoral Assistance (IDEA)/CEE Network for Gender Issues Conference. Budapest, 22–23 October 2004.

Hubert, Agnès and Maria Stratigaki (2007). 'European Gender Institute: New Opportunities for Connecting Expertise, Policies and Civil Society.'. Paper presented at the European Union Studies Association (EUSA) Tenth Biannual International Conference, Montreal, 17–19 May.

Hughes, Melanie (2007). 'Complications at the Intersection: Overcoming the Challenges of Cross-National Research on Minority Women's Legislative Representation.' Paper presented at American Political Science Association Annual Meeting. Chicago, IL, 30 August – 2 September , 2007.

Jacquot, Sophie and Cornelia Woll (2003). 'Usage of European Integration: Europeanization form a Sociological Perspective.' *European Integration Online Papers* 7 (12).

JämStöd (2007). *Gender mainstreaming manual.* Swedish Government Official Reports SOU 2007:15. Stockholm: Edita Sverige AB.

Jeffreys, Sheila (1997). *The Idea of Prostitution.* North Melbourne: Spinifex.

Jenson, Jane (2008). 'Writing Women Out, Folding Gender In: The European Union "Modernises" Social Policy.' *Social Politics: International Studies in Gender, State and Society* 15 (2): 131–53.

Jørgensen, Knud Erik, Mark A. Pollack and Ben Rosamond (eds) (2007). *The Handbook of European Union Politics.* London: SAGE.

Kaelble, Hartmut (2003). "Gibt es eine europäische Zivilgesellschaft?"In Gosewinkel Dieter, Dieter Rucht, Wolfgang van den Daele & Jürgen Kocka (eds), *Zivilgesellschaft. National und transnational.* Berlin: Sigma.

Kakucs, Noémi and Andrea Pető (2008). 'The Impact of EU Accession on Gender Equality in Hungary.'In Silke Roth (ed.), *Gender Politics in the Expanding European Union: Mobilization, Inclusion, Exclusion.* New York and Oxford: Berghahn Books.

Kantola, Johanna (2006). *Feminists Theorize the State.* Basingstoke: Palgrave Macmillan.

Kantola, Johanna (2006a). 'Transnational and National Gender Equality Politics: European Union's Impact on Domestic Violence Debates in Finland and Britain.' In Sirkku Hellsten, Anne Maria Holli and Krassimira Daskalova (eds), *Women's Citizenship and Political Rights*. Basingstoke: Palgrave Macmillan.

Kantola, Johanna (2009a). 'Women's Political Representation in the European Union.' *Journal of Legislative Studies* 15 (4), 379–400.

Kantola, Johanna (2009b). '"Tackling Multiple Discrimination": Gender and Cross-cutting inequalities in Europe.' *The Making of European Women's Studies*, Volume IX, Athena Network.

Kantola, Johanna (2010). 'Feminist Perspectives on the EU.' In Egan, M., Nugent, N. and Paterson, W. (eds) , *Research Agendas in EU Studies: Stalking the Elephant*. Basingstoke: Palgrave Macmillan.

Kantola, Johanna (2010a). 'Sifting institutional and ideational terrains: The impact of Europeanization and neoliberalism on women's policy agencies.' *Policy & Politics*, forthcoming.

Kantola, Johanna and Hanne Marlene Dahl (2005). 'Gender and the State: From Differences between to Differences within.' *International Feminist Journal of Politics* 7 (1): 49–70.

Kantola, Johanna and Kevät Nousiainen (2008). 'Pussauskoppiin? Tasa-arvo- ja yhdenvertaisuuslakien yhtenäistämisestä.' *Naistutkimus-Kvinnoforskning* 2/2008: 6–20.

Kantola, Johanna and Kevät Nousiainen (2009). 'Institutionalising Intersectionality in Europe: Legal and Political Analyzes.' *International Feminist Journal of Politics* 11 (4), 459–477.

Kantola, Johanna and Kevät Nousiainen (2009a). 'Institutionalising intersectionality with a separate strands approach: The case of Finland.'Paper presented at the ECPR Joint Sessions, Lisbon, 14–19 April 2009.

Kantola, Johanna and Joyce Outshoorn (2007). 'Changing State Feminism.' in Joyce Outshoorn and Johanna Kantola (eds), *Changing State Feminism*. Basingstoke: Palgrave Macmillan.

Kantola, Johanna and Judith Squires (2008). 'From State Feminism to Market Feminism?'Paper presented at the International Studies Association Annual Convention in San Francisco, March 2008.

Kantola, Johanna and Judith Squires (2010). 'The New Politics of Equality.' In Colin Hay (ed.), *Political Science in an Age of Interdependence*. Basingstoke: Palgrave Macmillan.

Keck, Margaret E. and Kathryn Sikkink (1998). *Activists Beyond Borders: Advocacy Networks in International Politics*. Ithaca & London: Cornell University Press.

Keil, Marion, Badrudin Amershi and Stephen Holmes (2007). *Training Manual for Diversity Management*. Brussels: European Commission.

Kelly, Liz (1987). 'The Continuum of Sexual Violence.' In Jalna Hanmer and Mary Maynard (eds), *Women, Violence and Social Control*. London: Macmillan.

Kelly, Liz and Jill Radford (1996). '"Nothing Really Happened": The Invalidation of Women's Experiences of Sexual Violence.' In Marianne Hester, Liz Kelly and Jill Radford (eds), *Violence and Male Power*. Buckingham and Philadelphia: Open University Press.

Kempadoo, Kamala (1998). 'Introduction: Globalizing Sex Workers' Rights.' In Kamala Kempadoo and Jo Doezema (eds), *Global Sex Workers: Rights, Resistance and Redefinition*. New York and London: Routledge.

Kennedy, Paul (2006). 'The European Court of Justice.' In John Peterson and Michael Shackleton (eds), *The Institutions of the European Union*. Second Edition. Oxford: Oxford University Press.

Kenney, Sally J. (2002). 'Breaking the silence: Gender mainstreaming and the composition of the European Court of Justice.' *Feminist Legal Studies* 10: 257–270.

Kilvington, Judith, Sophie Day and Helen Ward (2001). 'Prostitution Policy in Europe: A Time of Change?' *Feminist Review* 67: 78–93.

Kingdom, Elizabeth (1991). *What's Wrong with Rights: Problems for Feminist Politics of Law*. Edinburgh: Edinburgh University Press.

Kodré, Petra and Henrike Müller (2003). 'Shifting Policy Frames: EU Equal Treatment Norms and Domestic Discourses in Germany.' In Ulrike Liebert (ed.), *Gendering Europeanization*. Brussels: Presses Interuniversitaires Européennes.

Kofman, Eleonore (2004). 'Family-related migration: a critical review of European Studies.' *Journal of Ethnic and Migration Studies* 30 (2): 243–62.

Kofman, Eleonore and Rosemary Sales (2000). 'The Implications of European Union Policies for non-EU Migrant Women.' in Mariagrazia Rossilli (ed.), *Gender Policies in the European Union*. Oxford: Lang.

Kohler-Koch, Beate and Berthold Rittberger (2006). 'The "Governance Turn" in EU Studies.' *Journal of Common Market Studies* 44: 27–49.

Koldinská, Kristina (2008). 'Multidimensional Equality in the Czech and Slovak Republics: The Case of Roma Women.' In Dagmar Schiek and Victoria Chege (eds), *European Non-Discrimination Law: Comparative Perspectives on Multidimensional Equality Law*. London: Routledge.

Koldinská, Kristina (2008a). 'OMC in the Context of EU Gender Policy from the Point of View of New EU Member States.' In Fiona Beveridge and Samantha Velluti (eds), *Gender and the Open Method of Coordination: Perspectives on Law, Governance and Equality in the EU*. Aldershot: Ashgate.

Koldinská, Kristina (2009). 'Institutionalising Intersectionality. Equality Bodies in New Member States and their Role in Intersectionality.' *International Feminist Journal of Politics* 9 (2), 547–63.

Kollman, Kelly (2007). 'Same-sex Unions: The Globalization of an Idea.' *International Studies Quarterly* 51 (2), 329–57.

Kollman, Kelly (2008). 'European Institutions, Transnational Networks and National Same-sex Union Policy: When Soft Law Hits Harder.' Paper presented at the PSA Women and Politics Conference, February 2008, University of Sussex.

Koukoulis-Spiliotopoulos, Sophia (2008). 'The Lisbon Treaty and the Charter of Fundamental Rights: maintaining and developing the *acquis* in gender equality.' *European Gender Equality Law Review* 1/2008: 15–24.

Křižková, Alena (2007). 'The impact of EU accession on the promotion of women and gender equality in the Czech Republic.' Paper presented at the ECPR General Conference 6–8 September 2007, Pisa.

Krizsán, Andrea, Maria Bustelo, Andromachi Hadjiyanni and Fray Kamoutis (2007). 'Domestic Violence: A Public Matter.' In Mieke Verloo (ed.), *Multiple Meanings of Gender Equality in Europe*. Budapest: Central European University Press.

Krizsán, Andrea and Raluca Popa (2007). 'A success for women's movement? Putting domestic violence on the policy agenda in countries of East Central Europe.' Paper presented at the ECPR General Conference, 4 September 2007, Pisa.

Kriszán, Andrea and Viola Zentai (2006). 'Gender Equality Policy or Gender Mainstreaming? The case of Hungary on the road to an enlarged Europe.' *Policy Studies* 27 (2): 135–51.

Kronsell, Annica (2005). 'Gender, power and European integration theory.' *Journal of European Public Policy* 12 (6): 1022–40.

Krook, Mona Lena (2002). '"Europe for Women, Women for Europe": Strategies for Parity Democracy in the European Union.' In John S. Micgiel (ed.), *Democracy And Integration In An Enlarging Europe*. New York: Institute for the Study of Europe.

Krook, Mona Lena (2009). *Quotas for Women in Politics: Gender and Candidate Selection Reform Worldwide*. Oxford: Oxford University Press.

Laatikainen, Katie V. (2001). 'Caught between access and activism in the multilevel European Union labyrinth.' In Amy G. Mazur (ed.), *State feminism, women's movements, and job training: Making democracies work in the global economy*. New York and London: Routledge.

Laforest, R. and M. Orsini (2005). 'Evidence-based engagement in the voluntary sector: lessons from Canada.' *Social Policy and Administration* 39 (5): 481–97.

Lang, Sabine (2007). 'Gender Governance in Post-Unification Germany: Between Institutionalization, Deregulation and Privatization.' in Joyce Outshoorn and Johanna Kantola (eds), *Changing State Feminism*. Basingstoke: Palgrave Macmillan.

Lavenex, Sandra (2006). 'Towards the constitutionalization of aliens' rights in the European Union?' *Journal of European Public Policy* 13 (8): 1284–1301.

Lawson, Anna and Caroline Gooding (2005). 'Introduction.' In Anna Lawson and Caroline Gooding (eds), *Disability Rights in Europe: From Theory to Practice*. Oxford: Hart Publishing.

León, Margarita (2009). 'Gender Equality and the European Employment Strategy: The Work/Family Balance Debate.' *Social Policy & Society*, 8 (2): 197–209.

León, Margarita (2005). 'Welfare State regimes and the social organization of labour: Childcare arrangements and the work/family balance dilemma.' *The Sociological Review*, 53 (2): 204–18.

León, Margarita, Mercedes Mateo Diaz and Susan Millns (2003). 'En(Gendering) the Convention: Women and the Future of the European Union.'Paper presented at the ECPR General Conference in Marburg, 18–21 September 2003.

Levitas, Ruth (1998). *The Inclusive Society? Social Exclusion and New Labour*. Basingstoke: Palgrave Macmillan.

Lewis, Jane (1997). 'Gender and welfare regimes: Further thoughts.' *Social Politics: International Studies in Gender, State and Society* 4 (2): 160–77.

Lewis, Jane (2006). 'Work-family reconciliation, equal opportunities and social policies: the interpretation of policy trajectories at the EU level and the meaning of gender equality.' *Journal of European Public Policy* 13 (3): 400–37.

Lewis, Jane and Susanna Giullari (2005). 'The adult worker model family, gender equality and care: the search for new policy principles and the possibilities and problems of a capabilities approach.' *Economy and Society* 34 (1): 76–104.

Liebert, Ulrike (1997). 'Gender politics in the European Union: The return of the public.'*European Societies* 1 (2): 197–239.

Liebert, Ulrike (2002). 'Europeanising Gender Mainstreaming: Constraints and Opportunities in the Multilevel Euro-Polity.' *Feminist Legal Studies* 10: 241–56.

Liebert, Ulrike (ed.) (2003). *Gendering Europeanisation*. Brussels: Presses Interuniversitaires Européennes.

Liebert, Ulrike (2003a). 'Between Diversity and Equality: Analysing Europeanization.' in Ulrike Liebert (ed.) (2003). *Gendering Europeanization* Brussels: Presses Interuniversitaires Européennes.

Liebert, Ulrike (2003b). 'Gendering Europeanization: Patterns and Dynamics.' In Ulrike Liebert (ed.), *Gendering Europeanization.* Brussels: Presses Interuniversitaires Européennes.

Liebert, Ulrike (2003c). 'Europeanization and the "Needle's Eye": The Transformation of Employment Policy in Germany.' *Review of Policy Research* 20 (3): 479–92.

Liebert, Ulrike (2008). 'The European Citizenship Paradox: Renegotiating Equality and Diversity in the New Europe.' In Birte Siim and Judith Squires (eds), *Contesting Citizenship.* London: Routledge.

Lindvert, Jessica (2002). 'A World Apart: Swedish and Australian Gender Equality Policy.' *Nordic Journal of Women's Studies (NORA)* 2 (10): 99–107.

Lister, Marjorie (2006). 'Gender and European Development Policy.' In Marjorie Lister and Maurizio Carbone (eds), *New pathways in development: Gender and civil society in EU policy.* Aldershot: Ashgate.

Lister, Ruth (2004). 'The Third Way's Social Investment State.' In Jane Lewis and Rebecca Surender (eds), *Welfare State Change: Towards a Third Way?* Oxford: Oxford University Press.

Lister, Ruth, Fiona Williams, Anneli Anttonen, Jet Bussemaker, Ute Gerhard, Jacqueline Heinen, Stina Johansson, Arnlaug Leira, Birte Siim and Constanza Tobio, with Anna Gavanas (2007). *Gendering Citizenship in Western Europe: New Challenges for Citizenship Research in a Cross-national Context.* Bristol: Policy Press.

Locher, Birgit (2002). 'International Norms and European Policy-Making: Trafficking in Women in the EU.' *CEuS Working Paper No. 2002/6.*

Locher, Birgit (2007). *Trafficking in Women in the European Union: Norms, Advocacy-Networks and Policy-Change.* Wiesbaden: VS Verlag.

Locher, Birgit and Elisabeth Prügl (2009). 'Gender Perspectives.' In Antje Wiener and Thomas Diez (eds), *European Integration Theory.* Oxford: Oxford University Press.

Lohmann, Kinga (2005). 'The Impact of EU Enlargement on the Civic Participation of Women in Central and Eastern Europe – The Perspective from the Karat Coalition.' *Czech Sociological Review* 41 (6) 1111–17.

Lombardo, Emanuela (2003). 'EU Gender Policy – Trapped in the Wollstonecraft Dilemma?' *The European Journal of Women's Studies* 10 (2).

Lombardo, Emanuela (2004). *La europeización de la política española de igualdad de género.*Valencia: Tirant lo blanch.

Lombardo, Emanuela (2005). 'Integrating or Setting the Agenda? Gender Mainstreaming in the European Constitution-Making Process.' *Social Politics* 12 (3): 412–32.

Lombardo, Emanuela (2007). 'Gender Equality in the Constitution-Making Process.' In Dario Castiglione, Justus Schönlau, Chris Longman, Emanuela Lombardo, Nieves Pérez-Solórzano Borragán and Miriam Aziz, *Constitutional Politics in the European Union: The Convention Moment and its Aftermath.* Basingstoke: Palgrave Macmillan.

Lombardo, Emanuela (2007a). 'The Participation of the Civil Society.' in Dario Castiglione, Justus Schönlau, Chris Longman, Emanuela Lombardo, Nieves

Pérez-Solórzano Borragán and Miriam Aziz, *Constitutional Politics in the European Union: The Convention Moment and its Aftermath.* Basingstoke: Palgrave Macmillan.

Lombardo, Emanuela (2008). 'Gender Inequality in Politics: Policy Frames in Spain and the European Union.' *International Feminist Journal of Politics* 10 (1): 78–96.

Lombardo, Emanuela and Petra Meier (2006). 'Gender Mainstreaming in the EU: Incorporating a Feminist Reading?' *European Journal of Women's Studies* 13 (2): 151–66.

Lombardo, Emanuela and Petra Meier (2007). 'European Union Gender Policy Since Beijing. Shifting Concepts and Agendas Europe.' In Mieke Verloo (ed.), *Multiple Meanings of Gender Equality in Europe.* Budapest: Central European University Press.

Lombardo, Emanuela, Petra Meier and Mieke Verloo (2009). 'Stretching and bending gender equality: A discursive politics approach?' In Emanuela Lombardo, Petra Meier and Mieke Verloo (eds), *The Discursive Politics of Gender Equality: Stretching, Bending and Policymaking.* London: Routledge.

Lombardo, Emanuela, Petra Meier and Mieke Verloo (2009a). 'Conclusions: A critical understanding of the discursive politics of gender equality.' In Emanuela Lombardo, Petra Meier and Mieke Verloo (eds), *The Discursive Politics of Gender Equality: Stretching, Bending and Policymaking.* London: Routledge.

Lombardo, Emanuela and Mieke Verloo (2009). 'Institutionalising intersectionality in the European Union? Policy developments and contestations.' *International Feminist Journal of Politics* 11 (4), 478–95.

Lombardo, Emanuela and Mieke Verloo (2009a). 'Stretching gender equality to other inequalities: Political intersectionality in European gender equality policies.' In Emanuela Lombardo, Petra Meier and Mieke Verloo (eds), *The Discursive Politics of Gender Equality: Stretching, Bending and Policymaking.* London: Routledge.

López-Santana, Mariely (2006). 'The domestic implications of European soft law: framing and transmitting change in employment policy.' *Journal of European Public Policy* 13 (4): 481–99.

Loudes, Christine (2004). *Meeting the challenge of accession. Surveys on sexual orientation discrimination in countries joining the European Union.* ILGA-Europe Policy Paper, April 2004.

Lovenduski, Joni (1995). 'An emerging advocate: The Equal Opportunities Commission in Great Britain.' In Dorothy McBride Stetson and Amy Mazur (eds), *Comparative State Feminism.* London: Sage.

Lovenduski, Joni (2005). *Feminizing Politics* Cambridge: Polity Press.

Lovenduski, Joni (ed.) (2005a). *State Feminism and Political Representation.* Cambridge: Cambridge University Press.

Lovenduski, Joni (2007). 'Unfinished Business: Equality Policy and the Changing Context of State Feminism in Great Britain.' In Joyce Outshoorn and Johanna Kantola (eds), *Changing State Feminism.* Basingstoke: Palgrave Macmillan.

Lovenduski, Joni (2008). 'State Feminism and Women's Movements.' *West European Politics* 31 (1-2): 169–94.

Lutz, Helma (1997). 'The Limits of European-ness: Immigrant women in Fortress Europe.' *Feminist Review* 57, Autumn, 93–111.

Lutz, Helma, Ann Phoenix and Nira Yuval-Davis (1995). 'Nationalism, racism and gender – European crossfires.' In Helma Lutz, Ann Phoenix and Nira Yuval-Davis (eds), *Crossfires: Nationalism, Racism and Gender in Europe*. London: Pluto Press.

Mabbett, Deborah (2005). 'The Development of Rights-based Social Policy in the European Union: The Example of Disability Rights.' *Journal of Common Market Studies* 43 (1): 97–120.

Mackay, Fiona (2003). 'Women and the 2003 elections: keeping up the momentum.' *Scottish Affairs* 44:74–90.

Macrae, Heather (2006). 'Rescaling Gender Relations: the Influence of European Directives on the German Gender Regime.' *Social Politics* 13 (4) 522–50.

Mansbridge, Jane (1999). 'Should Blacks Represent Blacks and Women Represent Women? A Contingent "Yes".' *The Journal of Politics* 61 (3).

Marston G. and R. Watts (2003). 'Tampering with the evidence: a critical appraisal of evidence based policy.' *The Drawing Board: An Australian Review of Public Affairs* 3(3): 143–63 .

Martinsen, Dorte S. (2007). 'The Europeanization of gender equality – who controls the scope of non-discrimination.' *Journal of European Public Policy* 14 (4): 544–62.

Masselot, Annick (2007). 'The State of Gender Equality Law in the European Union.' *European Law Journal* 13 (2) 152–68.

Mateo Diaz, Mercedes (2004). 'The Participation and Representation of Women in the Debate on the Future of the European Union.' *South European Society & Politics* 9 (1) 208–22.

Mateo Diaz, Mercedes and Susan Millns (2004). 'Parity, power and representative politics: The elusive pursuit of gender equality in Europe.' *Feminist Legal Studies* 12: 279–302.

Mazey, Sonia (1995). 'The Development of EU Equality Policies: Bureaucratic Expansion on Behalf of Women?' *Public Administration* 73: 591–609.

Mazey, Sonia (1998). 'The European Union and Women's Rights: from Europeanization of national agendas to the nationalization of a European Agenda?' *Journal of European Public Policy* 5 (1): 131–52.

Mazey, Sonia (2001). *Gender Mainstreaming in the EU: Principles and Practice*. London: Kogan Page.

Mazey, Sonia (2002). 'Gender Mainstreaming Strategies in the E.U.: Delivering an agenda?' *Feminist Legal Studies*, 10: 227–40.

Mazey, Sonia and Jeremy Richardson (1997). 'Policy framing: Interest groups and the lead up to the 1996 intergovernmental conference.' *West European Politics* 20 (3): 111–33.

Mazur, Amy (2002). *Theorizing Feminist Policy*. Oxford: Oxford University Press.

Mazur, Amy (2009). 'Comparative Gender and Policy Projects in Europe: Current Trends in Theory, Method and Research.' *Comparative European Politics* 7 (1): 1–11.

Mazur, Amy and Dorothy McBride (2008). 'State feminism.' In Gary Goertz and Amy Mazur (eds), *Politics, Gender and Concepts: Theory and Methodology*. Cambridge: Cambridge University Press.

Mazur, Amy and Mark Pollack (2009). 'Gender and Public Policy in Europe: An Introduction.' *Comparative European Politics* 7 (1): 12–36.

McBride, Dorothy and Amy Mazur (2006). 'Measuring Feminist Mobilization: Cross-National Convergence and Transnational Networks in Western Europe.'

In Myra Max Ferree and Aili Mari Tripp (eds), *Global Feminism: Transnational Women's Activism, Organizing and Human Rights*. New York and London: New York University Press.

McCall, Leslie (2005). 'The Complexity of Intersectionality.' *Signs: Journal of Women in Culture and Society* 30 (3): 1771–99.

McCrudden, Christopher (2003). 'The New Concept of Equality.' Paper presented at the conference "Fight Against Discrimination: The Race and Framework Employment Directives" in Trier 31 March–1 April 2003.

McDowell, Linda (2008). 'The New Economy, Class Condescension and Caring Labour: Changing Formations of Class and Gender.' *NORA – Nordic Journal of Feminist and Gender Research* 16 (3): 150–65.

McGlynn, Clare (2000). 'Ideologies of Motherhood in European Community Sex Equality Law.' *European Law Journal* 6 (1): 29–44.

Meehan, Elizabeth (1993). *Citizenship and the European Community*. London: Sage.

Meehan, Elizabeth and Evelyn Collins (1996). 'Women, the European Union and Britain.' In Joni Lovenduski and Pippa Norris (eds): *Women in Politics*. Oxford: Oxford University Press.

Meenan, Helen (2007). 'Introduction.' In Helen Meenan (ed.), *Equality Law in an Enlarged European Union: Understanding the Article 13 Directives*. Cambridge: Cambridge University Press.

Meier, Petra, Elin Peterson, Karin Tertinegg, and Violetta Zentai (2007). 'The Pregnant Worker and Caring Mother: Framing Family Policies across Europe.' In Mieke Verloo (ed.), *Multiple Meanings of Gender Equality in Europe*. Budapest: Central European University Press.

Millns, Susan (2007). 'Gender Equality, Citizenship and the EU's Constitutional Future.' *European Law Journal* 13 (2) 218–37.

Millns, Susan and Mercedes Mateo Diaz (2004). 'Parity, Power and Representative Politics: The Elusive Pursuit of Gender Equality in Europe.' *Feminist Legal Studies* 12 (3): 279–302.

Moghadam, Valentine M. (2000). 'Transnational Feminist Networks: Collective Action in an Era of Globalization.' *International Sociology* 15 (1): 57–5.

Moghadam, Valentine M. (2005). *Globalizing Women: Transnational Feminist Networks*. Baltimore: Johns Hopkins University Press.

Montoya, Celeste (2008). 'The European Union, Capacity Building, and Transnational Networks: Combating Violence Against Women Through the Daphne Program.' *International Organization* 62, Spring, 359–72.

Morgan, Kimberly J. (2008). 'Towards the Europeanization of Work-Family Policies? The Impact of the EU on Policies for Working Parents.' In Silke Roth (ed.), *Gender Politics in the Expanding European Union: Mobilization, Inclusion, Exclusion*. New York and Oxford: Berghahn Books.

Morgan, Kimberley J. and Kathrin Zippel (2003). 'Paid to Care: The Origins and Effects of Care Leave Policies in Western Europe.' *Social Politics* Spring 2003, 49–85.

Mósesdóttir, Lilja and Rósa G. Erlingsdóttir (2005). 'Spreading the Word Across Europe. Gender Mainstreaming as a Political and Policy Project.' *International Feminist Journal of Politics* 7 (4) 513–31.

Mulinari, Diana, Suvi Keskinen, Sari Irni and Salla Tuori (2009). 'Introduction: Postcolonialism and the Nordic Model of Welfare and Gender.' In Suvi Keskinen,

Salla Tuori, Sari Irni and Diana Mulinari (eds), *Complying with Colonialism: Gender, Race and Ethnicity in the Nordic Region*. Surrey: Ashgate.

Nelsen, Brent F. and James L. Guth (2000). 'Exploring the Gender Gap: Women, Men and Public Attitudes toward European Integration.' *European Union Politics* 1 (3): 267–91.

Nielsen, Ruth (2008). 'Is European Union equality law capable of addressing multiple and intersectional discrimination yet? Precautions against neglecting intersectional cases.' In Dagmar Schiek and Victoria Chege (eds), *European Union Non-discrimination Law. Comparative Perspectives on Multidimensional Equality Law*. London: Routledge.

Norris, Pippa and Joni Lovenduski (1995). *Political Recruitment: Gender, Race, and Class in the British Parliament*. Cambridge: Cambridge University Press.

Nousiainen, Kevät (2005). 'Tasa-arvon monet kasvot: Kansainvälisistä vaikutuksista Suomen tasa-arvo-oikeudessa.' *Lakimies* 7-8: 1188–1209.

Nousiainen, Kevät (2008). 'Utility-based equality and disparate diversities: from a Finnish perspective.' In Dagmar Schiek and Victoria Chege (eds), *European Union Non-discrimination Law. Comparative Perspectives on Multidimensional Equality Law*. London: Routledge.

Nousiainen, Kevät (2008a). 'Unification (or not) of Equality Bodies and Legislation.' *European Gender Equality Law Review* 24–33.

Nousiainen, Kevät (2009). 'Double subsidiarity: EU as a polity for allocating care responsibilities?' Unpublished manuscript.

O'Connor, Julia S (2005). 'Employment-anchored social policy, gender equality and the open method of policy coordination in the European Union.' *European Societies* 7 (1): 27–54.

O'Connor, Julia S. (2008). 'The OMC and the EES: Broadening the Possibilities for Gender Equality?' In Fiona Beveridge and Samantha Velluti (eds), *Gender and the Open Method of Coordination: Perspectives on Law, Governance and Equality in the EU*. Aldershot: Ashgate.

O'Connor, Julia S., Ann Shola Orloff and Sheila Shaver (1999). *States, Markets and Families: Gender, Liberalism and Social Policy in Australia, Canada, Great Britain and the United States*. Cambridge: Cambridge University Press.

Okin, Susan Moller (1999). 'Is Multiculturalism Bad for Women?' In J. Cohen, M. Howard and M. Mussbaum (eds), *Is Multiculturalism Bad for Women?* Princeton: Princeton University Press.

Olsson Blandy, Tanja (2004). 'The Europeanization of Gender Policy: New Opportunities for Domestic Equality Agencies? The Case of Sweden.' Paper presented at the ECPR Second Pan European Conference on EU Politics, Bologna 24–26 June 2004.

Olsson Blandy, Tanja (2005). 'Equal pay and the impact of the European Union.' In PerOla Öberg and Torsten Svensson (eds), *Power and institutions in industrial relations regimes. Political Science perspectives on the transition of the Swedish model*. Worklife in Transition 2005: 12. National Institute for Working Life.

Orbie, Jan (2006). Gender in the Euro-Mediterranean Partnership.' In Marjorie Lister and Maurizio Carbone (eds), *New pathways in development: gender and civil society in EU policy*. Aldershot: Ashgate.

Ostner, Ilona (2000). 'From Equal Pay to Equal Employability: Four Decades of European Gender Policies.' In Mariagrazia Rossilli (ed.), *Gender Policies in the European Union*. Oxford: Lang.

Ostner, Ilona and Jane Lewis (1995). 'Gender and the Evolution of European Social Policies.' In Stephan Leibfried and Paul Pierson (eds), *European Social Policy: Between Fragmentation and Integration.* Washington DC: Brookings.

Outshoorn, Joyce (2004). 'Introduction: Prostitution, Women's Movements and Democratic Politics.' In Joyce Outshoorn (ed.), *The Politics of Prostitution: Women's Movements, Democratic States and the Globalisation of Sex Commerce.* Cambridge: Cambridge University Press.

Outshoorn, Joyce (2005). 'The Political Debates on Prostitution and Trafficking of Women.' *Social Politics: International Studies in Gender, State & Society* 12 (1): 141–55.

Outshoorn, Joyce and Johanna Kantola (2007). 'Assessing Changes in State Feminism over the Last Decade.' In Joyce Outshoorn and Johanna Kantola (eds), *Changing State Feminism.* Basingstoke: Palgrave Macmillan.

Outshoorn, Joyce and Jantine Oldersma (2007). 'Dutch Decay: the Dismantling of the Women's Policy Network in the Netherlands.' In Joyce Outshoorn and Johanna Kantola (eds), *Changing State Feminism.* Basingstoke: Palgrave Macmillan.

Pascual, Amparo Serrano (2008). 'Is the OMC a Provider of Political Tools to Promote Gender Mainstreaming?' In Fiona Beveridge and Samantha Velluti (eds), *Gender and the Open Method of Coordination: Perspectives on Law, Governance and Equality in the EU.* Aldershot: Ashgate.

Paxton, Pamela and Melanie Hughes (2007). *Women, Politics and Power: A Global Perspective.* London: Sage.

Pedersen, M. N. (1996). 'Euro-parties and European Parties: New Arenas, New Challenges and New Strategies.' In S. S. Andersen and K. A. Eliassen (eds), *The European Union: How Democratic is it?* London: Sage.

Penttinen, Elina (2007). *Globalization, Prostitution and Sex Trafficking: Corporeal Politics.* London: Routledge.

Pfister, Thomas (2007). 'Mainstreamed away? The European Employment Strategy and its Gender Equality Dimension.' Paper presented at the Biennial EUSA conference, Montreal, 17–19 May 2007.

Phillips, Anne (1998) .'Democracy and Representation: Or, Why Should It Matter Who Our Representatives are?' In A. Phillips (ed.), *Feminism and Politics.* Oxford University Press.

Phillips, Anne (1999). *Which Equalities Matter?* Cambridge: Polity Press.

Phillips, Anne (2007). *Multiculturalism without Culture.* Princeton and Oxford: Princeton University Press.

Pietilä, Hilkka (2007). *The Unfinished Story of Women and the United Nations.* New York and Geneva: United Nations.

Pillinger, Jane (1992). *Feminising the Market: Women's Pay and Employment in the European Community.* Basingstoke: Macmillan.

Plantenga, Janneke (2004). 'Investing in childcare. The Barcelona childcare targets and the European social model.' Speech prepared for the conference: Childcare in a changing world, 21–23 October 2004, Groningen.

Plantenga, Janneke and Chantal Remery (2006). *The gender pay gap. Origins and policy responses. A comparative review of thirty European countries.* The co-ordinators' synthesis report prepared for the Equality Unit, European Commission.

Plantenga, Janneke, Chantal Remery and Jill Rubery (2008). *Gender mainstreaming*

of employment policies: A comparative review of thirty European countries.
European Commission. Directorate-General for Employment, Social Affairs and
Equal Opportunities, Unit G1.

Plantenga, Janneke, Chantal Remery, Hugo Figueiredo and Mark Smith (2009).
'Towards a European Union Gender Equality Index.' *Journal of European Social
Policy* 19 (1) 19–33.

Platero Méndez, Raquel (2008). 'Intersecting Gender and Sexual Orientation: An
Analysis of Sexuality and Citizenship in Gender Equality Policy in Spain.' In Birte
Siim and Judith Squires (eds), *Contesting Citizenship.* London: Routledge.

Pollack, Mark A. and Emilie Hafner-Burton (2000). 'Mainstreaming Gender in the
European Union.' *Journal of European Public Policy* 7 (3): 432–56.

Prechal, Sacha (2008). 'EU Gender Equality Law: a source of inspiration for other EU
legal fields?' *European Gender Equality Law Review* 1/2008, 8–14.

Prügl, Elisabeth (2007). 'Gender and EU Politics.' In Knud Erik Jørgensen, Mark A.
Pollack and Ben Rosamond (eds), *The Handbook of European Union Politics.*
London: SAGE.

Prügl, Elisabeth (2008). 'Gender and the making of global markets: An exploration
of the agricultural sector.' In Shirin Rai and Georgina Waylen (eds), *Global
Governance: Feminist Perspectives.* Basingstoke: Palgrave Macmillan.

Puwar, Nirmal (2004). *Space Invaders: Race, Gender and Bodies out of Space.*
Oxford: Berg Publishers.

Radaelli, Claudio M. And Romain Pasquier (2008). 'Conceptual Issues.' In Paolo
Graziano and Maarten P. Vink (eds), *Europeanization. New Research Agendas.*
Basingstoke: Palgrave Macmillan.

Radford, Jill and Elizabeth A. Stanko (1996). 'Violence against women and children:
the contradictions of crime control under patriarchy.' In Marianne Hester, Liz
Kelly and Jill Radford (eds), *Women, Violence and Male Power.* Buckingham:
Open University Press.

Rai, Shirin (2002). *Gender and the Political Economy of Development: From
Nationalism to Globalization.* Cambridge: Polity Press.

Rai, Shirin and Georgina Waylen (eds) (2008). *Global Governance: Feminist
Perspectives.* Basingstoke: Palgrave Macmillan.

Randall, Vicky (2000). 'Childcare Policy in the European States: Limits to
Convergence.' *Journal of European Public Policy* 7 (3): 346–68.

Rees, Teresa (1998). *Mainstreaming Equality in the European Union: Education,
Training and Labour Market Policies.* London: Routledge.

Rees, Theresa (2005). 'Reflections on the uneven development of gender mainstreaming in Europe.' *International Feminist Journal of Politics,* 7 (4): 555–74.

Regulska, Joanna and Magda Grabowska (2008). 'Will it Make a Difference? EU
Enlargement and Women's Public Discourse in Poland.' In Silke Roth (ed.),
*Gender Politics in the Expanding European Union: Mobilization, Inclusion,
Exclusion.* New York and Oxford: Berghahn Books.

Reuter, Silke and Amy Mazur (2003). 'Paradoxes of Gender-Biased Universalism:
The Dynamics of French Equality Discourse.' In Ulrike Liebert (ed.), *Gendering
Europeanization.* Brussels: Presses Interuniversitaires Européennes.

Reynolds, Andrew (1999). 'Women in Legislatures and Executives of the World:
Knocking at the Highest Glass Ceiling.' *World Politics* 51 (4): 547–72.

Richardson, D. (2005). 'Desiring sameness? The rise of a neoliberal politics of
Normalization.' *Antipode* 37(3):515–35.

Richardt, Nicole (2005). 'Europeanization of Childcare Policy: Divergent Paths towards a Common Goal?' Paper prepared for the American Political Science Association Conference, Washington D.C., 1–4 4 September 2005.

Roggeband, Conny and Mieke Verloo (2006). 'Evaluating Gender Impact Assessment in the Netherlands (1994-2004): A Political Process Approach.' *Policy & Politics* 34 (4): 615–32.

Rolandsen Agustín, Lise (2008). 'Civil society participation in EU gender policy-making: Framing strategies and institutional constraints.' *Parliamentary Affairs* 61 (3): 505–17.

Rolandsen Agustín, Lise (2008a). 'Consensus or contestation in a discursive battlefield? Ideational changes in the development of EU policies on gender-based violence.' Paper presented at the 4th Pan-European Conference on EU Politics 25–27 September 2009, Riga.

Roseberry, Lynn (2008). 'Religion, ethnicity and gender in the Danish headscarf debate.' In Dagmar Schiek and Victoria Chege (eds), *European Union Non-discrimination Law. Comparative Perspectives on Multidimensional Equality Law*. London: Routledge.

Rossilli, Mariagrazia (2000). 'Introduction: The European Union's Gender Policies.' In Mariagrazia Rossilli (ed.), *Gender Policies in the European Union*. Oxford: Lang.

Roth, Silke (2007). 'Sisterhood and Solidarity? Women's Organizations in the Expanded European Union.' *Social Politics: International Studies in Gender, State & Society* 14 (4): 460–87.

Roth, Silke (2008). 'Introduction: Gender Politics in the Expanding European Union. Mobilization, Inclusion, Exclusion.' In Silke Roth (ed.), *Gender Politics in the Expanding European Union: Mobilization, Inclusion, Exclusion*. New York and Oxford: Berghahn Books.

Rubery, Jill (2003). 'Gender mainstreaming and the open method of coordination: is the open method too open for gender equality policy?' Presented in an ESRC seminar on gender mainstreaming, Leeds, October 2003.

Rubery, Jill (2005). 'Reflections on gender mainstreaming: an example of feminist economics in action?' *Feminist Economics* 11 (3):1–26.

Rubery, Jill, Damian Grimshaw and H. Figueiredo (2002). *The gender pay gap and gendermainstreaming pay policy in EU Member States*. Manchester: EWERC.

Rubery, Jill, Damian Grimshaw, Mark Smith and Hugo Figueiredo (2004). *Gender Mainstreaming and the European Employment Strategy*. Manchester: EWERC.

Rubery, Jill, Mark Smith and Colette Fagan (1999). *Women's Employment in Europe*. London and New York: Routledge.

Rubery, Jill, Mark Smith, Colette Fagan and Damian Grimshaw (1998). *Women and European Employment*. London and New York: Routledge.

Sacksofsky, Ute (2008). 'Religion and equality in Germany: The headscarf debate from a constitutional perspective.' In Dagmar Schiek and Victoria Chege (eds), *European Union Non-discrimination Law. Comparative Perspectives on Multidimensional Equality Law*. London: Routledge.

Saharso, Sawitri (2008). 'Headscarves: A Comparison of Public Thought and Public Policy in Germany and the Netherlands.' In Birte Siim and Judith Squires (eds), *Contesting Citizenship*. London: Routledge.

Saharso, Sawitri (2008a). 'Multicultural feminism: Finding our way between universalism and anti-essentialism.' *IPW Working Paper 3/2008*, Institut für Politikwissenschaft, Universität Wien.

Sainsbury, Diane (1999). 'Introduction.' in Diane Sainsbury (ed.), *Gender and Welfare State Regimes*. Oxford: Oxford University Press.

Sainsbury, Diane (2001). 'Gendering dimensions of welfare states.' in Janet Fink, Gail Lewis and John Clarke (eds), *Rethinking European welfare: transformations of Europe and social policy*.SAGE.

Sauer, Birgit (2009). 'Headscarf Regimes in Europe: Diversity Policies at the Intersection of Gender, Culture and Religion.' *Comparative European Politics* 7 (1): 75–94.

Sawer, Marian (2007). 'Australia: The Fall of the Femocrat.' In Joyce Outshoorn and Johanna Kantola (eds), *Changing State Feminism*. Basingstoke: Palgrave Macmillan.

Scharpf, F. W. (2002). 'The European Social Model: Coping with the Challenge of Diversity.' *Journal of Common Market Studies* 40 (4): 645–70.

Schiek, Dagmar (1998). 'Sex Equality Law after Kalanke and Marschall.' *European Law Journal* 4 (2): 148–66.

Schiek, Dagmar G. with Victoria Chege (2008) .'From European Union non-discrimination law towards multidimensional equality law for Europe.' In Dagmar Schiek and Victoria Chege (eds), *European Union Non-discrimination Law. Comparative Perspectives on Multidimensional Equality Law*. London: Routledge.

Schierup, Carl-Ulrik, Peo Hansen and Stephen Castles (2006). *Migration, Citizenship and the European Welfare State. A European Dilemma*.Oxford: Oxford University Press.

Schimmelfennig, Frank and Ulrich Sedelmeier (2008). 'Candidate Countries and Conditionality.'In Paolo Graziano and Maarten P. Vink (eds), *Europeanization. New Research Agendas*. Basingstoke: Palgrave Macmillan.

Schmidt, Verena (2005). *Gender Mainstreaming – an Innovation in Europe? The Institutionalisation of Gender Mainstreaming in the European Commission*. Opladen: Barbara Budrich Publishers.

Schoutheete, Philippe de (2006). 'The European Council.' In John Peterson and Michael Shackleton (eds), *The Institutions of the European Union*. Second Edition. Oxford: Oxford University Press.

Seppanen Anderson, Leah (2006). 'European Union Gender Regulations in the East: The Czech and Polish Accession Process.' *East European Politics and Societies* 20 (1): 101–25.

Shackleton, Michael (2006). 'The European Parliament.' in John Peterson and Michael Shackleton (eds), *The Institutions of the European Union*. Second Edition. Oxford: Oxford University Press.

Shaw, Jo (2000). 'Importing Gender: The Challenge of Feminism and the Analysis of the EU Legal Order.' *Journal of European Public Policy* 7 (3): 406–31.

Shaw, Jo (2001). 'European Union governance and the question of gender: a critical comment.' Jean Monnet Working Paper No. 6/01.

Shaw, Jo (2002). 'The European Union and Gender Mainstreaming: Constitutionally Embedded or Comprehensively Marginalised?' *Feminist Legal Studies* 10: 213–26.

Shaw, Jo (2004). *Mainstreaming Equality in European Union Law and Policymaking*. Brussels: ENAR.

Siaroff, Alan (2000). 'Women's Representation in Legislatures and Cabinets in Industrial Democracies.' *International Political Science Review* 21 (2) :197–215.

Sifft, Stefanie (2003). 'Pushing for Europeanization: How British Feminists Link with the EU to Promote Parental Rights.' In Ulrike Liebert (ed.), *Gendering Europeanization*. Brussels: Presses Interuniversitaires Européennes.

Siim, Birte (2008). 'The Challenge of Recognizing Diversity from the Perspective of Gender Equality: Dilemmas of Danish Citizenship.' In Birte Siim and Judith Squires (eds), *Contesting Citizenship*. London: Routledge.

Skjeie, Hege (2006). '"Gender Equality": On Travel Metaphors and Duties to Yield.' In Sirkku K. Hellsten, Anne Maria Holli and Krassimira Daskalova (eds), *Women's Citizenship and Political Rights*. Basingstoke: Palgrave Macmillan.

Skjeie, Hege (2008). 'Multiple equality claims in the practice of the Norwegian anti-discrimination agencies.' In Dagmar Schiek and Victoria Chege (eds), *European Union Non-discrimination Law. Comparative Perspectives on Multidimensional Equality Law*. London: Routledge.

Skjeie, Hege and Trude Langvasbråten (2009). 'Intersectionality in practice? Anti-discrimination reforms in Norway.' *International Feminist Journal of Politics* 11 (4): 513–29.

Sloat, Amanda (2004). 'Legislating for Equality: The Implementation of the EU Equality Acquis in Central and Eastern Europe.' *The Jean Monnet Program*. Jean Monnet Working Paper 08/04. New York University School of Law, New York: NY, USA.

Sloat, Amanda (2005). 'The rebirth of civil society: the growth of women's NGOs in Central and Eastern Europe.' *The European Journal for Women's Studies* 12 (4): 437–52.

Smart, Carol (1989). *Feminism and the Power of Law*. London: Routledge.

Smith, Anne Marie (2007). *Welfare Reform and Sexual Regulation*. Cambridge: Cambridge University Press.

Sobritchea, Carolyn (2006). 'Gender in European Union Development Cooperation in Asia.' In Marjorie Lister and Maurizio Carbone (eds), *New pathways in development: gender and civil society in EU policy*. Aldershot: Ashgate.

Sperling, Liz and Charlotte Bretherton (1996). 'Women's Policy Networks and the European Union.' *Women's Studies International Forum* 19 (3): 303–14.

Squires, Judith (1999). *Gender in Political Theory*. Cambridge: Polity Press.

Squires, Judith (2005). 'Is Mainstreaming Transformative? Theorizing Mainstreaming in the Context of Diversity and Deliberation.' *Social Politics*, 12 (3): 366–88.

Squires, Judith (2007). *The New Politics of Gender Equality*. Basingstoke: Palgrave Macmillan.

Squires, Judith (2008a). 'The Constitutive Representation of Gender: Extra-Parliamentary Re-presentations of Gender Relations.' *Representation* 44 (2): 187–204.

Squires, Judith (2008b). 'Negotiating Equality and Diversity in Britain: Towards a Differentiated Citizenship?' In Birte Siim and Judith Squires (eds), *Contesting Citizenship*. London: Routledge.

Steinhilber, Silke (2002). 'Women's Rights and Gender Equality in the EU Enlargement. An Opportunity for Progress.' WIDE Briefing paper. October 2002.

Steinhilber, Silke (2006). 'Gender and Post-socialist Welfare States in Central and Eastern Europe: Family Policy Reforms in Poland and the Czech Republic Compared.' In Shahra Razavi and Shireen Hassim (eds), *Gender and Social Policy in Global Context: Uncovering the Gendered Structure of 'the Social'*. Basingstoke: Palgrave Macmillan.

Sterner, Gunilla and Helene Biller (2007). *Gender Mainstreaming in EU Member States: Progress, Obstacles and Experiences at Governmental Level.* Ministry of Integration and Gender Equality, Sweden.

Stifft, Stefanie (2003). 'Pushing for Europeanization: How British Feminist Link with the EU to Promote Parental Rights.' In Ulrike Liebert (ed.), *Gendering Europeanization.* Brussels: Presses Interuniversitaires Européennes.

Stratigaki, Maria (2000). 'The European Union and the Equal Opportunities Process.' In Linda Hantrais (ed.), *Gendered Policies in Europe: Reconciling employment and family life.* London: Macmillan.

Stratigaki, Maria (2004). 'The Cooptation of Gender Concepts in EU Policies: The Case of "Reconciliation of Work and Family."' *Social Politics* 11 (1): 30–56.

Stratigaki, Maria (2005). 'Gender Mainstreaming vs Positive Action: An Ongoing Conflict in EU Gender Equality Policy.' *European Journal of Women's Studies* 12 (2): 165–86.

Stubb, Alexander, Helen Wallace and John Peterson (2003). 'The Policy-Making Process.' In Elizabeth Bomberg and Alexander Stubb (eds) ,*The European Union: How Does it Work?* Oxford: Oxford University Press.

Sullivan, Barbara (2003). 'Trafficking in Women. Feminism and New International Law.' *International Feminist Journal of Politics* 5 (1): 67–91.

Swenden, Wilfried (2004). 'Is the European Union in Need of a Competence Catalogue? Insights from Comparative Federalism.' *Journal of Common Market Studies* 42 (2): 371–92.

Tarrow, Sidney (1995). 'The Europeanization of Conflict: Reflections from a Social Movement Perspective.' *West European Politics* 18 (2): 223–51.

Tarrow, Sidney (1998). *Power in movement: Social movements and contentious politics.* Cambridge: Cambridge University Press.

Teghtsoonian, K. (2004). 'Neoliberalism and Gender Analysis Mainstreaming in Aotearoa/New Zealand.' *Australian Journal of Political Science* 39 (2): 267–84.

Tesoka, Sabrina (1999). 'The Differential Impact of Judicial Politics in the Field of Gender Equality. Three National Cases under Scrutiny.' European University Institute Working Paper RSC No 99/18.

Theorin, Maj Britt (2001), 'Statement.' In Laura Keeler (ed.), *Recommendations of the E.U.: Expert Meeting on Violence Against Women.* Helsinki: Ministry of Social Affairs and Health.

Thorbek, Susanne and Bandana Pattanaik (eds) (2002). *Transnational Prostitution: Changing Global Patterns.* London and New York, Zed Books.

Threlfall, Monica (1997). 'Spain in Social Europe: A laggard or compliant member state?' *South European Society and Politics* 2, 1–33.

Trubek, David M. and Louise G. Trubek (2005). 'Hard and Soft Law in the Construction of Social Europe: the Role of the Open Method of Co-ordination.' *European Law Journal* 11 (3): 343–64.

True, Jacqui (2003). 'Mainstreaming Gender in Global Public Policy.' *International Feminist Journal of Politics* 5 (3): 368–96.

True, Jacqui (2008). 'Gender Mainstreaming and Regional Trade Governance in Asia-Pacific Economic Cooperation (APEC).' In Shirin Rai and Georgina Waylen (eds), *Global Governance: Feminist Perspectives.* Basingstoke: Palgrave Macmillan.

True, Jacqui (2009). 'Trading in gender equality: gendered meanings in EU trade policy.' in Emanuela Lombardo, Petra Meier and Mieke Verloo (eds), *The Discursive Politics of Gender Equality: Stretching, Bending and Policymaking*. London: Routledge.

True, Jacqui and Michael Mintrom (2001). 'Transnational networks and policy diffusion: The case of gender mainstreaming.' *International Studies Quarterly* 45 (1): 27–57.

Valenius, Johanna (2007). *Gender Mainstreaming in ESDP Missions*. Chaillot Paper 101. Institute for Security Studies, European Union.

Vallance, Elizabeth and Elizabeth Davis (1986). *Women of Europe*. Cambridge: Cambridge University Press.

Van Doorninck, Marieke (2002). 'A Business Like Any Other? Managing the Sex Industry in the Netherlands.' In Susanne Thorbek and Bandana Pattanaik (eds), *Transnational Prostitution: Changing Global Patterns*. London and New York, Zed Books.

van der Vleuten, Anna (2005). 'Pincers and Prestige. Explaining Implementation of EU Gender Equality Legislation.' *Comparative European Politics* 3 (4): 464–88.

van der Vleuten, Anna (2007). *The Price of Gender Equality: Member States and Governance in the European Union*. Aldershot: Ashgate.

Velluti, Samantha (2005). 'Implementing Gender Equality and Mainstreaming in an Enlarged European Union – Some Thoughts on Prospects and Challenges for Central Eastern Europe.' *Journal of Social Welfare and Family Law* 27 (2): 213–25.

Velluti, Samantha (2008). 'Gender Equality and Mainstreaming in the Re-articulation of Labour Market Policies in Denmark and Italy.' In Fiona Beveridge and Samantha Velluti (eds), *Gender and the Open Method of Coordination: Perspectives on Law, Governance and Equality in the EU*. Aldershot: Ashgate.

Verloo, Mieke (2001). 'Another velvet revolution? Gender mainstreaming and the politics of implementation.' IWM Working Paper No. 5/2001. Vienna: IWM.

Verloo, Mieke (2005). 'Displacement and Empowerment: Reflections on the Concept and Practice of the Council of Europe Approach to Gender Mainstreaming and Gender Equality.' *Social Politics*, 12 (3) 344–65.

Verloo, Mieke (2006). 'Multiple Inequalities, Intersectionality and the European Union.' *European Journal of Women's Studies* 13 (3): 211–28.

Verloo, Mieke (ed.) (2007). *Multiple Meanings of Gender Equality: A Critical Frame Analysis of Gender Policies in Europe*. Budapest: Central European University Press.

Verloo, Mieke and Anna van der Vleuten (2009). 'The discursive logic of ranking and benchmarking: Understanding gender equality measures in the European Union.' In Emanuela Lombardo, Petra Meier and Mieke Verloo (eds), *The Discursive Politics of Gender Equality. Stretching, Bending and Policy-making*. London: Routledge.

Vogel-Polsky, Elianne (2000). 'Parity Democracy – Law and Europe.' In Mariagrazia Rossilli (ed.), *Gender Policies in the European Union*. New York: Peter Lang Publishing.

Waddington, Lisa (1999). 'Testing the Limits of the EC Treaty Article on Non-discrimination.' *Industrial Law Journal* 28 (2): 133–51.

Waddington, Lisa (2000). 'Article 13 EC: Setting Priorities in the Proposal for a Horizontal Employment Directive.' *Industrial Law Journal* 29 (2): 171–86.

Wahl, Angelika von (2005). 'Liberal, Conservative, Social Democratic, or... European? The European Union as Equal Employment Regime.' *Social Politics* 12 (1): 67–95.

Wahl, Angelika von (2008). 'The EU and Enlargement: Conceptualizing beyond East and West.' In Silke Roth (ed.), *Gender Politics in the Expanding European Union: Mobilization, Inclusion, Exclusion.* New York and Oxford: Berghahn Books.

Walby, Sylvia (1999), 'The European Union and Equal Opportunities Policies.' *European Societies* 1 (1) 59–80.

Walby, Sylvia (2004). 'The European Union and Gender Equality: Emerging Varieties of Gender Regime.' *Social Politics* 11 (1): 4–29.

Walby, Sylvia (2005). 'Gender Mainstreaming: Productive Tensions in Theory and Practice.' *Social Politics: International Studies in Gender, State and Society* 12 (3): 321–43.

Walby, Sylvia (2005a). 'Introduction: Comparative Gender Mainstreaming in a Global Era.' *International Feminist Journal of Politics* 7 (4): 453–471.

Wallace, Helen (2000). 'Europeanization and Globalisation: Complementary or Contradictory Trends?' *New Political Economy* 5 (3): 369–81.

Wallace, Helen (2005). 'An Institutional Anatomy and Five Policy Models.' In Helen Wallace, William Wallace and Mark A. Pollack (eds), *Policy-Making in the European Union.* Fifth Edition. Oxford: Oxford University Press.

Wallace, Helen, William Wallace and Mark A. Pollack (2005). 'An Overview.' In Helen Wallace, William Wallace and Mark A. Pollack (eds), *Policy-Making in the European Union.* Fifth Edition. Oxford: Oxford University Press.

Warleigh, Alex (2001). '"Europeanizing" civil society: NGOs as agents of political socialization.' *Journal of Common Market Studies* 39 (4): 619–39.

Waylen, Georgina (2007). *Engendering Transitions: Women's Mobilization, Institutions and Gender Outcomes.* Oxford: Oxford University Press.

Waylen, Georgina (2008). 'Gendering Governance.' In Gary Goertz and Amy G. Mazur (eds), *Politics, Gender and Concepts: Theory and Methodology.* Cambridge: Cambridge University Press.

Weichselbaumer, Doris (2003). 'Sexual Orientation Discrimination in Hiring.' *Labour Economics*, 10: 629–42.

Weldon, Laurel S. (2002). 'Beyond Bodies: Institutional Sources of Representation for Women in Democratic Policymaking.' *Journal of Politics* 64 (4): 132–54.

Weldon, Laurel S. (2008). 'The Concept of Intersectionality.' In Gary Goertz and Amy Mazur (eds), *Politics, Gender and Concepts: Theory and Methodology.* Cambridge: Cambridge University Press.

WES – The European Network to Promote Women's Entrepreneurship (2005). *Activities Report 2004.* Brussels: WES.

West, Jackie (2000). 'Prostitution: Collectives and the Politics of Regulation.' *Gender, Work and Organization* 7 (2): 106–18.

Westlake, Martin and David Galloway (2004). *The Council of the European Union.* London: John Harper.

Wiener, Antje and Thomas Diez (2004). *European Integration Theory.* Oxford: Oxford University Press.

Wiener, Antje and Thomas Diez (2009). *European Integration Theory.* 2nd edn. Oxford: Oxford University Press.

Wiercx, J. and Alison Woodward (2004). *Vernieuwend transnationaal gelijkekansen beleid: Sociale bewegingen en organisaties en hun rol in het gelijkekansenbeleid op*

Vlaams en Europees niveau: de voorbeelden van de vrouw- en holebiebewegin-gen. Brussels: Centrum voor Vrouwenstudies Vrije Universiteit Brussel & Steunpunt Gelijkekansen.

Williams, Fiona (2003). 'Contesting "Race" and Gender in the European Union: A Multilayered Recognition Struggle for Voice and Visibility.' In Barbara Hobson (ed.), *Recognition Struggles and Social Movements: Contested Identities, Agency and Power*. Cambridge: Cambridge University Press.

Woehl, Stefanie (2008). 'Global Governance as Neo-Liberal Governmentality: Gender Mainstreaming in the European Employment Strategy.' In Shirin Rai and Georgina Waylen (eds), *Global Governance: Feminist Perspectives*. Basingstoke: Palgrave Macmillan.

Women and Equality Unit (2006). *Minority Ethnic Women in the UK. Factsheet.* Communities and Local Government. October 2006.

Woodward, Alison (2003). 'European Gender Mainstreaming: Promises and Pitfalls of Transformative Policy.' *Review of Policy Research* 20: 65–88.

Woodward, Alison (2005). 'Gender Mainstreaming: An Example of Open Methods Co-ordination or a Challenge?' Article prepared for inclusion in A. Menon, K. Kassim and B. Guy Peters (eds), *Coordinating the European Union*.

Woodward, Alison and Agnés Hubert (2007). 'Reconfiguring State Feminism in the European Union: Changes from 1995–2006'. Paper presented at the EUSA Tenth Biennial International Conference, 17–19 May 2007, Montreal.

Yeates, Nicola (2009). *Globalizing Care Economies and Migrant Workers: Explorations in Global Care Chains*. Basingstoke: Palgrave Macmillan.

Young, Brigitte (2000). 'Disciplinary Neoliberalism in the European Union and Gender Politics.' *New Political Economy* 5 (1): 77–98.

Young, Iris Marion (1990). *Justice and the Politics of Difference*. Princeton: Princeton University Press.

Young, Iris Marion (2000). *Inclusion and Democracy*. Oxford: Oxford University Press.

Yuval-Davis, Nira (1997). *Gender and Nation*. London: Sage.

Yuval-Davis, Nira (2006). 'Intersectionality and Feminist Politics.' *European Journal of Women's Studies*, 13 (3): 193–209.

Zappone, Katherine E. (ed.) (2003). *Rethinking Identity: The Challenge of Diversity*. Belfast, Dublin, London, Manchester: Joint Equality and Human Rights Forum.

Zartaloudis, Sotiros (2008). 'Gender Equality in Greek Employment Policy: A Story of Europeanization?' Paper presented at the ECPR Fourth Pan-European Conference on EU Politics, 25–27 September 2008, Riga.

Zippel, Kathrin (2004). 'Transnational Advocacy Networks and Policy Cycles in the European Union: The Case of Sexual Harassment.' *Social Politics* 11 (1): 57–85.

Zippel, Kathrin (2006). *The Politics of Sexual Harassment: A Comparative Study of the United States, the European Union and Germany*. Cambridge: Cambridge University Press.

Zippel, Kathrin (2008). 'Institutionalizing Social Movements through Expertise.' Paper presented at the American Sociological Association Meetings, Boston, 1–4 August, 2008.

Zippel, Kathrin (2008a). 'Violence at Work? Framing Sexual Harassment in the European Union.' In Silke Roth (ed.), *Gender Politics in the Expanding European Union: Mobilization, Inclusion, Exclusion*. New York and Oxford: Berghahn Books.

Zippel, Kathrin (2009). 'The European Union 2002 Directive on Sexual Harassment: A Feminist Success?' *Comparative European Politics* 7 (1): 139–57.

Zwingel, Susanne (2005). 'How Do International Women's Rights Norms become Effective in Domestic Contexts? An Analysis of the Convention on the Elimination of all Forms of Discrimination against Women (CEDAW)'. Unpublished PhD Thesis, University of Bochum.

Index